Also by Donna Williams

Nobody Nowhere
Somebody Somewhere

Like Color to the Blind

Like Color to the Blind

Donna Williams

TIMES 𝕿 BOOKS

RANDOM HOUSE

The names and identifying characteristics of every person in the book have been changed to protect their privacy.

Grateful acknowledgment is made to Future Education, Inc. for permission to reprint nine lines from "Emotions" by Donna Williams from *Not Just Anything*, published by Future Education, Inc., Arlington, Texas. Reprinted by permission.

Library of Congress Cataloging-in-Publication Data

Williams, Donna
    Like color to the blind / Donna Williams.—1st ed.
       p.   cm.
    ISBN 0-8129-2640-4
    1. Williams, Donna, 1963– —Mental health. 2. Autism—Patients—
Biography.   3. Love—Psychological aspects—Case studies.
4. Intimacy (Psychology)—Case studies. I. Title.
RC553.A88W547 1996
616.89′82′0092—dc20
[B]   95-40979

Manufactured in the United States of America
9 8 7 6 5 4 3 2
First Edition
Book design by Susan Hood

To my husband Paul ("Ian"), a person no less special than anyone else for being an anybody anywhere and so much more special than most for seeing the anybody in me and showing me that one does not need to be exceptional in the eyes of the world in order to be special

Why does it happen? Where is it going?
Is this happy? Is this sad?
The context, often absent, passed us by.

Emotions in reply, they tumble
in response to echoed thoughts,
raised in situations left behind.

Who can tell what is this feeling
in the absence of its meaning.
Like sound in deafness or like color to the blind.

—From the poem "Emotions," featured
in the book *Not Just Anything* by
Donna Williams, published by Future
Education.

"I don't want to be special bad *or* special good," I explained to Bryn, hoping I'd get through to him that I didn't want to be outstanding and I didn't want to be put on a pedestal. "I just want to be an anybody anywhere."

"I hate to be the one to tell you this," said Bryn jokingly. "You blew it in a big way."

Like Color to the Blind

I lived in limbo as a nobody nowhere, unable to share selfhood with a world that I perceived as a place of cheap tricks. "The world," the world people moved in beyond the internal place of "my world," had been little more than a big stage I'd been made to play on where the semblance of a life was the performance and where one got Academy Awards for acting "normal."

Then, I lived as a somebody somewhere, sharing a selfhood that I had never known the hows or whys of sharing. I was only beginning to understand that "the world" *did* have some corners of meaning and belonging and dignity and integrity if you worked hard enough and long enough to find them, asking the right people the right questions, once you knew what they were.

That once despised and mistrusted place, "the world," opened its doors to me and offered me celebrity. It offered me the ears of experts and the eyes of the public and the hearts of supporters and comrades from one side of the globe to the other. Somewhere, though, between this side and that, between being a nobody nowhere and a somebody somewhere, was the place in the middle. That was the only place I'd never been to, the place where I could be an anybody anywhere.

———

To be an anybody anywhere is to be giving without charity and taking without selfishness. It is to live a life of one's own without having to be a hermit. It is to be able to simply be, without having to be an example to those who'd look to you for one. It is to be able to be like "everyone else" without conformity or performance.

To be an anybody anywhere is to look into the eyes of someone who matters to you and know that they don't care what or who you are, where you've been, or what you've achieved. To be an anybody anywhere is to look into those eyes and know that if you see love there, then you've earned it, not for being a walking achievement or an interesting case or a social inspiration or a charity cause, but just for being yourself. That is the gift of the ordinary person—an anybody anywhere.

The manuscript for my second book, *Somebody Somewhere,* was almost finished; it was a photo album of my journey from "my world" to "the world," in which I took the reins out of the hands of my autism and took control of my life.

There was both sadness and relief in settling down to life here in England, ten thousand miles from the place in Australia where I was born.

There was relief at not being caught up anymore with damaging people who took my triggered behavior to be real responses and then expected me to live by those responses as though I'd meant or even understood them. There was sadness for the loss of the familiar smell of sun-baked earth, muddy dams, and coarse squawking birds, of flaky gum trees and spritzy cheerful, yellow wattles and tall, dried golden grass.

Here in England, with its rows of narrow houses in narrow streets with well-kept front gardens, lush green rich lawns, and delicate twittery birds, the feel was nice but unfamiliar and though I was safe, I felt I was in something of a self-imposed exile.

Letters arrived every day from all around the world, making me feel less of a migrant and more like one of so many people in a vast fish tank called "the world"—the external world people think of as "reality" in which most of them buy into something they call "normality."

Through a small hole in my front door these letters came in response to my first book, *Nobody Nowhere,* in which I had described my life as a child with autism. The book had been translated into fourteen different languages and sold worldwide.

There were letters from parents saying thank you because they had found understanding, direction, hope, or self-forgiveness. There were letters from professionals, confessing ignorance and arrogance or writing to say they'd finally found support for their "out on a limb," nonignorant, nonarrogant, unconventional approaches.

There were letters from the public, who'd been wrapped in cotton wool and wrote to say thank you for the journey they went on in reading the first book.

There were letters from people who wrote to say the book had inspired them to return to education, speak up about things that happened to them, or leave damaging situations to risk the unknown.

There were books and manuscripts sent by people who were writers, people who hoped to be writers, and people who represented writers, hoping to get some feedback from me about their books and some little positive quote to say I enjoyed their book. What was so ironic was that they were sending their manuscripts to someone who, though a best-selling writer, was unable to read books for pleasure because of a reading disability that meant that I could flatly speed-read their books, but would generally have no idea of what I thought about them.

There were letters from auties, diagnosed and not, some in the closet in fear of exposure, some free in exposure but also in ridicule at the hands of arrogant people with heavy ego baggage and "I'll fix you" "the world" ideas.

There were people who wrote that they'd never had a friend. There were people who wrote that they'd had many apparent friends and had become every one of them and that nobody in fact knew them at all.

There were packages full of the chronicles of lives lived: desperate people pouring their lives out as they come out of the closet to me, the first person they felt will understand what they have lived through.

There were other packages. These were sometimes exhausting, desperate, and greedy attempts to have me play autie-expert via post free of charge to parents who sent chronicles of the lives and records and reports of their children.

I'd sit alone in my cottage and some of these letters would make me smile from inside. Some left me feeling like the wind in the midst of a symphony of dancing leaves to which it is oblivious. Some would bring brotherhood and sisterhood through that hole in the door and some would bring memory and turmoil and pass through another hole in a door in my mind. Some would pluck at the strings of emotion and some would pluck at the strings of commitment (and I would reach back via the fire-engine red post box on the corner of the street). Others would pluck only at the strings of responsibility and I would heavily plod through the chronicles of their children and their diarrhea of endless questions and the total absence of acknowledgment of Donna as a person with any wants of my own.

I answered each one as a personal interview: five pages, seven pages, ten pages. Then, having received those, some of these people would write again, sending another chronicle and then a third to the walking autie textbook. Sugared with "the world" compliments, nothing on the surface confirmed the twisting repulsed wordless feeling inside: I was being used.

I wanted to help people, didn't I? Everybody had thanked me for writing the book, for helping them, for helping others, for sharing my life with them. What else, if not caring, was the acceptance of publication for? What else was my compliance at accepting the suggestion of publication for, if not want? What else was my justification in the face of these weak knees of mine for, if not belief and interest and the personal want to "share"?

When I felt I couldn't be so greedy as to deny the publication of a book that would be helpful to others like me, was I not giving to myself? When I reasoned that it would be freeing and that it would mean I'd be out of the closet if I had the book published, did that reasoning not make these my wants? Could I have really found theoretical reasons, theoretical morality, theoretical versions of "what a person wants when . . ." and held on to them as my own, to justify my inability to say "No, I don't care" or "No, my privacy is worth more than their need or want or interest"? Was my commitment to the publication of the book and to answering these letters merely my way of pretending I had some control over my life when I did not?

Was it the want of my heart or had it been the compulsion of my fear to burn the manuscript of *Nobody Nowhere* after coming out of the closet to just one person who would read it? After all, that one person would have merely been a symbol of the whole world anyway, as any external "the worlder" was. Or was it the want of my child-heart? Perhaps my adult heart had a want that went beyond this, cradled in the arms of a sense of humanity and morality that evaded my child-heart, like the view on the other side of the walls of a prison that evades the prisoner contained within them.

What I called this child-heart had been born of an inward-focused view where my self was its own world and all things external were merely a wind blowing outside. There was never any call to stop and try to comprehend a wind. The commitment of this adult heart still felt intermittently external. This half-brought-up inner child had stood facing "the world," trying to stand firm on shaky legs. I swung between reaching back to "the world" from my own heart and reaching back from theoretical emotions when my own heart was nowhere to be found.

— ◂

Music composed itself with the help of my hands at a rate of about one piece per week. I worked on some and kept a note or recording of it, like some captured emotion I might need to lis-

8

ten to sometime to remind myself that I had had it. Compositions lay in piles on top of so many others that had gone before: "Enemy Lines," "Beyond the When," "Shoes We're Going to Berlin," and "Nobody Nowhere," the song. A classical storm would rage one day and a sunny skip-along tune the next. Words flowed out of some of them, others never spoke. In some ways, the music that came from so many corners of my soul brought me together as a whole.

When I first met Ian, he was working in a shop selling pianos. I had recognized him in the first five minutes as being "like me." My acquaintance with this tall, thin, gentle but intense, simple and complex man-boy had grown from comradeship to special-ship over the past few months.

Ian had been hired by the shop because of his skills as a musician. It was wrong to say that Ian, like me, was self-taught, because both of us had merely sat down at the piano and begun to play—there'd been no self-teaching involved. Music was inside and it came out. But Ian and I were different. He composed music from his mind—a technical mind. I composed music from my emotions—ever changing and unstructured. Left brain stuff and right brain stuff.

When Ian called me, it had been with the view to write music together. Five months of friendship later we had barely shared any. Another friend, Olivier, faxed me lyrics with an over-whelming passion for what he wrote and the tunes he had in his head, but he had no playing ability. Ian had all the playing ability he could have wanted, but none of emotional self-expression through music.

I walked about the cottage in Ian's coat trying to make sense of why I no longer tried to "disappear." Though disappearing—losing my grip on my sense of self—still happened automatically, over the years, disappearances shrank in length from hours to minutes to seconds. It was what happened in between episodes that had changed. I no longer craved being swept away like this in the all-consuming tide of total mental and sensory blankness, where "the world" stood irrelevant and uncountable leagues away.

Ian and I had been sharing a room in my little cottage for a few months now but every day he marched out the door to his job as a piano salesman, looking as starchy and non-him as the suit and tie he'd left in. Every week, I went to work within the cottage answering letters, sticking things irretrievably into a very "Donna" filing system (where taxation is found under "M" for "Money things"), looking over new contracts as my two books journeyed from country to country and dealing with publicity, editing, translations, publishers, and agents.

I took a bath in the tall-sided, scratchy, old white tub. The sky through the trees was so intense: deep blue–indigo diamonds playing background-foreground with light and dark green tickling it. It made me laugh. I stared for some time and disappeared in the hypnotic effect as the bath got cold. I got out of the bath and went for the mirror out of habit.

I had originally painted it with a rose-garden boundary and long grass, so that when I sat in front of it, it looked as though I was sitting in a garden with someone else who looked like me. That was how I had experienced "company," which I could never really find in the company of most others. The sense of self or other almost always gave out or, at best, was very inconsistent. The concept of company in "the world" had always seemed like a joke that I was meant to play along with. By my experience, it was always "me" plus "them" minus "them" or "them" plus "me" minus "me." One plus one generally added up to one. With Ian though, as with a handful of others "like me," it was different. I sensed "with" instead of in front of or around.

I had always dried myself in front of the mirror and, when there was no mirror, I had either lain down and waited for my body to dry or had put my clothes on over my wet body.

Mirrors had always been part of my life. In the attic I had lived in as a child, my room was tiled in mirrors wall to wall and ceiling to floor. The living room wall, too, had been mirrored the same way, and there were mirrors in the bathroom so you could see yourself using the toilet from all angles. There was one thing, for sure: if nothing else encouraged me to spend time in a room, mirrors did. The bigger the mirrors, the more space in the room I felt free to use. Seeing that my mirror reflection was with me in every corner of the room made me feel safe and understood and gave me confidence.

Without an internal feeling of personal connection to my body, I had felt I had little idea where all its bits were without seeing them in a reflection. Reflection somehow framed them, made them less disembodied, a visual disqualification of what perception in "the world" told me.

I went into my room and sat there wet but in towels. My emotional awareness was high, as were my senses. I could hold on to my thoughts for whole connected minutes and they didn't drift away like fluffy intangible clouds. I was a bundle of disembodied emotion, senses, and thought, with lumps of flesh and blood and bone in my immediate vicinity, which I knew from experience would follow me if I left the room.

Cold sometimes came from somewhere, as did pain, and I had learned how to look for signs of the source and how to beat cold and why it was in my interest to do so. Still, most of the time I continued to feel like a baby-sitter to the body I carried around.

I had come forward. I now had enough fragments of inner experience to question the assumptions my faulty perception had built. As much as mirrors had made me confident enough to take action, I hadn't identified with most of those actions I had seen my reflection do; furthermore, I was starting to realize that it was probably more than coincidence that the less I relied on mirrors, the more consistent became my inner body sense. I had overrelied on outer body image at the expense of developing inner body sense.

———

Ian was back and it was time to sleep. He and I brushed our teeth.

It was strange to feel a consistent sense of physical self without having to boost my visual impressions of self to hold the sense of it in memory. I wished I could see my own face, if only bit by bit, but if I couldn't, then Ian's would do.

Being with my mirror image usually made me "disappear" and cut me off not just from the world around me, but also from my own emotions. Without doing everything with my reflection, I could feel my feelings now—even if I didn't know what a lot of my feelings were.

As far as visual security blankets go, I no longer had my reflection but I had the things around me and I had Ian. I now went places with Ian, avoiding the compulsion to look at and touch window reflections as I walked along, and, instead, accepting security in the developing familiarity of his face, even if I couldn't see mine. I thought of how it was Ian who could see my face as I could see his and then I felt safe; this was relative symmetry, I thought.

"Relative Symmetry" was a concept by which we could accept being ourselves without needing to be a copy of the other person or to have them be a copy of us. A need for symmetry meant that a right could only go with a right and a left could only go together with a left. But our concept of Relative Symmetry meant that we could combat the anxiety of our defenses by bargaining with them to accept incongruity—provided that, whatever anomalous combination happened at one point, the combination would be exactly reversed at some other point. Left and right could be accepted as long as right and left would happen next time.

It was well past dinnertime and neither of us had got the mechanics working to get a meal going and my hypoglycemia had me in the mind-numbing state of a sugar-low. We went out to get some food.

We parked the car and got out to stand on the sidewalk of the busy main street. "Pink streetlight!" I exclaimed, racing across the street, oblivious to all else, to stand stock-still beneath this fifteen-foot illuminous God.

Ian checked the traffic before crossing as fast as possible to me. I stood beneath the God-like symbol, getting hypnotically further and further "inside" of it. The effect on my conscious awareness was comparable with the addictive feeling that happens when deep sleep doesn't creep up on you but actually grabs you and tugs you into itself and it is too hard to fight and you don't even know if you want to fight it. This was "buzzing."

These streetlights were yellow with a hint of pink but in a buzz state they were an intoxicating iridescentlike pink-yellow. My mind dived deeper and deeper into the color, trying to feel its nature and become it as I progressively lost sense of self in its overwhelming presence. Each of the colors resonated different feelings within me and it was like they played me as a chord, where other colors played one note at a time.

It had been the same for as long as I had known. My obsessions changed and got channeled into ever more socially rewarded and "acceptable" forms of "disappearing." Despite so many leaps forward, some things hadn't changed that much since I was an infant swept up in the perception of swirling air particles, a child lost in the repetition of a pattern of sound, or a teenager staring for hours at colored billiard balls, trying to grasp the experience of the particular color I was climbing into.

Over twenty-eight years, I had managed to awaken my sleepwalking mind to the acceptance and acknowledgment of the me within. But, even though I was now committed to staying aware and involved in the world around me, this other automatic pilot was still a renegade, changing sides unpredictably when I least expected and taking temporary control of my ship.

Ian stood nearby, saying my name again and again, trying to draw my attention away from this symbol that had turned him from inseparable best friend to redundant, external, yet acceptable thing among many in "the world." He watched my eyes fixed upon the light like a moth to a flame. He watched obsession eat my soul as autopilot sought a futile misperception of "freedom" in solving an unsolvable paradox.

It was in this moment that escape from all known troubles seemed to lie only in solving the puzzle of this color, as though if I could find that key I would feel assured that I could find anything—even the key to all the concepts that remained ungrasped and all the experiences unattainable and all the connections unmade.

He called my name. I swung around to glare at him like he was some kind of last-minute obstacle to entering through the gates to heaven.

To say he looked at me would be misleading, for in such a high-pitched buzz state there is no me and, yet, no one else either; too far over the edge of mania, I would become the buzz itself.

It didn't matter if a buzz involved compulsively regurgitating some stored academic hoo-ha, finishing the tracing of an interrupted pattern, or melding with a pink streetlight. They were all essentially the same dynamics. The road to compulsion was a dangerous one in which you lost yourself. In the total attainment of the compulsion, there is no self left to reason with. The world was full of heebie-jeebie "spiritualistic" types who'd have given the world for a taste of this "attainment." Free of the grip of such a state, I'd have given the world to be rid of it.

For the purpose of expressing in "the world" language (which defies conveying this reality accurately), I shall say that "I" looked at this person who was Ian. "I" felt a wildness. My soul was screaming and my eyes flashed manically.

"Come on, Donna," said Ian, "the restaurant is just over here." I was standing at the gates of eternal bliss, for at the edge of nothingness the "disappearing" seems almost always a "forever" and here was this someone yabbering at me about a restaurant. And yet within, this someone's efforts stirred the part that wanted to stay "being there in the world." This was the part that strained for mental images within the intrusive words flooding from this someone's mouth into my ears. This was the part that searched this someone's eyes for something to make it care enough to turn from oblivion and clutch awareness.

I no longer grasped the concept of food or hunger or my own body beyond the theoretical dictionary definitions, which now seemed empty and personally irrelevant, countless leagues away. Ian's words fell upon meaning-deaf ears.

"Who is this?" said Ian urgently, pointing to himself, his eyes big and almost panicking—a child left on the doorstep of a children's home. I looked blankly at this person. There was no rejection but nor was there interest. Everything was irrelevant and even "irrelevance" was a non-concept.

"Who am I?" he repeated. I looked deeply into his eyes with no "I" within me with which to know me in relation to him. I knew in theory that I could have looked for words and found blurtable answers but that all seemed so far away. Ian was effectively talking to a sleepwalker in a state where "the world" was redundant. My eyes felt like the flames of a raging fire as I fought back against the impulse to "become" the pink streetlight. "Ian," I blurted, speaking the mental words and turning back to the light.

The anxiety was climbing and the light no longer made me ticklish all over as the impulses within me were now at war with each other. I swung between "worlds" like the sped-up pendulum of an unbalanced clock. The sensory tickle I was addicted to was turning spasmodically to a pain I could not escape. "It hurts," I blurted out loud, before the next rush. "It hurts."

"Look at me," said Ian gently, "who is this?" "Ian," I replied, searching for the meaning of the word I merely knew fitted the picture but didn't know why. "Who is Ian?" said Ian. I picked up his hand and looked at it closely. I traced it with my eyes from the fingers to the shoulder, from the shoulder to the eyes, down to the nose and mouth. Ian was a jigsaw of bits that my mind was in no state to make sense of as a whole. I put his hand to my face and smelled it: familiarity. Ian put his head down holding strands of hair up. I touched the wispy strands and smelled: familiarity. "Ian's hair," I exclaimed; my manic face crumbled as my soul hit the ground like a rocket returned suddenly from the moon. I put my hand to Ian's face and covered it. "Familiar," I said. That was who Ian was. Ian was Familiar.

Ian and I sat quietly in the living room of the cottage. It was late, about one o'clock in the morning. The TV was going blah-blah, breaking at regular intervals into predictable commercials with their familiar jingles: "Mr. Muscle loves the jobs you hate," "Jif Micro liquid, where are you?"

The heavy sound of metal against wood made us both jump as the cast-iron knocker hit the door with a sudden "whack" and we heard the sound of footsteps running away. Willie, the character I hid behind when I needed to challenge the world, jumped straight out of the chair and bounded across the room, opening the door and bounding out into the street with the fluidity of a single move. Mentally, I was still sitting on the chair even though my body was well out of the door pursuing a cause I was only now beginning to fathom. A real life sit-com reply had been triggered and Willie was playing his part on cue before I'd even had time to work out what was happening or what to do about it.

Robyn and I ran about the flats in the darkness as I knocked on doors and ran away. It was something I'd learned from other kids some years before and I'd figured it was a game that was part of friendship. It was a game that I knew and I was sharing it with Robyn.

A woman kept answering one of the doors I knocked at. She was wild and animated and shouted and stormed about when I knocked and ran. This woman's reaction created a stir in Robyn and the hype of it all make me knock on this woman's door all the more. Night after night, it was becoming a ritual.

I went out to knock as usual. This time, the woman chased me and caught me. She threw my body about in her grasp and shouted words in my face. Her words were full of hate and full of "shouldn'ts." It was clear that she was telling me that what I did was very very wrong. Robyn told the woman we were sorry. The game ended there and was never played again.

Ian ran after Willie, who was oblivious to all but the cause—an unstoppable 3-D video on fast-forward. People aren't meant to knock on doors and run away. People should know they did the wrong thing and be stopped.

By now, my body was around the corner and behind a derelict shop in a street full of tumbledown fences. Willie stood there with a hard chiseled expression and a stony stance, poised for violence. "They're in here," shouted Willie in a broad, tough Australian accent, a voice with the power and force of a verbal bull terrier, undeniably masculine. "They're hiding in here," he shouted. "I can see them. They haven't even got the guts to come out and face us," he went on loudly, sounding like something from a gritty western.

Two people in their early twenties emerged from the shadows like a pair of rats from the gutter. Briskly, they marched out from the yard at the rear of the shop, and walked straight up the road without looking back or acknowledging Willie's challenge. Willie was silent. They'd paid their price in humiliation. Society's rule book was safe. Willie, having fulfilled the role, had politely disappeared. I stood there shaking, like a someone watching myself in an unstoppable dream until I'd suddenly had the cold water of realization thrown on me.

Back at the cottage, safe inside the front door again, anxiety broke through and took the reins of my runaway horse. I stood there, five foot two and a half inches, little more than a hundred pounds. Willie was a giant who had challenged a pair of unknown yahoos from out of a derelict premises in a dark and deserted side street. My heart was racing.

"So that was Willie," said Ian. I felt ashamed. I had had no choice in what had happened. No decision had been made. There was no awareness. Everything had simply been triggered. I felt like a puppet. "That was Willie," I echoed.

— ◄

My masks for the world were the tough-talking Willie and the flirtatious, compliant Carol, who borrowed her vocabulary from sit-coms to make herself liked. These "faces" were triggered in certain situations but it had been my choice not to fight them. I was now trying to control the overload that triggered the shifts and to respond to the world as myself, not as these "faces." Ian had his own triggered masks. If he could expose them to himself and to me, perhaps he could control them and reclaim his life. "Name your images," I told Ian, "name them to yourself or symbolize them with something; a name, a shape or color, anything."

Ian and I sat down on the floor in the bedroom in front of boxes and albums of old photographs. Ian had wanted to see how far back his own "faces" had gone. He wanted to see where each "face" began and ended and where and when he had started hiding and left himself behind in the shadows.

Ian went through his photos, taking some out: a photo of a baby turned side-on staring expressionlessly into space as the mother tickled it; another of an infant sitting with its sister, the sister, smiling and animated in contrast to the doll-like infant next to her.

In his older photos, a three-year-old looked as strikingly solemn in one photo as it did manic in another and distracted in the next. In another photo, crowds of people focused on the photographer, the surroundings and one another, while Ian looked alone in the crowd, as though no one and nothing else mattered or perhaps made enough sense to matter.

There were photos of a four-year-old with a crumpled brow, unsure smile, and eyes that seemed to defy the camera; one eye obedient, the other not. A photo of a five-year-old, by contrast, showed a forced square grimace and the eye obedient now but dead, the body surrounded by "friends" at a birthday party that was expected to be "fun."

The five-year-old's grimace withered gradually into a six-year-old's closed broad smile, as though the old one was erased and the new one drawn on. The head was cocked to the side. Was this another legacy of sit-com TV? The smile gradually softened over the years; seven, eight, nine.

Then something else seemed to appear. A much harder face emerged gradually from the scattered photos: tougher, bolder, forced, and manic and then replaced again with an impression of "outgoing," but with the eyes dead. The caricatures were almost too easily categorized. We sat before individual piles of what now appeared to be the distinct lives of five different characters. Each had his own version of "happy," or "sad," or "angry," or "close" and each version was almost chillingly distinct from its cousins.

A further pattern emerged and a transition could be seen from one to the next, each "face" used in relatively distinct social situations. Two characters seemed to dominate.

What I was seeing was too close to what I'd battled with in my own life. The realization provoked an equally strong need to run and a need to stay. Though I had known Ian was "like me" and seen his "faces" in transient glimpses, the photographs were like a stain I could not wipe away or overlook, a stain that reminded me of the dangerous side of characters and their unpredictability.

Awareness was the key to getting control over his "faces." Ian's was a life where time was a disconnected scramble and sleep was plagued with teeth-grinding nightmares of all the things he might have done in the black holes of time lost.

Had he robbed a bank? Had he hurt someone? Being constantly triggered by others, with little time to process, let alone identify with his own actions, Ian had little idea of what he'd done in any day. He wanted an end to other people pushing the buttons for him. Identifying, understanding, and gaining ownership of his characters, he hoped, would be the beginning of his holding the remote control of his own broken TV set.

Ian taped the photos from each of the categories onto five large boards. Each board looked like a distinctly different person. Each board depicted a different "face" and spanned childhood and adulthood and a range of "emotions."

Ian looked at each of his "faces" and named them. Richard the perfectionist, domineering, bossy, opinionated, and managerial, was named after a sleazy salesman Ian once knew. Nigel the comedian, appearing laid-back and cool, was named after a race car driver. Chris embodied the stored role of the romantic and lover. Homeboy was the family face and "darling son" of "loving Dad." Simon, crumbling, unstable, melodramatic and victimlike, was named after someone Ian had known whom "the world" bit off, chewed up, and spat out.

Ian wrote out a list for each of these faces. He described their stances, voice, likes, dislikes, friends, principles, goals, strong points, weak points, the situations they appeared in, philosophy on life, and every other identifying feature he could find. Finally, he could begin to see where they overlapped and to see what was "missing" in the makeup of each so that it was necessary to create (allow) each one in the first place.

I challenged him to privately, deliberately imitate each one if only for a few moments each day. It would give him a sense of control over them as "performances," making them voluntarily retrieved rather than involuntarily triggered. I felt that voluntarily imitating them at will would help him to understand how they appeared to other people and to consciously experience what *he* thought and felt in response to each one (for better or for worse). I felt it would help him to choose which bits of these characters that he could accept as parts of the real Ian—who would one day be the only Ian. I felt it would make it easier to eventually disregard those he didn't like, because they would slowly go from being alternate personalities to deliberate acts and Ian could take control of choosing whether or not to perform them, to be on the stage of life or not.

"I know *you,*" I told him in writing the next day. "I have also seen glimpses of all the others. I know where the you begins and ends. I know you will end up integrating bits of various other images. I want you to know that my friendship for you will not change because of this. It will just grow with it. This means you don't have to be anyone with me except for who you are and who you will be."

Ian's knowing who he was and who he wasn't was one thing. Letting anyone else know was another thing altogether. His father would still sit down next to Homeboy and squeeze his hand, playing the part of "loving Dad" as Homeboy played the part of "loving son," expressing feelings he didn't have but knew he was supposed to, to a man he felt torn between understanding, being indifferent to, and feeling threatened and pressured by.

Dissociated from his body and emotions, Ian went through the ritual scenarios, like playing a part in his own TV show. Ian's father seemed equally on automatic pilot, running an endless series of what seemed so clearly stored repertoires. Someone this far in the closet wasn't going to budge an inch and Ian knew it. To challenge the exposure of his son would be to challenge the exposure of himself. As far as Ian's father was concerned, there was nothing wrong with his son. He'd have noticed, wouldn't he?

It's hard to notice much when your body and mouth are on automatic pilot, your emotions are on the run, and your soul is in the closet hiding in the shadows. "Yeah, yeah, normal, right."

Ian would drive to his father's house and collect the perfectly ironed shirts with the creases running just so, the way his father had ironed them. It was a smooth household—somehow too smooth. Everything "as it should be" right down to the "tatty-bye," always exactly the same wave from exactly the same place at exactly the same window. It seemed like life in a vacuum: people expressing without self-expression. Real life has wants and likes and interests that just don't slide along so smoothly within the rigid boundaries of "should be." Though undiagnosed, Ian had already come to the conclusion that he had Asperger syndrome (a developmental social communication disorder related to autism), and that it was genetic in his case. Yet there was no way his father would ever bring this up, even if Ian felt it needed to be. Ian had raised the subject in a sort of "between the TV commercials" manner and it was discussed briefly and casually and impersonally with a weather-report feel to it. The topic just wasn't on the "should be" list.

Nigel found it difficult to get off to work but would bounce through the door and play "buddies" with all the people who scared, threatened, or overloaded Ian to the point of dissociation. He would play music demonstrations, just like he'd been taught to play for family entertainment, and engage the interest of "friends." He would eat packets of biscuits, drink Cokes, and smoke cigarettes. Behind Nigel, it didn't matter if Ian couldn't fluently understand speech as other noises competed on an equal level with words.

Richard set out to work like a robot programmed with a disk labeled workaholic manager. He did the accounting and ordering and handled difficult customers, drank coffee and hardly ate at all. Between the two of them, they were killing Ian, who was over six feet tall and fast on the way to anorexia with an autoimmune system on red alert.

At the end of the workday, with no wants, interests, or likes coming from himself, Ian's "faces" dove headlong into more of the same. Ian's body went to work from 8:30 A.M. to an extended day of 9 or 10 P.M. on a commission-based salary of 5 percent of sales. Though there were rarely any sales after 5:30, Ian's body went to work double-time. It was a way of avoiding something much worse: being real and facing up to having social communication difficulties with no idea of the solutions. His bosses rewarded his "enthusiasm" with chummy shit-stirring and asking him for more "favors." "Sure," Nigel would say, smiling. "Not a problem," Richard would say firmly, each of them giving away a life he didn't own.

Each night after work, Ian would return to the cottage. He'd knock at the door like some dejected stray, never using his key. I'd open the door to him, his eyes like the pits of a man with no soul on the run from a compulsive enemy that had worked him like a slave all day. This was the price he paid each day for being unable to manage the diversions of his own fear. He'd come in like something returned from the war, just to go off to it again the next day. At least he didn't have to come home as Chris anymore, to play the part of domestic prostitute.

It was hard for me to watch Ian still living the same kind of life that I had escaped. Somehow it was as though destiny had brought this to my door. For my first twenty-six years, I had had trouble experiencing my life because I'd been too busy performing it to feel or be aware of any of it beyond disjointed fragments. Watching Ian's life did what reading the manuscript of my first autobiography had done. It joined it all together and put it right in my lap, so that I could experience it all as a whole from the position of onlooker.

— ◣

Eating at restaurants was one of Ian's routines. Not being able to cope with nightclubs and parties, he had found that going to restaurants was the easiest way to be social with the women in his life. When you had your mouth full, you didn't have to talk or be interested or curious or amused or anything else you weren't motivated to be or do. When food-talk was exhausted, there were certainly enough restaurant scenes from television to do an endless series of reruns.

I was glad that nightclubs and parties were no longer on the agenda, but was unable to tell Ian just how hard restaurants were for me. I would mention the time and that we should eat. Ian would mention a restaurant. Next thing, we were going there.

Ian would order what he'd learned to order, order what I was having, or ask me or the waiter to pick something for him. The waiter would ask him if he wanted a drink. Ian would assume he wanted "what men in restaurants always want to drink"—lager-top—and would go into his ever-the-same word-and-action demonstration of how much beer and lemonade. It was like watching a computer program set to run when the waiter pressed the "would you like a drink" button.

I would order what my food allergies allowed me to have and what I'd learned was good for me, which usually didn't leave much choice.

We would sit there uncomfortably with grimacelike smiles, eating food that we had no personal idea whether we liked or not. We could describe its taste, even though half the time that description was a theoretical regurgitation of how we'd been told something tasted. We could describe its theoretical likability based on stored information of "what people like," "what they like it with," and "how they like it cooked," but no judgments came from our selves. Occasionally, Ian would ask, "Do you like that?" or "Is it okay?" Knowing I was supposed to feel something for the experience, I'd mousily reply, "It's okay." If it wasn't making me vomit, I guess, in a way, it was okay.

More and more, Ian noticed me moving away from the waiters and waitresses as they fluffed about trying to put napkins on my lap, push my chair in, or put knives and forks on the table. More and more, I noticed Ian unable to notice what he was eating or understand what I said to him with all the background noise, music, movement, lights, and smells competing for his attention.

Slowly, we began to talk about it: about the lights, the noise, the proximity of the other tables, the movement of the body parts around us. One week we would move the table away from the other tables and our bodies would relax and we'd breathe more. Another week, we would have the light turned off next to our table and we'd stop squinting, mapping everything out, and being so compulsively symmetrical. A third week, we would have the roar of the air conditioner extinguished and we'd notice what we were eating, chew it and explore its taste, and understand each other's words as we spoke between mouthfuls. During another visit, we'd have the music turned down. All this was new to Ian who, like me, had spent a whole life dissociating on almost every level rather than working out how to change things. Now, after twenty-five years, he was daring the exposure of harmlessly asking "the world" to alter itself, for the moments we were there, enough to have a whole experience of something as simple as a meal.

One day, the noise was too loud for him. He took cotton wool out of his pocket and put it in his ears, able to relax again. The texture was awful but the mental relief was great. We paid the cashier, who talked too fast for either of us to make much sense of. "Can you speak slowly, please?" said Ian. "We have a communication disability." Ian was on the road to reclaiming what was his: a life.

━ ◄

"I'm coming over" said Mr. Dawson on the phone. "I'll be bringing Alex with me. Is that okay?" "Yes," I replied automatically as usual, having only half understood the words. Unless someone gave me an explicit choice—"Do you want to do this *or not?*"—I usually felt compelled to go along, not understanding that I in fact had a choice. "Mr. Dawson's coming over," I said to Ian after I got off the phone. "He's bringing Alex with him."

The Dawsons lived only fifteen minutes from us and I had met them when I'd initially come to the United Kingdom to promote the first book. They'd heard about me and wondered if I'd meet them and their son, Alex, a big, bouncy, blond teenage puppy who had autism.

Mr. Dawson was a big tall man who was a warm but rigid person beneath an easygoing façade, but humorous and so eager to please and be helpful that he seemed to hand his life about on a serving tray. Mrs. Dawson had soft edges, was quiet and painfully shy but with a very strong will and endurance. They were nice, lighthearted, down-to-earth, nonusing people. Despite their eagerness to ask me an encyclopedia's worth of questions, they had tried to let me simply be. When I was looking for a home in the U.K., Mrs. Dawson had found the cottage where Ian and I now lived.

Ian had never met Alex but he had read his faxes to me. Alex's writing was typed via a method called facilitated communication, in which he received physical assistance in order to type. His writing was almost overwhelmingly deep, sweepingly poetic, and shatteringly real—the words of a teenager and a genius trapped in the straitjacket of autism.

Ian had been touched and awed by Alex's letters. Gradually, Alex's faxes were sent as much to Ian as to me. Ian had found one person, beyond me, with whom he dared to be himself—with whom, in fact, he dared not be anything much but his real self.

Ian and Alex stood on opposite sides of the fence. Ian had a lifetime of compliant façades that made him appear high functioning and near "normal"—at the cost of his own realness. Alex had a lifetime of labels and special schools because he could not comply and instead lived with the almost unbearable vulnerability of being so rawly himself. Ian had spent his whole life pushed to refine the art of "seem." Alex had spent his entire life fighting off cheap expectations, fighting instead to refine his ability to "be" despite appearances. To have looked at each other may have been each one's greatest nightmare: one might see the death of self that came with "the world" success, the other would see the shattering depth of self that came with being real at the cost of being thought "a failure."

At the prospect of Alex's visit to our cottage, Ian's walls went up. The more I knocked Ian's walls down, the more I saw that Ian was in the grip of a severe panic attack at the thought that realness would knock on his door and stare him in the face. Closer and closer, his huddled mass edged itself tightly into the corner of the bedroom trembling almost convulsively, his eyes full of tears. He was pleading with me not to let Alex in as though he were an antelope in a zoo and I was the zookeeper about to put a lion into his cage. I promised him I would keep him safe. I would tell the Dawsons they couldn't see him because he wasn't well.

Perhaps it was the fear of seeing himself reflected in Alex that was filling Ian with dread. It is a scary thing to look into the mirror of one's own fear.

Alex's own list of fears was endless. I had asked him to write them down, to get to know them and plan to challenge each one. A partial list he'd once written included the following:

- Frightened, except automatically, autism is certainly, myself, not the person I wish to be.
- Frightened to friends trust.
- Frightened, always, questions to answer and ask.
- Frightened to information, also to decide to learn and share with friends.
- Frightened to ascertain help from friends.
- Frightened, too, to people be with.
- Frightened to care about anything.
- Frightened to care about anyone.
- Frightened to have feelings.
- Frightened to a true self be.

The knock came. "Yes," I promised Ian, "no one will come through the bedroom door." I reassured Ian that the bedroom door would not be opened and that he was safe in there in his cage.

Alex's large hefty presence entered with his father and tore loose to explore "Donna's house," as he had once or twice before when Ian wasn't there. From the bedroom, Ian, huddled in his corner, heard him. Alex tried the bedroom door. I stopped him and eventually Alex and his father left.

After they'd gone, I opened the bedroom door. With his eyes huge and bulging, his body shaking uncontrollably, Ian looked like a sparrow with a cat in the house.

— ◂

We had an appointment in London. "Do you want to meet Olivier?" I asked Ian. He didn't know. Nor did Olivier know if he wanted to meet Ian. I decided for the both of them.

We met at Olivier's hotel. The two of them, each as quiet as the other, said nothing. Me, no master of handling social triangles, opted out, walking along in my own company on the fringes of theirs. Ian picked some lavender. Olivier smelled it. Olivier crumbled an autumn leaf by his ear. Ian found one and did the same, sharing in the experience.

We all went to the park. Trees hung over us and pathways snaked around us in every direction. Leaves rustled, squirrels scampered. Olivier walked off ahead, I walked on my own. Ian followed both of us, deeper and deeper into the park.

Olivier met a squirrel who jumped out at him; his tall willowy frame folded gently down to meet it with a pocket full of peanuts. As he chattered away to the squirrel, we disappeared from Olivier's mono world.

Ian and I stood surrounded by the squirrel's compatriots, yet aware of each other's company, to the squirrels' exclusion—a sign of things to come.

Olivier walked on toward the gardens. Lines of shrubs sprawled out before us in grand uniformity as we three stood on the head of the steps, like royalty at the gates of the realm of Symmetry and Order.

We descended in a flowing silence past the rows of shrubs in green, rust, and gold before turning the corner around a wall.

Colors exploded at us. Big lions' heads with shaggy velvet manes of pink, red, yellow, and peach called us to ruffle and nuzzle the tall and wild flowers. This was Olivier's favorite place.

Olivier sat quietly on his own on a bench as Ian and I faded further and further into an external "us" as we raced from flower to flower like oversized bees among four- to five-foot-tall plants. I squealed with delight at each new discovery. Ian nuzzled and touched, at one with the plants. Around forty plants later, we looked up, remembering Olivier, who remained on the bench silent and almost motionless. A nameless cloud washed over us.

We walked on in silence past a rose garden, its smells calling us back to a world of equal sensory delight. Olivier walked ahead of us both, somber, as though he led a funeral procession for an unnamed corpse.

Around a corner, we passed under an archway that led to a tunnel, like the tunnel Olivier and I had shared in the days before I had met Ian—in days when I had been Olivier's mirror and he my comrade in a world where all others were laughably external. Olivier turned sharply around. "Our tunnel," he announced out loud with a steely secrecy. I walked along guiltily thinking, oil and water, oil and water.

Three is an awkward number, lacking in symmetry and swing. People make the oddest of all triangles. With three, there are either triangles or sandwiches. I was feeling rather sandwichy.

"I have to go back to work," said Olivier. A silent, allergic sentence hung on the air, a feeling of "you two can return now to your sacred 'us.' " And yet, we'd had no "us" until then. We were just two people who spent all our time together. We'd never seen our "two" because we had never seen it enfolded within a "three": oil and water, oil and water.

Olivier became an ever more distant shadow. I knew that one had to move beyond having a mirror. I just hoped he'd find another albatross like himself to take the mirror's place.

＞　＜

A letter came from an organization on the Welsh-English border called B.I.R.D., which stood for Brain Injury Rehabilitation and Development. This group had helped many children with learning difficulties, cerebral palsy, autism, hyperactivity, and other brain-damage-related disabilities. The letter was from Sue, a woman with a background in pediatric nursing who worked at the center with people with all sorts of developmental disorders. She had read *Nobody Nowhere* and felt we could learn from each other. She had sent a pile of professional gobbledygook, among which were references to something called infantile reflexes and their connection to learning difficulties and other developmental disabilities. She invited us to visit.

For some reason, this was one of the offers we took up and we packed the car for the long trip from Essex to Wales.

The center was clinical and dentistlike but I had wanted to come here in case they had answers—not about what was called autism in general, but about the pile of sensory, perceptual, cognitive, emotional, and metabolic parts it was made up of in my case.

Sue was a finch who looked at me in flitting glances which, though short, were intense and piercing. Her movements were few and deliberate, but staccato; her voice was sure, despite the brittleness as she sat opposite me, perched on the edge of her chair looking doctorish.

Ian sat in the corner, curled in toward the window, intensely fixed upon some detail into which he progressively disappeared as he tuned out the blah-blah and the compelling mathematics of the multicolored patterned carpet.

My perceptions through sight, sound, and touch didn't seem incomprehensible or surprising to Sue, even if hearing them verbalized did. Most of them came down to recognizable faults where my brain had strayed off its developmental tracks or different parts of my brain hadn't gotten to know their neighbors or weren't on speaking terms.

Sue felt sure that I still had infantile reflexes; these should have been inhibited pre-birth and in infancy to make way for the development of new ones. She thought that I had learned to compensate for what didn't happen right, and that this put everything else out of sync and things had snowballed from there. It sounded feasible, but more than that, if she was right, it was an indication of something I had always felt but never been sure of. It would indicate that things had gone wrong before anyone ever laid a hand on me, that nobody's behavior had caused my difficulties.

Sue wanted to do some tests and also asked permission to touch me. It is hard to have someone touch you when you can't make proper consistent sense of where all your parts are or where you and the room and other people begin and end, but I wanted to know. I needed to know for my past, for my present, and for the direction of my future.

If I gave in to unwanted touch, either I could cut myself off from what was happening and from connection with my body, selfhood, and emotions, or I could go through all of this as myself in a state that would push me close to overload. I would need Ian's help to handle what was going to happen with a "me" intact. Ian got down onto my level like someone on my side of the war, forced to cooperate with the enemy. He held my gaze as my body shook and convulsed as this stranger manipulated my limbs and tested my reflexes.

Sue did a series of reflex tests, designed to see how my different body parts speak or don't speak to one another.

What she found was that as far as my brain was concerned, I was cut up into quarters. One of my quarters had developed "normally" and showed that I had inhibited the old infantile reflexes and developed in their place the ones that would carry me to adulthood.

Two of the other quarters showed signs of partial inhibition of some of these reflexes; the last quarter showed signs that the original infantile reflexes were still there in full force.

Sue explained the original purposes of each of the infantile reflexes still present. I asked when these various infantile reflexes were meant to have been inhibited and replaced naturally with more advanced reflexes. Some were meant to have been abandoned at around ten months of age. Others were present that were meant to have left by the time I was born. For instance, on one side of my body was an uninhibited, pre-birth, infantile hip reflex that had to do with wriggling out of the womb. On the other hip I had, at nearly thirty years of age, almost outgrown this and developed normal reflexes in its place.

It was as though I was only half born. I realized that this feeling, which threaded itself through emotion and mind, had probably originated in body. I also realized that no amount of harsh words or brutal behavior had caused the first slips from the rails of my development.

— —

Ian and I headed up country in the car. Ian had already begun to come to terms with why he was "like me" but his defenses still held on to the myth that they were "normal." And so they appeared to be—as long as no one got too close and as long as they could control the movements of everyone in his life, so that no two situations blended or merged and people from no two separate situations compared notes. Mirrors need no insight.

Until he had met me, the circle of people around Ian had cushioned an allergy to insight. The people around him never questioned that "to seem" was the same as "to be"; that had suited everyone.

We arrived at an autistic community to which we'd been invited and were shown around. It was a big country property with houses that had about six people in each. Here they worked, made things, and lived out of reach of a community where tolerance of "difference" is too often at the mercy of ignorance.

Samantha came down the stairs as Ian and I entered the house. She had never seen or heard of us in her life. She took me by the hand and led me to her room. "Do you want to see my things?" she asked with a plastic "adoptable" smile. She seemed to be "playing Carol" and was "jumping out of the cupboard before anyone opened the door."

> "Would you like to see Donna's room?" the visitors were asked without the option of choice. The visitors climbed the stairs to the attic and they were given the tour: the chandeliers, the dolls, the coordinated purple decor, the wardrobe full of "pretty" clothes, and wall-to-wall mirrors. The visitors looked out at the view of the city in the distance. They were so impressed that they never seemed to notice they were looking out through bars. They never noticed the dolls were all perfectly dressed without a hair out of place or that the room was impeccably neat, too neat for a lived-in child's room. Carol sat on the bed with a plastic smile on her face. "What a lucky girl you are," a voice had said, like so many other voices who'd taken the tour, "all those dolls and lovely clothes."

The jump-out-of-the-cupboard-before-they-open-the-door strategy had been a means of combating surprise, exposure, and invasion. It works the same as the salesperson who meets you at the entrance to the shop with a handshake. You are disarmed. If people were going to try to get you to massage their egos and show them they were special by making you speak to them, you could save yourself the defeat by storming into the room and yabbering at them before they had the chance. Nine times out of ten you'd have them trying to get under the table faster than you were.

Tony crept around the hallways behind us like a shadow as we went from room to room. When we looked at him, he suddenly found an intense desire to study marks on the wall and ceiling. He seemed to be a social person trapped in an asocial body.

Jeffrey approached us cautiously, head cocked to the side. "Are you a tarantula?" he riddled, crawling his hand over Ian, who seemed somewhere between freezing and bolting. "Or an airplane?" He seemed pleased with himself, as if he were the manager of an exclusive club where only those who spoke his special language were members. Were we people who creeped and crawled invasively with unwelcome touch? Or were we evasive, flying away, disappearing, or hiding like him?

Carl sat under a tree alone. Ian stood stock-still looking at him. Ian had never seen anyone who sat as he did: his knees in front of him, his calves splayed out to either side, perpendicular to his thighs, like some hinged foldaway picnic table.

"Feel free to wander around," said the woman who managed the place. Ian and I wandered down to the craft center.

A big dark giant approached me and put his hands gently on my shoulders as he leaned forward and stared intently, but gently, into my eyes. I felt his warmth and his realness and I guess he was looking for mine.

A worker approached us. "Say hello, Cleo," said the woman in the sort of irritating patronizing singsong you sometimes hear from teachers working in special education. Cleo's eyes grew wide and manic, a plastic push-button smile sprang instantly across his face. "Hello," came the robotic words booming from his mouth. The worker, having done her job, walked away. The smile left along with the performance and so did Cleo.

He walked over to Ian and put a hand on his shoulder. Ian put one of his own hands on Cleo's shoulder and they searched each other's eyes in silence. The worker bounded over again like some vigilante with a save-the-world-martyr purpose. "Say hello," she prodded Cleo as he stood with Ian. Cleo jumped away from Ian and the same manic smile sprang to his face. "Hello, how are you?" came the robotic, though animated, words just as before. He waited for no answer. Performances don't need answers unless they, too, are in the learned script. The worker took Cleo's hand and led him into the craft room like a pup on a leash.

I saw some paint on the light switch. Feeling out of control, I felt compelled to even it up. "Leave the light alone," came the voice of one of the workers there. When she realized I wasn't turning it off after all, her voice changed. "Oh, you *like* light switches," she said as though speaking to a very small child. "We have other light switches."

Ian and I walked to the other side of the room. "No misunderstanding, no misinterpretation, no misunderstanding, no misinterpretation," a man repeated. He was talking to everyone and no one at an ever increasing, anxious, increasingly unintelligible pace, though to others he probably looked like he was talking to himself. He came over to where we were standing and finally fell silent.

Cleo approached us and stood silently in Ian's company. Another worker came over. "Say hello," she prodded Cleo. "He's already said hello in *his own way*," said Ian, fed up with the same robot-training theatrics he'd seen enough of in his own life. The first worker bounded over to join us. "We encourage them here to be polite," she said authoritatively. "You want to be polite, don't you, Cleo?" she said at Cleo.

Cleo stood like a stunned child in the center of a domestic dispute. The noise from the others in the room grew restless. The room felt like a cage full of birds with a cat in it. Ian explained his views on treating people as puppets. The woman reached out and took hold of Cleo's chin with her hand. She waggled it from left to right as though he was a toy. "He doesn't understand anything, though, do you, Cleo?" she said in that sickening singsong, as though she was speaking to a plant. Even in this place that was meant to be a haven, there were corners of perversity, arrogance, and ignorance.

Ian and I felt bad and went to leave. A woman with autism made a beeline for the door. On her way, without looking at me, she reached out and patted me gently on the shoulder. Her silence spoke so loudly.

Ian and I took a room at a nearby hotel for the night. The manager of the community had phoned ahead for us. "Yes, this is the way to the room," said the woman slowly, showing us up the stairs. The phone rang out in the corridor. "Excuse me," said the woman.

"We've got two *disabled* people staying with us," she said into the phone in a gossipy loud whisper. She pronounced the word "disabled" in the manner some people use when speaking about things to do with sex organs. Ian and I looked at each other. "Disabled people," we whispered jokingly.

— ⸺

Among the children with autism I had met a year before was a pretty little seven-year-old called Lucy.

Lucy had make-believe friends, but they were not friends with whom she played. Instead, she became them. She had told her mother some of their names, as well as some signs by which she would be able to tell if Lucy was one or the other.

Lucy and her mother had an interesting relationship. It was like they were sisters, as though the mother was in some ways just a big version of Lucy and each of them knew it.

There was something else, something different about their relationship. It looked as if the person with the control wasn't the mother, but Lucy. It felt as though some sort of spell existed between them and the power to make or break it was in Lucy's hands, as though Lucy wrote her mother's script.

Lucy seemed, on the surface, more verbal than a lot of able children with autism and more emotionally expressive. She pouted, giggled, skipped, and smiled enough, so that people who didn't know her well thought she couldn't be autistic at all and scoffed at her mother's seemingly ludicrous insistence that there was something "wrong" with her.

I was invited to a birthday party for a six-year-old boy with Asperger syndrome, a high-functioning, mild condition related to autism. Some of the children there had autism and some did not; they were all equally noisy and quiet, equally animated and reserved.

The children were seated in front of a small stage for a puppet show. As the curtains parted, Lucy was there in the audience along with the other children, staring straight ahead at the puppet show before her. At the sound of other children's laughter, she would laugh on cue with a barely noticeable delay. This was an impressive instance of echolalia, her laughter triggered automatically by the sounds of the other children's. Nothing registered in her eyes, no puzzlement, no interest, no amusement. The smile on her face seemed disconnected, pulled by invisible, mentally programmed strings.

Once the paid puppet show was over, the children played with toy bikes and cars, which they pushed about and rode around the interior of the large hall. Lucy ran along behind a toddler's plastic ride-in car. Smiling and squealing on cue to the sounds of the other children, her eyes were frozen and expressionless. They looked straight ahead as she pushed the car around with no apparent sense of where the other children were around her, nor any sign that she knew why she was doing it.

"Lucy's having fun," I heard someone nearby remark casually, chalking up some points for the autism success-story files. Lucy's mother ignored the remark, looking doubtful. For that moment, it felt as though only she and I had any real idea of what a difference there was between "to appear" and "to be."

Lucy went to a regular school and had "made friends." Despite the fact she was constantly called mad or weird, some of the children apparently found her funny or interesting. Seeing her flash from one character to another, her voice, stance, and facial expression changing repertoires like a television with a dodgy remote control, I felt that anyone who "made friends" with "Lucy" had really made friends with the TV programs and other people she'd gathered these patchworks from.

———

I invited Lucy's mother to bring Lucy to visit where I lived. She seemed relieved that someone acknowledged what she already knew: that the child people saw was not Lucy and that Lucy was by now, at the age of seven, so many people that she was hardly ever herself anymore. I could see it scared her mother, and I guessed that some of what scared her was that she had a feeling the same thing had happened in herself. It was clear that Lucy's mother could function, but she confided that she was just now starting to find inner feelings and get a glimpse of a stranger inside her who she suspected might be her own real self.

Outside of the train station, Lucy greeted me with a practiced greeting that would almost have got her a part on a cheap American sit-com as somebody's "adorable" child. Then, with a sort of suddenness, she showed the indifference toward me that, I felt sure, she had had all along. Skipping away from us, talking to herself in a collection of voices, perhaps she thought that her façade had disarmed me as it had others. Perhaps she thought that was all anybody was doing—going through the motions using stored repertoires.

As we walked around a park, over hills and around trees, I confronted Lucy a few times and got a different face, different movements, different pace and pitch, a different Lucy every time: one comically firm and formal, one sugary sweet and sickly, one cartoonlike and bouncy, one wispy and aloof.

"Do you think she has true emotions?" I asked her mother. Emotional problems had, she said, run in her family and she had thought a lot about what she was seeing in Lucy. She could vividly remember the last time she had seen true emotions in her daughter, she told me, as though remembering a funeral where the person was never seen again.

Though Lucy was only seven years old, it had been more than four years ago since she shared real emotions. Her mother remembered how Lucy had seemed terrified of the enormity and incomprehensibility of her own feelings. After that, she had seemed to have closed the door on them. Though she would play "frightened," "concerned," "sad," "happy," or "excited," her mother knew it was an empty act and said she could see that in Lucy's eyes, or see what it was not.

It was very clear that Lucy knew she was meant to feel all sorts of things, and she seemed to take every opportunity to use her mother like a familiar stage prop in what looked like an old melodrama. Lucy had stored "expressions," stored "emotions," stored "conversations," stored "interests," and a stored "sense of humor." With luck, in the absence of emotions to develop any of her own expression or interests, she would at least develop stored "theory-morality." That, at least, would be better than none at all.

As her mother described some of these things, a feeling crawled over me. The mother went on to tell about some of the things that Lucy seemed to find amusing or interesting: for example, an announcement of "Mommy, wouldn't it be funny if we took the cat by the neck and threw it down the stairs?"

> The adult was talking aloud in the presence of a child who seemed never to listen. It was one of so many stories from the woman's childhood. This one was about skipping home cheerfully after seeing her sister hit by a car. She had believed that her sister was dead and had burst boldly into the house and announced to her parents that they could all be happy now because the sister was dead. She was recalling her shock that they hadn't been pleased that one of their daughters was dead.

I could hear a vulnerability and brittleness in Lucy's mother's voice. Then she confirmed what the feeling was telling me: despite understanding her and caring about her, she was afraid of her own small daughter—she was afraid of Lucy.

A sick feeling began inside of me. A feeling like dark rain clouds, the "just around the corner feeling." Lucy reminded me of someone and the picture wasn't nice. Lucy reminded me, for some reason, of an adult monster I had known.

Could amorality or even immorality stand back to back with naïveté? Could a label associated with a kind of saintly naïveté ever be linked with the lack of personal morality of a sociopath or even a sadist? Yet was saintliness not sometimes just a misread inability to comprehend? And if inability to comprehend is merely a difficulty processing information at a simple level, could it be that a milder version of this at a less simple level might show itself in a difficulty processing information for personal signifi- cance or affect? If events have no personal significance or affect, could amorality or immorality occur in the absence of develop- ing stored "theory morals"? In some cases or environments, could a condition related to autism develop an ugly face? I hoped Lucy wouldn't grow up to wear it.

Lucy and her mother caught the train. They were going to come back another time.

I had talked to her mother about keeping a dialogue going with Lucy about her characters, so that Lucy wouldn't lose sight of how it all started and where it all began and ended. I also talked to her about getting Lucy to use her characters as performances instead of using them as substitute selves, so that she wouldn't burn all the bridges to her true self and the potential to salvage her emotions one day. We discussed encouraging outward signs of Lucy's characters to keep them from "going underground" and encouraging the use of costumes and accents, but giving their "performances" designated times and situations. We talked about keeping scrapbooks of the achievements and photos of Lucy's different characters that she could look through when she was older, when the impact of being a patchwork person might hit her hardest. Deep down, my fear was that, without some thread to emotions and identity, compulsion and obsession would be like weeds in fertile soil. As I watched their train leave, inside I whispered to myself, "Please God, no. Don't let there be another one."

Ian arrived home to find me lifeless and haunted. For a few days, I couldn't really get my feelings out. When they did come out, we both decided what not to do. My fear was like a moth to a flame and my life had been driven by such compulsions. I didn't wish Lucy luck, I wished her self, without which she wouldn't need luck. But I wouldn't see Lucy again.

＿ ＿

When Ian had first begun to stay with me, his defenses refused to acknowledge that he lived in the cottage even though he never spent a night anywhere else. To Richard, Nigel, Chris, Homeboy, and Simon, he was just staying over on an extended basis.

Richard was just here because he was "helping." Simon was here because he was being "helped." Chris, who rarely appeared, was here probably because he wasn't in a relationship anywhere else. Homeboy made himself useful and Nigel was just passing through. Making it much easier for them to consider Ian's stay temporary was the fact that, even after several months of sharing a room, Ian was still sleeping on the floor in a sleeping bag, while I slept in the only bed, a ten-pound secondhand bed from the rough-and-ready bargain shop around the corner.

Every morning or evening, Ian's defenses would lead him back to the room he had at his father's house to pick up a newly ironed pair of trousers or a shirt. At other times he would strategically remember that he needed to travel back there, three suburbs away, to shave. It was always because the lighting was better or there was an adapter over there or the mirror was better or there was a wastepaper basket to catch the whiskers over there.

His defenses never acknowledged it had a lot to do with finding excuses to get out of any challenging situation or with confirming that they still had the escape hatch of a push-button life—a life jumping to the well-defined cues of others.

My defenses were just as guilty. They had a vested interest in letting Ian's defenses believe what they wanted to believe. To do otherwise was to give a damn and show Ian he meant something to me. Though they could wave their flags, my defenses weren't very good at backing up their flag waving.

Ian had been sleeping on the floor for almost four months now while he waited, casually, for the arrangements on his new flat to be completed. Finally, our defenses decided to get a pair of single beds. It would be the first new bed and mattress I had had since I was a child.

Our defenses were probably under pressure from us from inside. Although they were our compulsions out of control, they were often subject to our feelings from inside—even if they simplistically misinterpreted emotional discomfort as something like needing to use the toilet. I am sure our defenses would never have wanted Ian and I to be friends, let alone share a room in any permanent way but . . .

We were driving our defenses to compromise in the attainment of our wants, even though our defenses made it a battle to access what our own wants truly were.

Our defenses had decided we could go halves financially on the pair of beds. That way another pair of beds would be bought later, when Ian finally moved into his flat. The significance of the buying of one set would be canceled out by the buying of the other set.

We had no idea of what we wanted, so we bought what we thought was right for an old cottage: wooden, spindly, colonial beds. We also ordered the other set, which we'd pay for once Ian got his flat.

Buying two sets of beds brought Richard out of the uncomfortable position of having received or accepted anything and brought Willie out of the uncomfortable position of the transaction's being anything personal. To them, it was merely a convenient material exchange.

Willie and Richard attempted to play our lives as a chess game. That was how life and friendships had always seemed in those emotionally detached and logical modes—a series of back-and-forth strategic moves.

I slept on my side of the room with Travel Dog, my stuffed toy dog. I lay in bed, flip-flopping like a pancake. Ian slept on his side with Travel Dog's friend, Orsi Bear, sleep-talking in the fluent gobbledygook of verbal dyslexia. Each of us lay in our new-smelling wooden beds with the new-smelling mattresses.

"Good night, Orsi," I said each night. "Good night, Travel," Ian would say every night in reply. "Good night, Ian," I'd go on. "Good night, Donna," Ian would reply. That was about the limit of our ability to converse as ourselves: structured, repetitive, predictable, and routine.

The next morning we'd sometimes look at each other as ourselves for just a moment. Then our defenses would take over like waves over sand. With their plastic expressions and dead eyes, Willie or Richard would find a reason to absent themselves because x, y, or z had to be done. Mornings were difficult, because they were times of disorder, change, and vulnerability as we crept out of the twilight zone of sleep.

We called what we had a "specialship" but we shared our selves with each other only in glimpses; the rest we gluttonized for ourselves, and the other person was either incidental or was significant merely in the reassurance that we were protected. Though we appeared to be doing things together, we were usually speaking in parallel monologues, sharing things with the familiar human-objects that went by our names and giving and taking without realization of significance or awareness of want.

We sneaked time to be ourselves in some lone activity or in a separate room, or to dare the occasional look at each other, as humans, with feelings and self intact. It was not for lack of want. It was for abundance of fear. Fear triggered our defenses beyond our control and imprisoned us within.

The Dawsons had called again. Ian had met Mr. Dawson already. I asked Ian if he now felt ready to meet Alex. He decided he would meet Alex on Alex's territory which, though unfamiliar, Ian and I were both free to escape.

We arrived at the Dawsons' house. Ian sat there in the car waiting to be prompted. I sat waiting for Ian to choose to go of his own accord. There was no way I was going to put myself in the position of a person forcing his defenses' compliance.

Ian's body and face changed and it seemed clear that his defenses, unable to blame me for his compliance in the absence of my prompts, had every intention of having him go into the Dawson's house fully clad in their defensive armor. "Ian," I said calmly but firmly, "you can do this as yourself." His face and body settled back into his real mood rather than the one the defenses had assumed. We got out of the car and, in a mental tug-of-war of who was leading and who following, who was complying and who was being forced and therefore meant to retaliate, we made it the twenty steps to the front door.

Ian and I stood there in a battle of wills regarding who would knock or ring the doorbell. I could see his defenses were by now on the verge of a new tactic, the "you make me do everything and you do nothing" angle. It was a no-win situation because if I knocked I would therefore be the one who had forced him to meet the Dawsons. I waited for him to take the action and went to do it at the same time. We knocked together.

Mr. Dawson answered the front door. Alex was typing, with Mrs. Dawson next to him. He had come a long way with a lot of opposition. He had fought with, bargained with, and challenged his own defenses all the way from pointing at words on a word grid to typing with physical support to now typing with relative independence.

He had gone from meeting expectations about playing with toys at his special school to telling his teachers what they could do with their toys. He had explained how he was not retarded as they assumed from his behavior, and that although they'd been attempting to teach him the alphabet for the past seven years and waiting for him to show them that he knew it, he had in fact already learned how to read by the time he was three.

He had come to ask them why they didn't teach him art history, literature, and physics. The school had finally conceded that they didn't have the resources to do this and had allowed him to attend a local college part-time.

Alex came bounding across to Ian and smelled his hair and offered him a biscuit. Ian was stuck to the spot where he stood and couldn't move, look around, or say anything. He shook all over and tears fell silently down his face.

Seeing his distress, Mrs. Dawson went to make Alex move away. Alex looked intently and searchingly into Ian's face as though he knew Ian was in there and having trouble connecting with his outsides. Ian looked back into Alex's eyes with the sadness and vulnerability of a deer. His hand came up and took the biscuit from Alex. "He's okay," I said to Mrs. Dawson.

There was a rapport between Alex and Ian that needed no words. It was as though each knew where the other had been and had walked through the other's soul.

After that visit, Ian and Alex began to communicate with each other directly through the fax. Alex's were the only letters I had seen that could make Ian cry. Ian respected the person in those letters and knew that that person was gutsier and had more self than Ian had been able to hold on to in "the world."

It was time for the American and Canadian publicity tours for my first book. Out of the blue there also came an invitation to Ireland for an event called Rose Week, which was in aid of autism and epilepsy.

Ian and I had not spent a day apart in five months. Although I had little fear about where I was going, I had no idea how to leave him behind—in my house.

My defenses wanted him left behind. Publicity was something between my defenses and me. Though I did the publicity, I had no awareness of motives or wants in doing so beyond those of the publishers and my own copied, stored, high-flying theoretical morality. Without a direction of my own, it felt inside like I was being dragged into the limelight by an invisible stage mother.

I wanted Ian with me but I had no idea how to manage his company along with everything else. I was too scared to rock the boat with publishers and agents or to draw attention to myself in any personal way beyond autism and the book. These people lived in a world where most people had already grown up or pretended they had—a world where growth happens a day at a time, and not in the leaps and bounds that I was going through and with the adjustments that my growing demanded. I wanted to blend in, perhaps mostly out of view of myself, so I wouldn't have to look at the grief of recognizing my own backwardness.

Ian agreed to come to Ireland. Two abnormal people together starts to make the whole idea of "normality" less unquestionable and more of a numbers game. Who would be abnormal among a group of people "like us"?

We tacked the Irish charity tour at the beginning of what would now be a three-week, three-country tour. I took little account of anything so personally immediate as the possibility of tiredness, mental exhaustion, or jet lag. Three weeks, three countries? No problem.

Ian sat rigid in his seat on the flight to Ireland, not daring to touch anyone. I sat stiffly beside him, not daring to touch Ian. The airport was a mass of fluorescent lights and moving feet and somewhere in there Ian became a body with a name and little more.

A smiling unfamiliar brown-eyed face approached us with the usual "I'm so privileged to meet you" author stuff. It all begged for a sit-com stored response of "playing celebrity." Something inside always jumped like I was on a quiz show, filling me with dread and drowning out whatever other feeling I might have had from what I was doing. Then, in the defiance of the compulsion, I could feel a furious inner temper tantrum compelling me to attack the person who had stopped it: me. I'd fight that, too, keeping my body stiff, trying to stay aware of the external happenings, and not indulging the internal ones.

"Yes," my mouth was saying automatically in response to the external blah-blah as the battle raged inside of me. I had no idea what I'd said yes to and was too distracted to even worry whether the yes would bring me bad consequences.

"Keep your thoughts to yourself." "If you haven't got anything nice to say, say nothing at all." "Try and think before you speak." "Do you even know what you are saying?" Memories of nagging reminders and digs that tried, in ignorance, to train me out of verbal diarrhea had worked enough to eventually teach me to keep my mouth buttoned on most of these triggered responses as long as I could get my body mechanics into action before the words came out.

Compliments of any sort still aggravated and confused me and this woman's compliments had stuck in me like pins I was meant to walk around with, with no time to take them out. Compliments were the stuff of sit-com responses and took me off track—with either confusion, fear, or distraction—from my already tentative grip on my place in the non-context of everyday life.

"What a pretty girl," said a stranger as I entered the kitchen. "Watch it," the stranger was warned. It was too late. Eleven-year-old ears had just begun to know such words with meaning but still didn't understand their significance beyond the fact that such words caused feelings to explode out of control, connecting her with an outside world that dared affect her. All of that was against the law, feelings and connection to "the world." Willie's hands were on the chair in a flash, picking it up, ready to swing it to ward off the threat. "Ooops, you've done it now," someone said to the stranger on the edge of a laugh at what had by now become predictable triggered theatricals. Exposed by the pre-empting of what he was about to do, Willie put the chair back down and stormed out of the room, his mind filled with all the things he "could have done" to that bastard who'd dared to compliment me.

As a child I had thrown things, sworn, and ripped things when complimented. The laughter and ridicule at these temper tantrums, together with the exposure of other people now preempting my response with a warning to the person about to make a compliment, had extinguished this response in me; nevertheless, this was like an open wound that had covered itself with new repertoires. If I couldn't attack with rejection and threat, I could distance with bullshit.

In the limelight, on the illusionary pedestals that each newcomer conjured up, Ian faded again and again into obscurity. With this, my lights went out and again and again and I became a walking autism textbook/case study, one that had learned to speak itself like a book on tape.

A talk was scheduled and I was one of the guest speakers. We were to go to dinner in a restaurant to meet one of the other people who would be speaking.

Across the table sat an Irish version of Jed from *The Beverly Hillbillies*. This hillbilly seemed equally as "privileged" to meet me as the woman at the airport. He thrust his hand across the table in my direction, like a picture shot out of a TV set. I pulled back in my chair at the object and ignored it.

The hillbilly spoke in ego-massaging waffle that more and more demanded recognition and reply. Finally, I replied via the woman accompanying us and, in doing so, referred to the hillbilly as "he."

He was furious. "You'll look at me when I'm speaking to you," spat the hair and lips, "and I'm not 'he.' I have a name, and you can give me a bit of respect."

I was under siege from a bundle of disembodied bits, sitting too close, talking too viciously in a restaurant full of noise and light and movement. "He," I managed to stutter under overload, "doesn't understand the real meaning of the word 'respect.' "

Ian looked to me and to the exit. We got up and left into the foreignness of an unknown Irish city at night. Past shops and lights and noise and traffic, Ian followed me as the rain beat down. Finally we came to a park in the darkness. The leaves of a tree overhanging the fence were a thread of familiarity and predictability among the chaos. The rain poured down on both of us as we huddled up against each other.

Before the big talk for Rose Week, we were hustled into a little cloakroom away from a crowded room of about seventy people who'd come to the launch of an anthology called *My World.* A poem of mine was one of several in the book, which also included drawings and anecdotes from people with autism, people with epilepsy, and well-known people in Irish society.

I stepped out onto the platform when it was my turn. Ian stood nearby so I could look at him and maybe thaw out a bit. I looked at the room and its seventy pairs of eyes upon me. The multitude of meaningless expressions scared me, an alien landed, alone.

I was so overwhelmed with the impression of other that my self was gone. I looked at my speech before me, but, for a moment, the mechanics of reading had gone AWOL.

Just read it, I told myself mentally. I began to read the words without meaning and the sands of meaning fell gradually back into my brain. I looked up momentarily at the people and waves of nausea swept over me like car sickness among their movement and proximity. When I glanced at Ian, the waves calmed.

I finished speaking and the room thundered. My face pulled into a grimace. Ian came and got me and we went quickly back to the little room. Ian lit the candles we had put in a pattern on the table.

My body was in tremors so intense that I looked almost like I was convulsing. "Relax," "breathe," came a voice. It was Ian. My body was tensing and relaxing with spasmodic jerks. The emotions were too big and too confusing and my senses were all up too high.

There was a knock. It was the woman who had organized the talk. Could we meet someone? It was out of the question. He was an autistic boy who wanted to meet me. Could I sign his book? Okay, I'd meet him.

A young, evasive little sparrow entered the tiny room with a book in his hands and stammered out his request. He had one of his pictures published in *My World* and I had a poem published in it. I signed his copy and asked him to sign mine.

We were returning home for an overnight stay before I would fly off to America and then Canada for more publicity, leaving Ian behind.

We arrived back in England, drove the two hours back to the cottage, and slept. Then it was time to drive back to the airport and fly again. It seemed that no sooner had one plane touched down than I was back on yet another one.

We faced each other, dead and cut off under the weight of stored, theoretical, social expectation that people were supposed to be emotional during good-byes. We both stood there determined not to do theatrical robotics and yet the theatrical robotics were so poised, so programmed, with so much energy put into just constraining them, that there was almost no energy left for any potential responses of our own. It was as though the whole thing was a monotonous everyday experience, and we were both going through the motions like a silent movie minus the melodrama.

Ian went back to the cottage, which his defenses would not allow him to call home. I got on a plane to go do publicity I had no want or personal interest in doing.

My body arrived in New York with me hovering about somewhere. I sat Travel Dog across the table from me and ordered up dinner in a fancy New York hotel suite. Later, I gathered up what I didn't eat and put it into a bag. Every morning I crossed Central Park West, putting the leftovers in the park for the people who lived there. Although I was fifteen floors up, I could see people living in boxes. From this height, the park appeared to have more human wildlife than animal.

Down in Central Park, the ground was covered in the rusts and reds and golds of autumn leaves that rushed over my feet

with a *whoosh*. I picked up leaves and threw them over me, together with Ian in my mind. I collected some leaves, rocks, and
bits of glass and put them into an envelope and sent them to Ian
in the post. If he could touch things from where I was, then he
was somehow here, or I was there.

Back in the hotel suite, I flicked through the TV stations: a
myriad of plastic faces, social façades, and *Dallas* hairdos; and a
multitude of "dial a this" and "dial a that" and "this will change
your life" commercials.

The first journalist who was scheduled to meet me had written to
me and sent me a book she'd written before I'd come over. It was
called *Wake Me Up When It's Over*. Feeling I'd lost my first
twenty-five years under the misperception that life was a performance you weren't meant to feel or experience, I could relate to
the title. Her name was Jean and I felt we had something in common, having both written books and done big book tours.

Jean had had a brother who was manic-depressive, and she had
written about her life and about him and about her experience
within a coma she had fallen into for over a week. She told me
that in the publicity for her book she'd come to be referred to as
"the coma lady."

Her brother had tried to share his world with her and with her
sister but had killed himself. I felt somehow—in Jean's intense
longing to understand him as himself, her shared situation of having coped with barrages of questions and requests to meet
strangers, and the way that the public had known her more for
her condition than for herself—that she was something of a comrade. Her experience while in the coma had also had some surprising connections with states of overload and shutdown, with
disconnectedness to body and to words and to visual image and
to the "appear" of what people called your self.

We walked through the park. There was a surety about her, an
older-childness without the dominance. There was also an only-
ness of an only child, without the lostness. I sensed that I could
trust her. Though she had a fierce hunger for understanding oth-

ers, she walked within her own space, somehow on the fringe of a world that she seemed to study more than live in. I couldn't help but wonder if some of her brother's genetics were in her in some other form.

Everyone was buzzing about with an idea to do an article for *Life* magazine. There was a photographer who, I was told, specialized in photographing people "like me." I was asked to meet her. She looked a bit like a non-hippie version of Janis Joplin and spoke like bubble bath under a waterfall, the words tumbling out all over one another at lightning speed, full of hills and valleys of wild intonation and branching like a wild stream into a multitude of tangents.

After walking around with me, the bubble bath came up to the hotel room with the Chinese food she'd helped me order. Her blah-blah poured down on me at a speed way beyond my ability to process consciously; it was triggering me all over the place.

My mouth had been letting vocalized air out for three hours and I was so far behind that I had little idea of what I'd said or what I was meant to have got out of it. Somehow in that three hours, this photographer had the certain impression that I had enjoyed my time with her and that I would agree to having her follow me about with a camera, photographing me for *Life* as I went about my daily doings, both here and in Toronto. "What about Ian?" she had suggested. "Could he come over?" It would be great for photos and publicity. There was talk of photographing us together as we handled publicity and ate and, and, and . . .

The bubble bath got back to the American publisher, who was excited. Jean would write the story to go with the bubble bath's pictures and Jean was excited. Everyone was saying things that amounted to it all being such a privilege and so exciting. I had no idea what I thought, so got swept down their stream like a salmon swept along by a torrent. I was drowning and hoped someone would throw me a branch to grab hold of, but had no time to think how or even why to shout for one.

"Ian," I asked over the phone "would you come over to Canada? They would like to photograph us both." Ian wasn't sure and was even less sure that I had had any time to think, un-influenced, about what I seemed to "want."

I thought about how to organize the photographer so she would be less intrusive and thought her into corners further and further out of my life, but I was still thinking within the bound-aries of her context. I had no idea how to set my own.

By the end of the week, I had had enough. I phoned the air-port. "How do I get on a plane home?" I asked before giving up under the weight of a pile of bureaucratic bullshit that was over my head. It didn't matter that the publishers had paid out thou-sands for hotels and flights, arranged itineraries and interviews with the leading journalists around the United States and Canada. It didn't matter that the Canadian publishers were expecting me in a few days time for more of the same of what I'd done here in New York.

I phoned my Canadian agent. She had had no idea of all the hoo-ha going on here in New York. "I want to go home," I told her. She asked me why and I told her.

Jean came to the rescue. She arranged to pick me up from the hotel and drive me back to her house in Connecticut. The sky-scrapers gradually gave way to water and sand and trees full of rusty, rustling leaves.

We pulled onto a little cowboy street and went into a shop with an old chunky wooden counter and raw, natural, wooden floorboards, like shops used to have before Formica and nylon and nonstick frying pans. I mapped the room and the walls up to the roof. Annoying fluorescent lights buzzed over my head and, even though I was wearing Jean's mirror rainbow sunglasses, I winced from them. It seemed like the gradual abolition of the natural in an unnatural world always happened in a stifling way from the top down, and not in a growing way by building from the bottom up.

Arriving at Jean's house was like driving into an American sit-com of suburbia. This was my first view of American houses in real life, a big difference from New York City.

Her house was orderly and homey and smelled good and natural. Nothing bombarded here and there was not much traffic on the quiet dead-end street. The guest room had its own door out to the backyard. I put Travel Dog out to observe the room.

Down the hall, I passed the phone on the wall. For the next two days, I would be without access to a fax machine. Ian was thousands of miles away and less tangible without the reassurance I could speak to him in written words through the phone. "Would you like to call Ian?" asked Jean.

The phone rang. It was the photographer. She had another "really good idea" of how to get this *Life* magazine thing done. . . . Jean hung up the phone and talked calmly and gently to me, looking for some me in my responses, beyond mindlessly mirroring the expectations of everyone else about *Life* magazine. She could see I didn't want to be part of it and prodded about until I confirmed this. Then she phoned the photographer and called it all off.

I spoke to Ian on the phone. His voice, warm but fragile, was like water in the desert and though I shook, it was a welcome relief to at least have some feelings again in all of the chaos. I got off the phone. I felt awful. My stomach felt bad, my throat felt tight, my heart pounded. I asked Jean what the feeling was. "I think you're in love," said Jean. "Oh no, not that," I said.

Jean's friend Lisa sat in the living room as the open fire crackled. She was dark and quiet with gentle brown eyes that contained a breeze of wilderness within them.

Lisa had been to madness and back and I wanted to know how she got there and what it was like. I couldn't visualize what she was telling me, so we picked nuts out of the nut bowl on the table and made different nuts stand for different things as she explained the mechanics of how her mind had worked at the time.

She had discovered a part of her mind that was deeper and more hidden than the rest of her daily-living mind. She had been compelled to explore it and had gone deeper and deeper into it. She found in there ever more deep, full meanings to everything, until she believed a whole array of things that were known to be "unbelievable" and "illogical" in the daily-living, so-called real world.

The daily-living world had still expected her to live as though its beliefs and purposes were believable and important. Eventually she could no longer contain this other world of hers within her mind alone. She began to live this other world as she went about physically in her daily-living until she was eventually seen to be dysfunctional and got committed.

Once she started talking about this other world with professionals, she was made to act like it did not exist. It was as though the only important thing was to get her to commit herself again to the daily-living world and its unquestionable "sane" beliefs and purposes.

Such was the expectation that conformity would solve things; all that was important in order to *be* non-mad was to *appear* non-mad. I felt you had to talk about the comparative value, purpose, and logic of the "real world" and the other world, so that you could decide which one you were more personally committed to and belonged in. Then, if the other world was still more appealing, I figured it was important to talk about what was missing in the experience of daily-living in the "real world" that made it such a second-rate choice.

Instead, like so many other apparent mental health "successes," Lisa had merely swept her other reality under the rug and showed the professionals how clean her room was. Though she was resigned to the apparent irrationality and dysfunctional nature of her other world, she hadn't been able to talk it through, mourn its loss, or cherish its wild creativity.

I wondered aloud whether having a world of one's own was always madness. She didn't know whether her world of her own was like my one. Both "her world" and "my world" were dysfunctional when one was pulled into these worlds and away from the daily-living place of "the world" or the "real world." Mine was dysfunctional because it lacked meaning, imagination, context, and interpretation. Hers was dysfunctional because it was too abundant in all of these things: the meaning too rich, the imagination too compelling, the context too oversignificant, the interpretation overanalyzed. If perceptual or mental worlds were products of hormones or chemicals, allergic reactions, or vitamin-mineral deficiencies, then maybe one of us had too much of something that the other had too little of.

What we did share in common was the societal reaction to having any reality other than its own unquestionably valuable one. But the question remained: If "the world" or the "real world," as a reality, was in fact so truly unquestionably valuable, why should therapists fear comparing it face-to-face with any perceptual or mental other world?

Jean watched me. I was tired and mentally bedraggled. She asked if I wanted Ian to fly to America to be with me. I did and called him. Once he called back to say that he had got the time off from work, Jean arranged his flight.

My weekend with Jean and her friend was over.

Jean drove me to the little airport and I boarded a small plane as the only passenger. The stewardess reeled off her safety speech facing straight ahead, as though the plane were full. Either she didn't notice I was the only passenger or it wasn't relevant.

The plane landed in Toronto. The Canadian publisher met me and I was whisked away to a hotel. Till the next day, when Ian would arrive, I was on automatic pilot.

The next day, I watched the clock, waiting for the time when the taxi would take me back to the airport to pick up Ian.

At the airport, I stood at the arrival gate waiting for Ian to come through the doors. It was his first major international flight—nine hours packed in with other people, sharing air, inhaling their smells, putting up with their noise, maneuvering past them, and eating unfamiliar, allergenic, plastic airline food.

We had been apart only seven days, but when I saw Ian in this unfamiliar situation, under different lighting, the only thing I recognized was his coat. Nor did he recognize me, except for mine. We were a pair of coats with names.

Though we were glad to see the coats, we approached the people in them not so much with relief as with caution. We looked at each other and saw almost nothing familiar.

We plonked ourselves down on the pavement outside of the double doors of the airport in the cold. Each of us waited for some familiarity to happen, each of us not too happy about feeling so little for our reunion. Each of us was emotionally anesthetized.

Sitting there on the pavement as taxis came and went, we weren't ready to leave together as strangers. Ian was holding Orsi Bear. I was holding Travel Dog.

Orsi Bear and Travel Dog had missed each other and said hello. We sat there like plasticine appendages to these animated stuffed toys. Then, like apes, we smelled each other's hair and clothing. "Donna," said Ian, referring to the smell. "Ian," I said, smelling him with equal relief. At least something was still roughly familiar.

The Canadian publicity kept me as busy as the American tour had. When I wasn't actually at interviews, I was looking over interview questions for interviews yet to come and writing all my answers on the computer for handing to the journalists scheduled to meet me. Answering in print was the only way to be aware of what I'd said and know I'd meant it. It was also the only way to stay on the track of each question, without running off onto stored tangents. And it was sensorily safe. Written interviews would avoid the overload of blah-blah and the exhaustion of mental and physical mechanics that occurred if I tried to speak complexly with a self intact for any ongoing amount of time. Writing my interviews left some amount of time for me to "feel" the person interviewing me and for them to get a "feel" of me as someone more than a walking autism textbook (which their questions often made me feel like). So in order for them to know me beyond my writing, I'd take them for a walk.

Like a ghost in the background, Ian accompanied me to interviews to make sure I didn't push myself beyond my limits and into automatic pilot, that I was experiencing, with some understanding, my interaction with these journalists.

"What's your favorite color?" "Do you like pets?" "Will you ever get married?" "What was sex like for you?" "How would you define autism?" "Why do autistic people . . . ?" When interviewers weren't insulting my intelligence, it seemed they were insulting my dignity, my humanity, and my wholeness.

Ian and I walked into a Canadian radio station for a preliminary meeting. The idea was to get used to the studio and the interviewer's voice before the interview itself, so I wouldn't freeze or be distracted by everything. I'd already been given the questions for the interview—another chorus of insults. Without Ian there, I probably would have tried to answer them uncomplainingly. But Ian was like a me outside of me: standing before him, I could get some idea of what I thought or wanted. In front of him, I could think for myself and not as my publishers, publicists, or interviewers wanted.

With Ian's silent support, I threw a wobbly and during the tantrum, I ripped up the page of stupid questions that I'd been given. The interviewer, Mr. Gzowski, conceded that the producer who wrote the questions had made a mistake. I could keep only those questions I liked and make up any others that I wished someone might ask me.

I mapped Gzowski out: his hairy face, his gentle stance, his warm and raspy voice. He resonated the feel of an old grandpa tree, and Ian and I felt at ease in his company and strangely unimpinged upon.

Once I finished with Gzowski, I turned my attention to the studio itself. After I mapped out the light and shadow, the echo and thud, the structure of the room, the placement of its things and what they were there for, and the pattern of Gzowski's movements, intonation, pace, and pitch, I was ready to leave. I'd go home and interview myself on paper and we'd return tomorrow.

The next day the publicist picked us up in a taxi. I clutched the five or so typed pages containing my responses as we walked into the studio. After Mr. Gzowski read them, we talked about the structure of the interview. He asked if it would be possible to talk freely a bit at the end.

I was a lone free-faller and certainly didn't trust the self-expressive free-fall of letting go of structure and control in front of anyone else. Yet the "feel" that both Ian and I got from Mr. Gzowski was that we were not in front of him, we were with him. We weren't rowing our boat with him watching us, he was in the boat, too, with his own oars. It was as though "speaking with" was not something he did to people, it was a place where he met them, without expectation or judgment. He owned himself. I looked at Ian. "We'll see," I said.

I walked around the studio with a microphone clipped on to me as we rolled through the questions I'd written and answered. I felt in control of my own life, listened to, respected—no longer a media puppet blindly answering questions within others' boundaries.

When we finished, Mr. Gzowski asked calmly and without expectation, with interest that was personal but expressed with detachment, if we could go on talking for about ten minutes. In the lack of expectation, I felt that I was intact enough to be aware of the want to say or not say anything. I felt that I could say nothing if I had nothing to say or thought nothing or had no want to say anything. So I agreed.

We talked freely, without structure, and I stayed on track with awareness as I continued to walk about the room, doing my own thing and explaining myself and my feelings as I would to Ian, but with more words. At the end of the ten minutes, we stopped as agreed. Surprisingly, I didn't feel used or exploited, dissociated, disoriented, or confused. I did feel tired, but I felt glad of what we'd done. I'd felt a part of things.

Ian and I had been invited to the house of the Canadian publisher. He was a quiet and tufty old teddy bear, formal and rigid in his social awkwardness, but a person with integrity and soft edges.

When we rang the bell, he opened the door and unobtrusively and quietly stepped away to let us in. He said very little and didn't try to make conversation. He wanted us to be free to simply be.

I went about looking at jangly and dangly things hanging from the ceiling and on the walls. A bowl of paper curls and another bowl of shells. I ran my hands through their *clack* and became part of their auditory shower. I looked through the curls to exhaust the number of variations among them.

Ian found his way into the turret at one end of the house; a tall round little room without edges.

The books on the shelves were so orderly and neat. The big shiny dining table looked edible. By contrast, the kitchen was lived in and chaotic. Cooking always takes big mechanics to get together, maybe that was why.

As we climbed upstairs in the dark to look at what was up there, I sensed there was something very wrong with Ian. He crouched down on the top stair in the darkness, shaking violently. Absolute and silent terror had come over him. He was frozen and could neither speak nor move. He felt too cripplingly real here to call to the fore stored actions and yet too exposed to dare or even find any of his own. Sometimes simply being—which should be so easy—is so incredibly hard to endure in the presence of others. I had oblivion on my side most of the time, but Ian was raw and vulnerable in his social awareness.

Sometimes, it is easier to be around plastic "the worlders." There is a kind of camouflage in knowing that no one is looking for the you in you and that so many people probably wouldn't see it if you showed them. This teddy bear's simple and unconditional acceptance was making the lines fuzzy.

Ian's shakes gave way to tears and he gradually freed up. I encouraged him back down the stairs like a fireman rescuing a kitten up a tree. But down there, in the living room, the cat was waiting. In some respects, it was not unlike the potential self-exposure involved in meeting Alex. This teddy bear was somehow not enough of a "the worlder" to trigger defensiveness and just enough of an autie-like (but very aware) "gadoodleborger" (someone with a distinct "my world" for whom "the world" is a secondary home) to leave Ian brutally able to be himself and so brittle in his exposure. This was the trail of being a somebody somewhere, and I was sure Ian was hoping I'd take a detour at the next crossroads.

Ian and I went off to meet the final interviewer. She was big and bouncy and covered in bright colors against a background of red. She looked like an advertising billboard. She was fumbling and bumbling all over herself, and, even in her self-restrained composure, she looked like a zipper about to burst.

"What is your favorite color?" "Do you like pets?" . . . I felt that to her I was as flat as a rug, a very interesting rug, but she could not grasp my personhood as she stumbled all over me with admiring yet muddy feet.

The tour was finally over. We left to catch our plane to England. It had been a long week. It had been a long three weeks.

At the check-in counter, we got our boarding passes and discovered that our assigned seats were at different ends of the plane. We would be separated in the air for nine hours amid a bundle of strangers.

"There's nothing we can do about it" seemed to be the prevailing attitude as we went from one part of the airport to another trying to get things rearranged and Ian became more determined not to fly. Inside of me, I'd already tumbled over the edge of a phobialike tantrum. I was ready to burst into something between tears, terror, and attack, and only my eyes expressed the wildness inside of me. Finally, the staff managed to swap one of our seats with someone else so we'd be seated together.

Quack, quack, went the speakers with the boarding call. Bodies herded through doors and down long pipelike tunnels and onto the plane, where stewardesses waited with their guiding arms outstretched, like smiling octopuses ready to touch us. Ian and I folded in upon each other, edging around the stewardesses, who looked all the more likely to touch us for our apparent discomfort. We were directed into a skinny row of three seats. Ian sat by the window, I sat next to him, and a perfumed woman sat next to me, boxing us in. My allergic reaction to her perfume made the inside of my nose feel like it had been walled up with clay up to my eyebrows. Her perfume burned my lungs; my mouth tasted like I had eaten a bunch of sickly smelling flowers. My emotions hated her for it; my mind told me to behave myself. Ian told me that she didn't know how she made me feel.

Still, it was sometimes better to be boxed in than on the aisle. Hostesses didn't tap you on the shoulder or lean across you to pass meals. People didn't hold on to your knee as they maneuvered past you on their way out. Being boxed did mean that either you had to stand up and grunt to give the message that you needed to get out or ask them to move if you could, or you needed to wait until the person on the aisle chose to go to the toilet.

Ian and I sat side by side tired, jet-lagged, and travel-sick. Compact seats are not made for tall lanky men and Ian's legs had had enough as he squirmed about for several hours before checking that I didn't mind if he stretched his long legs out into my space. In exchange, he offered that I could stretch myself over into some of his space. As the hours went by, we huddled more and more into the window seat, away from the perfumed stranger. She was the enemy armed with stink and we were retreating from the battle lines as best we could.

Ian padded a sweater on his shoulder to put something between us and make it all right for me to put my body near his. "There," he said, indicating I could use his shoulder because, after all, it wouldn't be like leaning directly on his body. Both of us scurried like rats behind the justification that "it was just for the flight." Both of us "knew" we didn't really want to be close to each other.

I leaned on Ian's arm but it went numb. He put it over his head. He put it behind his neck. He looked for anywhere else noninflictive to put it. Could he put his arm around me? It wouldn't be personal.

More than finding that these arrangements weren't an uncomfortable infliction, we found them comfortable and comforting, both of us becoming painfully embarrassed with the emerging realization and admission. By the time the plane landed, we had to uncurl ourselves from the nest we had made of each other, which we did with a defensive attitude of "glad that's over." But inside, the undercurrent had its own message: I wasn't so glad to lose something that felt so nice.

We had been living together, sharing a bedroom, for six months. We'd done "mirror hands," which is what we called putting one's hands up against the other's, like mirror images. We often smelled each other's hair, and sometimes brushed it. We'd very occasionally stood up against each other when one or the other was very upset—but without hugging. The plane trip was the first time we had cuddled like this, so overtly and directly; we were both aware that, for whatever reason it had begun, it felt good emotionally and physically.

We slept in the taxi on the way home. Back at the cottage, night fell and we lay on the living room floor under the scratchy army-type blankets we called camels. We lay there under the blankets, away from "the world." We lay there with the smell of each other's clothed bodies and looked into each other's eyes, but here—with no excuse to hide behind—we couldn't cuddle.

We couldn't cope with the freedom, because freedom was

without end or beginning, without rules or guarantees or repertoires or performances, and our defenses demanded all those
things all the time. Freedom was about choice, and that was
about awareness and self; as always, these things were difficult and
even harder in the company of someone else. To imagine life
without defined beginnings or ends, rules or guarantees was to
imagine a bottomless pit or an endless void and *that* seemed crazy.

Ian went back to work a few suburbs away in his crisp perfectly
ironed shirts. I went from room to room doing one thing after
another on automatic pilot.

Things that were out of place got moved without thought.
Light switches were cleaned without thought of the wet cloth
being used. Carpet got taken up from entire rooms without
thought to move the furniture first. My inability to maintain attention and complete a task meant the house and I were often
both in turmoil by the time I'd realize what I'd done.

Hardly a week went by when Ian didn't return home to find a
wall of hacked-off plaster, a floor covered in torn-down wallpaper, used paintbrushes and rollers in the bathtub and me covered
in paint, or the house filled with dust or fumes and me with
asthma.

With a sledgehammer and a chisel I had begun to break through
the bedroom wall on the off chance a fireplace was concealed in
there somewhere. The room was choked with dust, the floor was
strewn with wallpaper and rubble. Bricks and blocks were pulled
out of the wall and the beds and furniture were coated with thick
orange brick dust.

I did find a fireplace, as well as a pipe running through its
brickwork. I hit brickwork away from it but the pipe just went
farther and farther along and into the wall. Damn, I thought, I
don't know how to pull this out.

"There's this pipe sticking out of the wall," I explained to Ian on the phone. "I don't know what to do with it."

"Don't touch it," warned Ian.

"Why?" I asked. "I've got to get it out so we can use the fireplace."

"You don't have to get it out," said Ian, trying to stay calm. "If you break that pipe you could blow the whole house up. If that's a gas pipe, you'll kill yourself."

I had taken the phone into the bedroom and stood looking at the pipe and the whole catastrophe with a mixture of awe, confusion, and anxiety.

The carpet had been torn up in the bedroom but now it had to go back down. After dragging the carpet back through the house to the bedroom and trying to roll it out and move beds and furniture, I got fed up and wrestled both of the beds out of the bedroom and into the living room. Our new beds now stood stacked half on top of each other like something thrown out at the dump. I stood there looking at them. Well, the living room furniture would have to go but it was a good idea. The beds would stay out in the living room.

I went back to the bedroom and relaid the carpet. That would make a good office, came a thought that was probably Willie's. Even though we had no need of one, the mere fact it would make a good office meant, logically, that that's what it would be.

Carpet laid, I turned to the beds and untangled them, the legs of one jutting between various slats of the base on the other.

Two tall single wardrobes already stood in opposite corners of the living room: Ian's and mine. Fine, I thought, the beds could go between them—one bed on Ian's side of the room, one bed on my side. I pushed everything into place. There was something wrong. There wasn't enough space for two sides to exist. With two wardrobes in the corners and two beds in the middle, the symmetry was fine, but there was no more Ian's side or my side. The beds next to each other, it now appeared, if not for separate duvets, that Ian and I slept in a double bed.

At that point, Ian came home. I was embarrassed. With a lot of opposition from our defenses, we decided to give it a go. We would leave the beds there, together. It was only temporary anyway, like everything else.

With the beds now in the living room, and no space left to sit and watch TV, we would watch TV at night from the beds. Ian would stretch out along the length of his bed and, being shorter, I would lie in front of him.

We would grab at invisible threads to cut away the invisible knots we could see each of us were tied up in. We would do "jubblie-ectomies," tearing out invisible "jubblies," our word for the knots that gripped our stomachs and made our minds race with anxiety and frustration. We would blow invisible peace into each other's ears to calm our troubled souls in the grip of jubbliedom. But all cuddling remained "incidental." Cuddling was just something that happened when two people with winter in their bones put their bodies in close proximity of each other and arms went around one another as a means of keeping these annoying appendages out of the way.

Day by day, week by week, we lay closer and closer to each other on top of the covers as we watched TV and the winter crept up on us. Every night, we would turn off the TV and climb into our single beds, each firmly tucked in and divided from the bed next to the other.

We had felt so secure and so much warmer lying next to each other while watching TV and so, eventually, we lay closer and closer to the respective edges of each of our tucked-in beds with the tucked-in duvets between us. Ian curled up with Orsi and I curled up with Travel. Everyone said good night to everyone and we all snuggled close to the gap where the duvet divided us all.

━ ━

Christmas crept up on us. It had been six months since Ian had brought up the idea about the wonderful Christmas we would have together if I didn't go back to Australia: a simply be Christmas. Tinsel and wrapping paper, a Christmas tree and lights, and good food. Now, as the day approached, I looked forward to my first Christmas in company as myself.

But, with each passing day as the holiday neared, Ian's walls grew thicker and thicker, and the idea of a simply be Christmas drifted off to the land of lost dreams.

Too much "kiss Aunty Joan," too much "isn't that lovely," too much "do you like it?" Too many presents bought flatly and given flatly based on stored rules of how to behave at Christmastime were haunting Ian. These were guidelines rigidly reinforced by a family whose reality was a world of rules where ability to rely upon practiced, predictable roles was an easier alternative to spontaneous self-expression.

For me Christmas had been different. In the house I'd grown up in, both my parents seemed to live in their own worlds in different ways, worlds that seemed ruled by roles and obsessions and the need to prove something to anyone but themselves. But, unlike Ian's parents, my parents seemed much more preoccupied with maintaining their worlds of guarantees than ensuring that I was part of it.

Despite the day-to-day exceptions, at Christmas and birthdays there seemed an assumption that there was no point asking Donna if she liked her present. Perhaps that was because I'd either insult them honestly, not answer, or disown the present because others seemed too interested in or focused on my reaction. The giving of presents was generally not from hand to hand. There was no kissy-kissy ego massaging and no demand of "gratefulness." In my family, presents were left in your territory for discovery and subsequent fascination or ignoring. It was only later that visitors would be taken on the usual "look what Donna owns" impressiveness tour.

As a child my Christmases were relatively simply be, even if I couldn't be myself in company. Even at mealtimes there was no real demand that food be eaten at a table—or even necessarily from a plate. There was no need for thank yous or ego feedback from me, or perhaps I just didn't perceive it.

Growing up, I had sometimes been more defiantly stubborn, mischievous, and generally less compliant than Ian; but for each of us compliance and defiance came at a price. The response to Christmas was just one of many symptomatic legacies of the different ways our environments had adjusted to our difficulties, and we to their demands or lack of them.

Too busy to talk or fax, Ian shrugged off his defensive evasiveness with the rush, rush, rush of managing a shop at Christmastime. In the hurry and the bullshit, this was Xmas more than Christmas.

More and more, I could feel him arming himself. As the days to Christmas became fewer, his face became more and more chiseled in its expression and he came home laden not with decorations or presents but with rules.

Ian's rules were the antithesis of his father's Christmas rules with alphabetical listing of who were meant to get cards. He seemed to be developing Christmas-phobia.

From each visit to his father's house he would return with a new rule. He had seen the card list at his father's house with his name listed among acquaintances and relatives. Ian didn't want a Christmas card from me, nor should I or anyone else expect one from him.

At his father's house, he had been engaged in the ritual family discussion of what present he "wanted," as well as where to get it and what brand it would be and how much would be spent buying each thing. He didn't want a present from me, nor should I expect one.

The rules went on and on, until the only thing allowable according to his Christmas rules was for me to give to myself and receive from myself and celebrate by myself in the presence of his tolerant physical form, which was allowing me to be. The message to me was loud and clear: Christmas hurt.

What about a Christmas tree? I didn't want a real one to be

killed just for me to look at. I had wanted a pretend one of some kind, and, while I didn't have a car to bring one home, Ian did.

Ian had spotted a fluffy white plastic tree. Would that do? "Yes" I replied, not convinced by his struggling efforts to raise himself beyond the murky dredge of compliance. He brought home some pink lights. We put up the tree and it was beautiful to look at, like something one would expect from a fairy tale. But the fairy tale was flat, two-dimensional, and without magic.

Ian won a few rounds in his battle against Xmas compliance and sellout, and I spent Christmas as I always had—alone, in company.

The phone rang. It was Susan, a cheerful but troubled teenager with autism who had been in touch with us now for about six months. She'd been calling almost weekly now, her life falling apart this way and that with teachers giving her a hard time for things she didn't intend and often couldn't help. Other times, Susan's mother was on the telephone and Donna became Donna-the-walking-autie-textbook and an on-call, free-of-charge social worker.

The phone would ring again and someone else would ask me why so-and-so did such-and-such. The post would come through the door with more reams of questions from parents who wanted to find the answers that they couldn't find, were too intimidated to look for from professionals, or couldn't pay for. I was feeling like a worn-out sponge.

Now I was getting ready for a weekly trip to London. I was on my way to meet Kath, the mother of an adult son with autism. She worked as a teacher of autistic children. I was also going to spend time with Anne, an autistic child who went to the school where Kath worked.

It took a long time to get to the school: two and a half hours on three trains, a bus, another train, and another bus. Recently,

I'd noticed that each week at the school I found myself spending less one-on-one time with Anne and more and more hours answering the enthusiastic questions of various staff members. In personal, one-on-one interviews I shook with the exposure, struggled to find the words, and fought the muscles of my throat, which seemed to want to strangle the words to stop them from coming out. By the end of the day, my throat would be sore and my lungs would hurt from my fighting them to expel words they didn't want to let out. My voice would be hoarse and my brain boggled.

That morning, as I stood in the living room, already exhausted, Ian prodded me about the trip. I was sick, my eyes tired, my throat still bedraggled, my spirit dangling, Not go? No way.

Once I'd said I was going to do something and shown up for the first and then second time, the pattern was set; there was often no way that my own compulsive commitment to follow through would allow me to back out. To break this rule was to allow weakness and fear to dictate the terms of my life.

Ian pointed out the defiance on the part of my body. It was loitering instead of making its way out the door. This had nothing to do with fear. It looked like a "not want." We reasoned it through, with me throwing weak, momentary, wobblies as Ian shook the dust from my rule book. In the end, I was agreed, not with Ian, but with myself.

I had left one life of blindly meeting expectation, only to have come full circle and be heading full speed ahead down a similar path with different faces and names. The path was a different one but it led to the same place, a place where self faded into oblivion as other became so foreground that I could no longer find the me in the picture.

Ian got on the telephone. "Donna won't be coming," he said. It would be "such a disappointment," he was told. Kath had told X, Y, and Z that I was coming. Everyone was so looking forward to meeting me. If only I could have admitted it consciously to myself, Donna was looking forward to spending time with Donna, too. "I suppose she'll be coming next week?" Kath asked

Ian. Ian looked at me like he was looking at a dog he'd freed from the circus: no, he didn't think I would be coming next week.

The phone rang again. "Could I just . . . It would mean so much. . . ." Ian looked at me and I looked at Ian. I retrieved the memory of what I'd just witnessed. "No," I said, loud and clear. "No, I can't."

— —

As we entered the new year, I knew this was the time Ian would move into his proposed new flat.

Inside, I had two sets of feelings—mine and those of my defenses. Mine were a combination of regret and sadness.

The sadness was at the loss of a friend. I knew I wouldn't be able to sustain our friendship if I had to take the initiative of going to Ian's new place. I also knew he wouldn't be able to sustain the prompting necessary to get me to come, daring my own self-expression. Ian's moving would, therefore, mean the loss of our friendship.

The regret was that I knew that he didn't yet have the awareness of his own wants, emotions, and identity in order to sustain life on his own as his real self. I knew it would soon be overrun with the directions of others as it always had been—a triggered life.

Meanwhile, my defenses were celebrating. Ian's upcoming move would mean freedom. They defined this according to prior experiences, where living with someone meant loss of my self and the triggering of their takeover. Therefore, unquestionably, by definition, Ian's moving out would mean that they'd get back "a life." But the life they wanted back wasn't one to do with feelings or self. It was the one they lost. It was one of hiding, of performing, and of cheap two-dimensional acceptance. It was a mockery to call it a life, since it was more like a living computer program or a long-playing improvised performance. They knew damned well that without Ian to keep me aware of where compliance and oblivion stepped in and I stepped out, they would have a chance to walk all over me. That was their form of security, a life without feelings or self to hurt.

Ian's solicitor got in touch with him. All was not well with his prospective purchase.

Ian didn't know quite what to do as he jumped between trying to trigger cues from me and following through with a "leaf in the wind" plan that had been put into action in the days before we met. There was some stored surface dramatics of "what am I going to do?" but generally he seemed detached from these displays and the whole "buying a flat" scene. It was as though, having started the direction, he was compelled to at least go through the motions of following it, unless otherwise stopped or redirected by someone else. Yet, at almost every turn, he seemed to be setting up conditions that would stop him from getting what, to most people, he appeared to have wanted.

The more he appeared to fight for a flat, the more something else in him ran it down. The more he gave up on the whole idea, the more fiercely he seemed compelled to force himself into it. It was like watching a vegetarian possessed and force-feeding himself animal meat.

He went looking for another flat and finally—in between determination to make an offer they wouldn't accept, determination to give them the exact asking price, put-downs of the property, and fantasies of what it could be—he found he had landed it. So after living together as best friends for seven months, it seemed certain that Ian was moving out after all.

As Ian began to buy things for the flat and talked about what would "look nice" (with no care for whether what would "look nice" was his taste or not), I felt sad for what now seemed wasted time. Despite all he had achieved in finding the self inside of him beneath his façades, it seemed he was going to move out, full steam ahead, without his self.

Ian went through the motions of telling me how welcome I was. We'd get two more beds for his place so that we would each choose where we wanted to stay. We'd know we were in each other's company by choice. But I knew his defenses had been pushed to the limits of realness and fear and he wasn't going to make it. I said yes, yes, yes, but inside I was saying good-bye and my defenses were saying good riddance. I'd go and find my dream farm and live there with a horse that simply was and fight my defenses not to turn the place into a circus or a welfare agency. Ian would move into his city flat because that was "what people dream of doing." He'd fill it with musical instruments because that was what people thought he was interested in, and play rearranged repertoires of other people's blues and soul music because that was what made people popular.

He had paid his deposit and was ready to sign his way into a predictable life of stored values and stored expression and stored images. I wished him well and gave him the stored line that I might see him some time. Inside I knew he would fade into a past of people with whom the journey had been good even if they weren't to be part of the destination. He had waited and waited for cues that didn't come—some sort of feedback of what Donna wanted, so he wouldn't have to act on his own wants. But I was bound and gagged and he got none.

I was struck with surprise when Ian suddenly pulled out of the deal. It was not that I was surprised that he had done so by himself or that he'd "decided" he didn't "want" a flat after all. I was surprised at my own elation that he was staying. He was staying but we'd have to get a bigger place.

━ ◢

As the weeks passed, each of our skinny bodies kept falling into the uncomfortable six-inch gap between the two beds. It was driving us both crazy. Finally, we gave up the two duvets, stuffed one of them into the gap and used the other one across the two beds.

It was more comfortable than falling down the gap, we told ourselves, and each of us now intermittently rolled across what was now a long lumpy cushion in the middle of "our bed" (an action for which our defenses drove us to apologize every other time).

We had dared to untuck the wall between us and sleep within reach of each other, but our defenses blocked all acknowledgment of the want it had come from. According to them, it was all merely a practical arrangement during winter, one to do with staying warm, and though it wasn't really so warm as before (with a whole duvet apiece to wrap around one), neither of us was able to admit it, even to ourselves.

As it got warmer and warmer, we wore less and less to bed. It was so much more comfortable, freer to sleep and, of course, we "knew" we weren't attracted to each other's bodies, so there was no inhibition. Bodies were just things to get us about; annoyances which demanded baby-sitting chores of washing, drying, feeding, and toileting. There was no question that our bodies needed physical touch, because there was not even the thought of the possibility and certainly no awareness of the want.

Our defenses apologized constantly for accidental touching and at the same time we both felt a craving for incidental touching that couldn't be admitted to. Every other morning became a debriefing session to do with redefining the rules and boundaries; half of it stuttered out by us, half of it waffled in stored hoo-ha by our defenses, each contradicting the other and leaving both of us confused.

Somewhere in there, we gradually broke through the defensive blockage and denial of curiosity or interest and began, fleetingly, to look over each other's bodies in the only way we could: as collections of disembodied bits.

Carol and Willie each played havoc. Falling into the role of the molested child, Carol would become nervous, chatty, evasive, and busy—as if Ian was something to avoid—without being able to admit it.

Willie would have things to do, suddenly finding compelling justification to keep getting up or to study, rather than watch, the television (keeping both of us on guard) as we lay snuggled up together.

More and more, I came to know that neither of these responses was my own. They could try to impose their stored structure on my experiences, but they could no longer sour them. Now that feelings were flowing freely from myself, they could no longer convincingly deny my reality and convince me of theirs.

A person can't be being molested when she is becoming more and more relaxed because of what is happening. A person can't have a true want to do something else when she has an undeniable aversion to leaving what she is already doing.

More and more, I was reaching out to Ian, daring to look into his eyes as we touched like a pair of young children, bathing in the feeling of security.

Like Robyn, a friend from my teenage years, Ian would sometimes brush my hair and tickle my back lightly before we went to sleep. I'd be enjoying the feeling, relaxing into it, aware I was with Ian and safe. And then my defenses would rebel, slashing through my safety net with every weapon at their disposal. I was coming to the horrifying realization that I was being attacked from within and that my defenses were not, as I had always thought, "on my side."

The more relaxed I became and the more I discovered security, the more my defenses would attack me. I was defying their "reality," a reality where closeness, emotions, and touch were against the law of a "my world" that I had turned my back on. My defenses weren't ready for it and they let me know it.

Suddenly and unexpectedly, I would go through emotional overload. A bundle of undefined emotions would explode all at once like some uncontrollable chemical attack. Like an internal earthquake, it would leave me disoriented and unsure about my self, my surroundings, and Ian.

Without any awareness that it was happening, I'd be tuned out by some repetitive pattern, leaving me in a zombie state. I would come to, as though from a trance, the victim of some kind of soul-rape that left me feeling unsure of the ownership of my own life.

When my defenses didn't get me one way, they got me the other. Unpredictable muscular attacks would make my whole body so uncomfortable, manic, and maddeningly restless that I couldn't sit still or bear anything near me—or even bear the physical awareness of my own body.

The worst attacks were groundless, wild impulses of self-destructiveness. My only weapon against these was to tell, and telling was sometimes impossible. When the last thing wanted by some compulsive force within myself was to have me helped, my voice would be tied up in knots.

Yet the more I defied my defenses, the more I shattered the self-delusion that they were on my side or ever had been, and the more I saw that the only person who could help was the one who could get close to me, beyond their clutches: Ian.

— —

With no flat on the horizon, Ian settled down to the idea that we were going to stay living together and "my plans" of moving to a farm in Wales became "our plans" of moving to a farm in Wales.

One of Ian's biggest fears was unemployment. So, since he had no idea how he'd get a job in Wales, he decided he would take his job on the road, buying and selling musical instruments.

Soon, with a bit of help from our compulsions, the old bedroom was filled, from floor to ceiling and wall to wall, with old instruments and various odds and ends bought cheap at second-hand shops. We decided to refurbish them and sell them at markets; this would be our day-to-day job as "real people."

As the contents of the old bedroom climbed closer and closer to the ceiling, more and more of our living happened in the living room, which was already our eating and sleeping quarters. Effectively, except for when Ian was at work, we were spending twenty-four hours a day with each other in a ten-by-seventeen-foot room (the small, skinny, kitchen and bathroom tacked on the back of the cottage each fit only one of us at a time). Every day, within these rooms, I worked on various matters related to my book and dealt with incoming letters, and we both cleaned and restored bits and bobs we would later sell.

To look for a farm together, we started with the yellow pages for the whole of Wales. We sent out a standard fax asking for details of country properties; soon there was a waterfall of envelopes cascading through the letterbox every morning. We rated them in terms of how they met our criteria and made appointments to view them. Then we packed up the car and went to see the ones that seemed best to fit us.

After a mind-numbing drive we arrived somewhat dazed to the appointments. Loud, singsong voices pierced our ears, sometimes two at a time, and barking dogs joined in, deafening us to the meaning of the people's words—which we were then meant to act like we had understood.

Hands were thrust out at Ian and guiding arms were slipped around our backs as people walked behind us up stairs and around corners as we viewed their houses. Often husband and wife and curious kids all scuttled about us, already with little sense of body and spatial awareness among the bombarding chaos.

The actions of these people from house to house were pushing various systems into overload, minute by minute. One minute, we'd lose our bodies, next minute they'd come back on line but we had by now traveled into a different room on automatic pilot with no awareness of how it joined to the room we'd come from. Then our hearing would go meaning-deaf, or our vision would go meaning-blind, or our emotions would be cut off, or we'd be cut off from any sense of self. The whole lot just shifted back and forth within us as these house owners blahed and poked and gawked and guided and tried to engage us in their social chitchat. We spent so much time and energy on coping strategies that by the time we left each house, we'd hardly taken anything in at all and felt nothing but a big blob of detachment and indifference.

Away from the houses, we were damaged, worn-out people, surveying the wreckage and sometimes taking some of the effects out on each other. Ian would be hyped up, way over the top, his systems in bits and dissociated from one another like he'd been through an internal bombing. I would be numb and half brain-dead. After the next house, it would all shift: different systems in each of us would now be a mess, I'd be the manic one, and he'd be numb and half brain-dead.

Finally, we made plans on how to assert our needs. We acted out potential scenarios in order to have responses ready, stored so we wouldn't get dragged off our tracks in the face of their bombardment. "We have a communication problem," said Ian. "It's the opposite to deafness. You'll have to speak quietly and slowly and one at a time. Also, please don't touch us. It cuts us off and we can't be aware of what we're doing."

"Can only one of you show us around and could you let us look around without commentary?" I said to one of the house owners.

The next arm thrust in Ian's direction was met with "Sorry, we're not into handshakes." The next time people tried to make chitchat, we put up with it for about a minute and then told them, "We have difficulty keeping up with social talk—could you just show us the house?"

As we drove along in drizzle to the last property on our list, we were tired out from the house hunting. We were disappointed that nothing had moved us and, without being moved, we were not able to decide where we were moving to. We felt compelled to make a choice that day. This next place was our last hope.

We drove along a very long, very green driveway surrounded by flowers and tall lush trees of all kinds. An older lady came out and met us at the entrance. She was peaceful, gentle, and unintruding. We walked up to the house, our noses filled with the smells of flowers and trees, our ears filled with the sound of birds, finally unbombarded by chaotic, intrusive human sounds and smells and movements.

After the exhaustion of all the other houses, we were totally worn out and our guard was finally down. Our emotions heaved a sigh. As we went around the gardens and from room to room, we were moved; we cried and smiled. Not knowing what else could have caused the pipes to unblock like this, we decided theoretically that these emotions must have been because we liked this house. We decided, based on this, that "Myr Cwymp"— Welsh for "falling walls"—would be our house. The lady made us tea and coffee and gave us a sprig of mint from the garden.

Back in the car, we looked at this house, figuring it would be our house and we would be its people. As the drive home to the shoebox cottage wound down motorway after motorway, Carol and Willie and Richard and Nigel all wormed a little of their own stored, copied, hidden agendas of "what we wanted from a house" into our open-book minds.

With no real ideas of what to do with a new house—*our* house—our defenses set about filling our heads with high-flying, copied possibilities, which were flippantly mislabeled as "wants." By the time our key was back in the front door to the cottage, unknown to us, our defenses had each secured a handful of guarantees that they would try and hold us to: guarantees by which they'd establish "their" place in the new house and leave our real selves behind. Each of us had been so tired out that we'd given each other's defenses relative free rein throughout the drive, acknowledging each flippant, un-thought-through "I'm going to . . ." with "yes," "yes," "yes."

We put everything into the hands of the accountant and solicitor. We were glad to be getting some space. Our defenses were glad at the prospect of using the move to reestablish a foothold of security in replaying their various copied "acting normal" routines. We would be out of the cottage within three months and, without our knowing it, our defenses had every intention of coming with us—and, if possible, of leaving us behind or squeezing us out. The only sign that anything subliminal was going on was the unusually strange inner calm about such a huge impending change.

Ian set a date for quitting his job at the music shop. Despite the huge amount of unpaid overtime and favors he had done for his bosses, and the month's notice he would give them, he felt guilty at quitting. His bosses seemed to play on that, becoming less chummy and hinting constantly of how he was "leaving them in the lurch" and "could he just . . ."

He had stopped going to his father's house for ironed shirts and his face became hairier and his shirts less starchy as his quitting date approached. When he left for work each morning, I paced about the cottage driven by a worrisome sense of urgency that two people stuck in one room day and night together might not work.

Ian came home from working his final day a freed man. The first week seemed easy but slowly the crowding and exposure took its toll. Richard no longer had a job. Nigel no longer had keyboards to demonstrate. Instead of spending more time with Ian, the stress and the change meant I was spending time with his "faces"—faces I neither trusted nor felt comfortable with (nor they with me).

The stream of fan mail and faxes continued. There were manuscripts to read through, editing to be done, contracts to look over, and publicity to plan. There were blurbs and covers to approve and photos to arrange, and there was something called taxation.

After realizing that most things I filed never came out again and that receipts were kept all over the place or not at all, Ian started working as my personal assistant. Publishers, agents, and publicists all began to hear a word they weren't used to hearing from me very often—no.

Since Ian didn't know how to be himself in a work situation,

Richard broke through and played at being my "manager." My walls went up and Willie broke through and retaliated with his own stored managerial repertoire. After spitting and door kicking, huffing and stomping, Richard would quit under the melodramatic guise of "lack of appreciation." Throughout, Ian remained unable to process his own feelings and could do nothing to express his turmoil or resolve it.

Willie carried on, working militantly with a performed, point-scoring, resentment, basking in the achievement of disarming "Ian" through exclusion, redundancy, and hopelessness (for they defined "Ian" by his defenses). In the chaos, Ian's faces raged and mine raged back like a pair of bratty melodramatic amateur actors compelled to play a barrage of roles we felt nothing for and didn't believe in.

After several nights of sitting up with Richard and Nigel, overload had been so ongoing and my walls had been up so consistently that Willie and Carol had moved back in on what seemed like a permanent basis.

After lots of self-abusive "but, this *is* me" and "I can't take this anymore," the characters owned up to what was going on. Carol introduced herself flippantly to Richard. Nigel introduced himself just as flippantly to Willie. Willie introduced himself brusquely to Nigel, and Richard introduced himself brusquely to Willie. Our characters introduced themselves to one another, announcing the obvious: that in the absence of any self-expression in word choice, voice, body language, or actions, Donna and Ian were gone.

I was staring into a mirror image of my own mother and father and I couldn't take it anymore. Job or no job, flat or no flat, I wanted out and said so.

Ian's face pulled into fierce sharp angles, his movements chiseled, his defenses raged into the old bedroom full of things and started to phone a moving service. They'd move all his belongings back to his father's house. There was only one thing amiss. It wasn't Ian who was wanted out, it was his defenses. They were more than happy to have got exactly what they were looking for—a way out. The only problem was that they were taking Ian's body with them.

My defenses had loved it all up until now, too. They wanted all the feelings gone and they wanted all the involvement gone and they wanted me alone where they could "protect" me (which involved running my life recklessly without any awareness of how reckless it was).

My heart felt like it was made of paper being torn to pieces. I didn't want everything to end like this. Somehow, my own feelings and the revulsion at how we mirrored my parents chipped at the hardened surface of my defenses and Willie encouraged Richard to put the phone down and try to talk things through.

We sat on the edge of the beds. Both of us broke through in glimpses, the stances and facial expressions crumbling, the words stuttering. These glimpses were enough to have hope. We had realized that things were way out of control. We didn't know how to fix them but we decided right there that we had to make a commitment to fight our defenses and not each other. We were agreed, and we went to war, this time on the same side.

———

A request came through the post asking if I would speak at an autism conference overseas. I had no idea. "Yes" sounded equally as probable as "no." How was one supposed to make such decisions? Which mind was one supposed to listen to?

There was the social mind, which reasoned that this was a privilege and privileges are supposed to make you grateful to accept. That one was a yes.

There was the logical mind, which reasoned that the place would be full of people and that they'd come up to you and try to chat blah-blah. There'd be bright lights and noise of all sorts from all directions and bodies everywhere and people pouring out emotions you'd feel nothing for and the semblance of emotions they'd feel nothing for and . . . That one was a no.

There was the moral mind, which reasoned that I had important things to say that people should hear. That one was a yes.

There was the humanitarian mind, which reasoned that if I spoke five times at such conferences simply by virtue of being known for my book then that would mean at least four other auties with equally important things to say wouldn't get the chance to be heard. That one was a no.

There was the paranoid mind, which reasoned that if you didn't go, people would say you didn't care and then everyone would think you were an asshole. That one was a yes.

There was the emotional mind, which reasoned that I didn't feel comfortable about going. And there was the body mind, which reasoned that the jet lag would be awful and I'd probably get sick from allergies to the food over there, or from people's perfume and things. Those were both no.

I felt like getting someone else to make the decision for me. Ian came home.

I showed Ian the invitation. "Are you going?" he asked. "No idea." I replied—so far the scoreboard was equal in the battle in my mind. Ian asked what I wanted personally. I hadn't done that one.

My personal mind reasoned that I dared to have a life of my own without guilt for doing so. That life was far removed from auditoriums and applauding crowds of people who would look up to me, study me, or pity me. That one, which I most associated with my identity that I called "I," was a no. I wrote:

Dear Madam,
I have been asked to give a lot of talks and have said no continually. It is not that I am a snob. It is not that I don't care. It is not that I am lazy.

I am very unsnobby and down to earth when I know and trust someone. I have strong feelings and beliefs about many things and a strong sense of justice. I work hard and seem usually to be busy.

I have just finished my second book, *Somebody Somewhere*. The tour for that book will take up the next three months or more and eat into my privacy and security and stability. Yet, I am committed to doing publicity for it because it is in the contract. Otherwise, I am a *very private* person and would keep to myself.

I have no interest in being applauded or interesting or important. I don't have those ego needs. I thought very hard but could not find a personal want to give such a talk.

Also, I feel very strongly that other auties should not be in my shadow. Please give the time that I might have spent being listened to to another much less known autie who deserves an equal hearing of what may possibly be an equally enlightening perspective.

Sure, I have lots to say. I say it to myself through my books and then after I have heard it I let other people eavesdrop by reading it. We all have our ways. That is mine.

Thanks for trying anyway. But I have no desire to talk to an audience. I have no desire to swap one version of life "on stage" for another one, nor do I want to be a bug under glass (even an applauded one), nor do I want to be put in the position as some kind of spokesperson on autism (I am an expert only on my own life, no one else's).

I know how to keep my head and life intact. Ego business confuses most people and I am no exception; I just see it coming and they often don't.

So, no thank you . . .
From Donna Williams.

Ian and I had both always reveled in our compulsions and obsessions, defining them as who we were, as our personalities. Ian was the person who lined everything up and made the arrangements of fruit in the fruit bowl symmetrical, no matter how empty or full. I was the person who automatically pulled my sleeves up at the glimpse of the kitchen sink, whether empty or full, on the way out the back door or to the toilet. We were the people who stood at the sink making sure that all the bubbles were gone before we could walk away.

We ate ritualistically, we slept ritualistically, we bathed ritualistically, and went to the toilet ritualistically. We watched TV ritualistically and read ritualistically and used phrases, stances, movements, and facial expressions ritualistically. Ian parked the car ritualistically, I dressed ritualistically, we sat ritualistically and entered and exited ritualistically. Ritual and compulsion didn't dominate our lives because it *was* our lives. The free-falling glimpses we saw through the cracks left us feeling shaky, unfamiliar, and vulnerable. Ritual and compulsion always came with guarantees and the only problems seemed to be the ways in which "the world" put up barriers to these things or forced them to be constantly reformulated and refined.

We had hellos for every time we saw each other in a doorway or crossed each other's path in a room. We had good-byes for going to the toilet or going for a bath, for going to get something to eat or for taking out the rubbish. The other person's rituals would not have been so blatantly obvious in a big house with a lot of rooms and chaos—it might have looked like a very smooth running household. However, we lived in a tiny one-bedroom house with a narrow kitchen, a bedroom filled with collectibles, and the living room functioning as sitting room, dining room, and bedroom all in one. Here, rituals that might have gone by, each passing for normal, had begun to look like a cartoon life. Worse, each of our compulsions were at odds with the other's compulsions.

Ian kept putting the cushions diagonal. I kept putting them square. I kept making the curtains meet in the middle. Ian kept opening them with an exact measurement of space in the middle. Ian kept putting things in pairs. I kept restoring everything to a symbolic world of one.

I kept putting symbolic boundaries between us, standing on a different piece of carpet or on the other side of the door frame, as though in another world. Ian would keep meeting me on my territory. I kept putting myself in symbolic company with objects, making him external and redundant. Ian kept matching me, making my compulsions acts of dialogue rather than exclusion.

I had compulsions to categorize and order for size and height, for tins, packets, or bottles, for color and for use. Ian had compulsions to give company to objects, making sure that the Rice Krispies or Ragu spaghetti sauce weren't lonely on the shelf. His system drove me crazy and looked haphazard, giving company to a tall box of cornflakes by placing it with a rolled-up plastic bag full of muesli. I would take this "friend" away and put it with the packets somewhere and Ian would get frazzled, not just because he couldn't find things but because something had been left on its own.

Everything I did, Ian felt compelled to redo. I would open and close a drawer. Ian would privately reopen it and close it without wanting anything in it. He was like a dog marking territory. If I cleaned something, he recleaned it. On the other hand, I did similar things in different ways. If he dropped something in a place that made sense to him, I picked it up and placed it strategically somewhere else. If he alternated something of his with something of mine, I removed all of his things to a different shelf, a different drawer, or a different side of the room. Things were clearly "my side," "your side."

We did singular rituals, repertoires of rituals, and strings of one ritual after the other. If the rituals ran to "joyous" completion, then everything was like a ticking clock. If a string of compulsions were stopped in midsentence, the house would be in chaos, the floor would be in chaos, and we would end up like either raging bulls or a jelly left in the sun: frazzled and confused in a state of overload or with a stomach full of knots, which we called jubblies.

When we weren't doing things by ritual we mirrored each other. Ian picked up his knife. My knife got picked up, even if my plate was empty. Ian opened a window. I went and opened a window, even if I was cold. If Ian wanted something he asked, "Do you want . . . ?" and I'd echo, "Do you want . . . ?" and neither of us had any answer but to repeat the whole thing and get agitated that the other person didn't respond.

I would make vague statements in midair: "There's melon in the fridge if you want it," which meant, "I want some melon"—

but Ian would reply, "Okay" and I would sit there unable to put my want into action. A few days later, I'd go to the fridge, misdirected, meaning to go to the cupboard to have Vegemite on Ryvita. I'd see the oldest thing in there, the melon, and eat it mechanically without want, because I had a rule that dictated that old food had to be eaten first.

Both of us were sad, both of us were trapped, and both of us could see it in each other though not in ourselves. Neither of us could set the other free from the straitjackets of compulsion and rote-learning, for to do so was to challenge the compulsions within ourselves. Without them, we had no idea how we'd even cross a room.

Things were sometimes so perfect they were imperfect. Being in the house with someone else with whom you were personally and emotionally exposed made even going to the toilet seem like a frightening act of self-expression. The sound of your own excrement hitting the water, its volume, intensity, duration, and pace, were personal trademarks to be hidden or disguised. Neither one of us could bear to make a noise in the toilet; we found out later that we had both been peeing or shitting into paper, acting like thieves caught in possession of bodily functions.

To make spontaneous noise had come to feel like an imposition on each other. This imposition was an act of sharing and that was something that was against "the law" because we didn't understand its mechanics, its boundaries, or its rights and wrongs. Though we couldn't make bodily functions happen at will, we could try to stop them from happening or put them on hold. To cough or sneeze, without prior announcement that we would, was emotionally almost impossible. Ian never blew nor apparently picked his nose, as though it were some magical appendage with evaporating snot. Neither of us would fart or belch, nor express the disembodied discomfort of stomach cramps from food allergies. We made yogis look like amateurs.

Ian washed and dried himself as thoroughly as a deodorant commercial. I brushed my teeth for exactly three minutes, just like on the Colgate commercial, because that was how long it said it took to remove plaque. We sat upright in our chairs, crisp and symmetrical, breathing with perfect timing and rhythm: a pair of starchy shirts reveling in order and self-containment. This was the house where Barbie and Ken didn't poo, and if they did, it didn't stink and that was good and normal and not to be challenged.

"But I *like* to do the dishes," I would say when Ian tried to make me roll down my sleeves and go where I was headed—to the toilet. "But I *like* straightening the fruit bowl," Ian would say as I stood there asking if he really *wanted* to do that on his way to open the post or make his breakfast. We asked how we knew that we liked these things. The answer for both of us was obvious, simple, and unquestionable: we'd always done things like this so we "knew" these things "were us."

"I don't think that *is* you," Ian started to say when I had launched into a triggered ritual, and he explained that I was on my way to get something to eat or to paint something or go to bed. "I don't think *that* is you," I started to say to Ian in a "you too" every time I saw him diverted and preoccupied, explaining that he had seemed on his way to watch TV or looked interested in the program he'd changed for one he had a ritual with.

"That's not you," "that's not you," we mimicked each other in fierce and bitter defensive attacks. After all, if all these things weren't "us," who the hell were we?

The alternative was even worse: If these things weren't likes, wants, or interests, how much of our lives had these rituals and compulsions stolen away? How constantly denied were we from the very simplest of connections between intended thought, emotion, and action? How many times had we been stopped from going to the toilet because a particular program was on? How many programs had we watched that we knew by heart, that actually bored us, frightened us, confused us, or helped cut us off from self and feeling with incomprehension, fear, or monotony? How many meals had we missed because we had been diverted by a lack of symmetry that joined to yet another lack of symmetry that joined to yet another lack of symmetry in need of our correction and control? How many connections with our bodies and sense of space had we missed, too preoccupied with ritualistic exits and intros? How much attachment had we lost in spending so much time doing rituals and so little being self? Even if we had formed "attachment rituals," we hadn't spent time getting to know the self who was meant to become attached. Ritual and compulsion were the mechanics of "characters" without the characters. This was who we were beneath the façades and it looked like a mess. This was life with a rain check, an IOU dated "eternity."

There were compulsions to hide self even from self. Self-expression in its most basic form was distorted, altered, inverted, and made its opposite. If I had the urge to eat, I went to the toilet. If I had the urge to go to the toilet, I ate. If I was cold, my sweater came off. If I was hot, another one came on. If I meant to say something nice, it came out nasty; the nastiness came out nice. The requests came out as statements and the statements as questions. The important came out glib and the glib came out stressed, melodramatic, and seemingly important. The stored came out disguised as self and the self came out challenged by my defenses as the stored they had conceded to be committed to vanquishing.

If I meant to say "paper," I said "pencil," "book," "big white square flat cr–cr–cr." If I meant to eat one food, I was compelled toward something in a similar category, something not wanted, or something that would make me sick. If I meant to go in one direction, my body headed in the other, my head still turned sometimes in the intended direction as my body walked blind in the compelled direction, off on a track of its own.

Sometimes the compulsions screamed too loud for awareness to compete. Sometimes the awareness made me want to cut my arms and legs off, pull my tongue out, and stitch my mouth up. If not for a sense of humor I might have killed my body outright in retaliation, but I couldn't do that properly and completely with intention, except as a replay of someone else. Without choice I had come to do the only real option possible. I convinced myself that compulsions were me and life and normality and that as long as they were roughly functional, I wouldn't fight them too much.

More and more, the unquestionable became questioned and a new compulsion developed—the compulsion to make the other person disarm and be self, consistently, and at any cost. We agreed to draw attention to each other's rituals, and we agreed that the person caught must admit to being caught and forfeit the compulsion there and then.

There was a lot of "but this *is* me." There were lots of "I am not compulsed." There were lots of "I'm enjoying this." There were lots of "but it *was* my thought." But there was also a lot of okays and tears and statements of "you know this is eating me alive."

The result was sometimes wobblies. The result was sometimes a furious character emergence ready to pack bags, catch trains, or find excuses to go out. The result was sometimes a glib and animated, stored "I can't help it," macabre in its perversity, the echo of a patchwork mosaic of a thousand cheap, plastic sit-coms. The result was sometimes the construction of an entirely new temporary character with the predictable but see-through intro of "okay, *this* is the real me." "Sure it is," we would say to each other in a stored line, fed up with trying and being met only with more of the same from a person so riddled with compulsion that he or she would be equally compelled to hold on to it at any cost—despite our pact.

When Ian was defeated and compulsion won, it was not he who felt the loss, because compulsion deadened him too much to care. It was I who felt his loss, because my defenses boldly scored points within me, rubbing my face in the dirt as they "joyously" watched the confirmation of hopelessness of efforts to combat the compulsions they hugged to themselves as "identity" and "life." When I was defeated and compulsion won, it was not I who felt the loss, because compulsion also deadened me too much to care. It was Ian who felt my loss, as his defenses were rewarded with what they wanted to see—the defeat of selfhood (which equaled the impending ultimate death of what his defenses called "themselves"). We fought for each other as though it was the battle for ourselves. Our defenses lapped up our defeats like cream in a cat's bowl, purring all the way.

Their celebration of our defeat was more than this though. There was something chilling about it in its echoing reminder. Their defensive, vindictive celebration of compulsion and ritual had us staring into the faces of two people we didn't want to be reminded of—our genetic leftovers. We had come face to face, not just with responsibility for facing our own realities, but for what we now saw as something that had been subtly passed down to us from the last generation and who knew how many generations before.

The ritualistic exits and intros, stances, lines, and smiles of Ian's father were staring back at him as he watched himself in me and regretfully knew who else it reminded him of.

I felt I could already acknowledge remnants of other difficulties in my father's side of the family and had come to terms with these and could accept them: difficulties in understanding what was said, performing and impressing in place of knowing how to be social, metabolic difficulties underlying manic behavior. But I had never examined the origins of compulsion. Consciously face to face with them now, I felt these came more from the other side of my family, a side I saw riddled with trademarks of compulsion, obsession, and phobia. The last thing I wanted to know or admit was that I had some of my mother in me.

I saw my defenses in Ian and Ian saw his defenses in me; we knew that we were like each other and that these mechanics, as bad as they seemed, could have other, not so pretty, sides.

This realization bashed us with a sense of hopelessness, self-rejection, and self-mistrust. We weren't just trying to undo two and a half decades each, but generations. We were trying to undo genetics that repulsed us, and the attempt seemed to threaten to tear each of us into two. As we approached that which repulsed us with a conviction to challenge and deal with these things, our gut instinct drove us to deny and turn away.

We had innocently resolved to climb Mount Everest in a day wearing oversized Wellingtons. With each minor defeat that we saw in each other, we felt like shaking each other with "how dare you be weak," "how dare you not win," "how dare you not have the strength and will to fight the jubblies in your gut and shatter the grip of your bastard defenses," "how dare your life be the living example of my own condemnation," "how dare you make me see what I cannot conquer."

There was something else, though, beyond this battle. Seeing these others within ourselves, knowing they perhaps had tried and failed, created within us feelings that we had no time and space for and no desire to admit: an element of the forgiveness that comes from understanding, a forgiveness for the ignorance they could never fly above, the obstacles they never challenged, and the defeat they'd never know living life in the cocoon of compulsion and ritual.

We heard back from the solicitor about the house we were buying. Myr Cwymp turned out to have more than just falling walls. The engineer's survey showed that it had a falling roof, too and, and, and . . .

We felt we should have felt upset, disappointed or something, but instead we felt very little at all about the darkening rain cloud hanging over our prospective new home. We knew logically that if we had felt so moved by this house and wanted it so much, then we must therefore logically be upset about things not turning out.

The portrayal of assumed disappointment didn't fit, and the

cameo performances fell flat on both of us. We finally conceded that, though perplexed as to why, we felt indifferent about the whole thing. We let the house purchase fall through, along with the walls and the roof and, and, and . . .

We were off house hunting again. This time we'd go armed with a better idea of what we did or didn't want from a house. We decided that we, as "a person," theoretically wanted a place with privacy and seclusion, tradition and simplicity. Theoretically, we, as "a person," wanted a place with a garage, some outbuildings, and one exclusive and escapable room each.

We found all of this on a hillside overlooking a town. The garage wasn't there but could be built. There were no outbuildings really, but there was a lopsided, falling-down, woodworm-infested old wooden barn that we figured we could do up. There were the right number of rooms. It was as simple as a five-hundred-year-old house with whitewashed stone walls, quarry tiles, and natural wood can get.

This house would suit "a person." We decided therefore that this house would suit us. Besides, the people who owned the house were nice people (by virtue of having left us alone to look around, not chatting to us too much nor trying to touch us) so it must have been the right place. "Mains water?" "Yep." "Privacy?" "Yep; nobody walks down that public footpath over there."

We returned to the cottage happy that we had made a decision and were moving.

Within the walls of the cottage, our battle against compulsions had escalated. We were like a pair of junkies going through withdrawal together, but we were winning. We shook from both the exhaustion and the overwhelming insecurity of sinking into a bottomless pit of unknown.

If our compulsions were about being quiet, we dared to make noise. If our compulsions were about doing things in a certain order, we dared to do them in any other order than the dictated one. If our compulsions were about cleaning or tidying, we dared to dirty and to mess. If we were compelled to wear a certain color or garment, we wore any other one. If our compulsions dictated the second choices, we made the other choose for us.

Ian dropped some spaghetti and a wobbly was on its way. I slopped some more onto the floor and sat down. Together we picked up the spaghetti, slopping it back down on the floor again and again, laughing at our defenses and at the jubblies in our guts. Like two naughty little children, we were scoring points together against our defenses. When compulsion drove us to pick the stuff up, we responded by making patterns ever wider across the kitchen floor. When compulsion made the texture feel unbearable upon our skin, we squelched it ever more through our fingers and over our hands. This was what our defenses had done to us all of our lives. We'd used awareness to study their weaponry and use it back against them. We had infiltrated the enemy lines. We were showing our defenses who was boss, for our present, for our past, for our history, and for our future. We felt strong, no longer groveling in submission for a life in glimpses.

Surely this pit had a bottom to it, I told myself mentally. Surely, beneath the rituals, there was connected self-expression. But the more we exorcised, the more demons we found and the earlier and earlier were their origins.

The more we freed ourselves up, the more time we had to think in new, more personal, less defensive ways. The more we freed ourselves up, the more we felt for the lives we had and the more self-love we felt. The more we freed ourselves up, the more we could see each other as more than familiar objects and unwitting accomplices in our rituals, and the more we saw ourselves as comrades on the same team. In the end, we were faced with what was left: a plate of scraps a mountain high with still no consistent us in sight.

We slowed down every movement, response, and utterance to a snail's pace and watched with alert minds as our bodies tried to take us as their captive passengers on autopilot. With everything slowed down, the stored and unintentional expression of my defenses broke through, now only in glimpses. I watched, with a mixture of alienation and distress, the unrecognizable stored swing of arms that were mine and the bounce in the step of feet that were mine, both disconnected from self in identity and intention. I was now watching my own physical dissociation, no longer from outside of my body, but from within it.

Ian tried to keep track of his face, as he felt his mouth attempt a multitude of mirrored, plastic smiles and an inquiring eyebrow minus the inquiry inside. The experience was like watching a whole pile of strangers in your body. What was now simultaneously both humorous and horrifying was that we could actually see and name who some of these things had been borrowed from. Many of these people were those we had feared, hated, or been used by; others were TV or cartoon characters. To finally watch this consciously and from within our own bodies was startling; if Ian hadn't gone through it with me, I'm sure my mind could never have stood the shattering impact of the realization. If this pathetic accumulation had become the threads of the straitjacket on my selfhood, no wonder I had felt allergic to being social with inner selfhood intact. To have shown self would have been to have lost it in a suffocating ocean of "other."

— ◄

Ian seemed to be becoming an ever more silent whirlpool of depression, anger, and shock at how far removed his appearance had become from his self within. Each Sunday, he would drive out to his father's house and his father would expect him to play the role he'd always played, a role encouraged and perfected from early childhood. Each Sunday, Ian would be determined to enter his father's house as himself and come out intact. Each Sunday, his father's comments about Ian's not being "his old self" stoked the flames of an unseen fire inside of him. Each Sunday, Ian became increasingly irritated and saddened by the fact that his father seemed unable and even unwilling to acknowledge even the small hints of his real self that he dared to trust enough to show. More and more, Ian would climb back into the car with bitterness, mocking the expectations of pretentiousness expected of him. More and more, Ian was giving up on the hope that he'd ever be able to be himself with his family, which would therefore make them no family at all.

Ian wrote his father a letter. If he couldn't speak to his father as himself, perhaps, he thought, the letter would speak for him. It spoke of all he'd gone through, how he'd finally come to understand why he'd spent his life mirroring everyone and jumping from one influence to the next with no sense of continuity between any two situations. He wrote of losing time from day to day, hour to hour, and even minute to minute as he shifted from one performance to another. He wrote of the realization that nothing he had thought of as "him" was "him" and that he needed to distance himself from the origins of some of his more entrenched, stored roles. He wrote of his sadness and his shock and also of his relief that there would now be hope that he could begin to develop enough of a self to finally feel some of the belonging and feeling that had evaded him all his life. He wrote the letter from a position of courage and trust and sharing. He wrote the letter in the hope it might be a beginning in relating to his father and his sisters, finally as himself and not a role.

We drove to Ian's father's house. Ian went upstairs and silently handed his father the letter in the hope it would be a new beginning.

Ian's father came downstairs. He said nothing but looked directly at Ian with understanding, smiled and nodded, seeming otherwise at a loss of what to do. Then he left again. Ian looked over to me and smiled, signing that he thought his father understood.

— ⸺

We heard back from the solicitor about the house we'd decided to buy. The house turned out to have no permission for mains water. The people turned out to have already promised the house to someone else. And we turned out to have second thoughts about the prospective privacy of a property with a public footpath running through it. Amid token gestures of expected disappointment, we were again resolved to the fact that we were fairly indifferent and still just as perplexed as to why we didn't really care.

Taking back control from our compulsions had seemed such a positive move and both of us assumed that what we'd find in its place was spontaneous self-expression. We were in for a shock.

Since we had now recognized their alienness, the actions of our defenses would be aborted midsentence as though someone switched off the electricity. A swinging arm would stop midair like a burglar caught in the act. Suddenly told it was invalid, a movement just died where it stood at the moment of external recognition. It was as though the movements themselves (or the part of the brain that was triggering them) had mistakenly believed that all the copies had been expression of self, in the absence of any connection of self with expression.

Raised eyebrows got stuck there, sometimes triggering another stored expression and that would get caught and stuck, too. We'd then find it hard to get these expressions to remove themselves. This was because there were probably no recognized or connected responses of what to do or use in their places.

Walking across a room, one leg would have one stored movement and get caught and the other would try a different one. I'd end up walking clumsily like two halves of two different people and getting tangled in legs that were meant to be mine, with one having stopped and the other continuing a step or two unaccompanied.

Ian would be crying because of the shock and distress of his physical helplessness as the corners of his mouth flickered like a bad fluorescent light. It looked like the mouth was trying to pull itself into one of the stored smiles that he had recognized as not being him. But without any other message, it seemed unsure what to do—to disassemble itself or try again. More and more the surface comedy of it all subsided and we saw the wreckage of what happens when you attempt an exorcism of intruders within your own body.

Here we stood with obviously dysfunctional bodies belonging to what were ironically thought of as "high functioning" autistic people. We had thought our own responses would step in in place of the stored ones but we had opened the drawer and found no files inside (or they were locked in a room without a key). We'd unwittingly created a dangerous recipe for helplessness. What was worse, the program we had set to run had, like everything else, gone to automatic and even if we had wanted to stop the stored actions from spontaneously aborting, we now couldn't. We had no idea how far stored behavior had gone back. It was obvious that some of it went back to early childhood, but what if it went back to infancy—or (the unthinkable and unimaginable) even earlier? We didn't know how much worse it would get, or whether we would ever be able to climb out and in what form.

Within the walls of the little cottage, we were more than overwhelmed with the amount of mess we'd made of ourselves. It was like we'd gone into a derelict building to tidy up with a brush and shovel. We'd opened a door in that derelict building and mountains of debris had fallen out on us, burying us. "Overwhelming" was an understatement when it came to describing what we were in the midst of. On top of this feeling, we felt regret that we'd probably destroyed what was at least functional. We'd destroyed it because we'd been selfish enough to want to feel we owned our lives as whole people.

There was also guilt and shame. "The world" had put me on its pedestal and people with autism from all around the world had trusted me like some light in the darkness. Ian had trusted me and followed me through this developmental tunnel. Our tunnel was looking like a dead end, and that light was almost extinguished underneath this mountain.

With the destruction of stored movement repertoires, trying to do the simplest of things soon became terribly hard. Making my way around the kitchen, I found my body was like a series of stills, each limb doing a different unsynchronized scene-fragment from my past, whether from real life or the TV.

My left leg might have stopped "doing my father" but my right leg was still keeping up the mimicry. My left leg, in the meantime, would start replaying someone else and my right arm another someone else and my head would cock to the side like Cindy from *The Brady Bunch*. Inside of me, my own program echoed mentally on autopilot: that's not you, that's not you. With each thief caught, another stored action came—an automatic punch or slap lashed out at the offending limb or part of face because something in me had learned that "that is what is done for disobedience."

"Stop hitting yourself," Ian was saying. "Help me. I can't help it," I would reply, a stored giggle tacked on the end because "that was what went with cartoons" and this slapstick certainly looked like one.

It was not that my mind was breaking apart; instead, the connection between my mind and my body had gone into the workshop for minor repairs, but were now getting a total overhaul. I hadn't gone crazy but my body had.

I found myself physically stuck and physically disconnected. I struggled to "remember" how to cross the room or open a drawer, but I was now trying to remember with my body and my body had little memory of moving as me. Inside of me I was thinking, Come on, leg, you know what to do. But it was like my body couldn't hear me, like I had no body-memory. I'd mentally visualize me and lose the context of the intention or surroundings or get the context or intention but lose the me. I had to do something that stored copied actions had made redundant: I had to use my mind.

"What do you mean you can't move?" Ian asked.

"I mean, I'm stuck here," I replied. "My legs won't listen to me."

"Just lift your leg and move it forward," said Ian simply.

I tried to lift but nothing happened and the word "lift" just fell emptily upon the air. I was crying now, hysterical and frightened at my helplessness. "It's okay," said Ian, "you'll get it," and, disembodied, he came across the room to help me.

Lifting a leg and putting it down in front of me, it connected with feeling. I had recently connected with the feeling of my leg but I still couldn't both feel it and use it consistently and simultaneously. I replayed the feeling rather than using compulsive, thoughtless mirroring; of what is called echopraxia. I still couldn't get the other leg going, so we worked on that one and we got it going, too.

But something odd was happening. My legs now connected with movement, but they didn't "know" how to move in cooperation with my hip sockets. Picking them up now caused the whole hip to rotate, jerking upward and over and down and making the whole act of walking difficult and ugly in its awkwardness. This was the woman who had once been a little dancing doll, even pirouetting, at the age of seven, in oversized point shoes, bulked out with cotton wool.

Six girls in a row, hands on the bar, the familiar music played to familiar rote-learned exercises.

The girl in front raised her leg. Mine raised itself in reply, rigid and stiff, nothing more perfect in ballet than the perfection of wooden legs that feel no fatigue nor pain. Her arm went out, my arm went out, not as a copy of her, but *as* her (for there was no "me"), yet without her humanness, and with it, her imperfections.

"You go to the front now, Miss Polly," said the dance teacher, as I went to the front of the line as reward for my "perfection." In my head was a void, an absolute nothingness of what to do or what was about to happen. There was no want in me, nor interest, no inquiry or enjoyment.

The teacher would press the button. The music would start, and the stored video would play; my body, on automatic, moving along with it; monkey see, monkey do—without the faults and without the ownership. Applause was for appearances and no one questioned the absence of "be," especially with stage-mother pride in the way.

I'd won over the rebellion of my body and though my links between body and mind were slow and tentative, my body now waited for instruction, like a child in a classroom where the rest of the class had long since grown up and graduated but the teacher had come back anyway to teach this class of one.

My defenses prodded me mentally with pointy sticks of stored mock-disgust at my awkward and ugly movements, which were far from the dainty movements of a technically perfect ballerina. Despite this disgust, I burst with pride that, though they were ugly by "the world" standards, these movements were mine and, in that alone, beautiful.

This defensive mock-disgust was an undercurrent to the tidal wave of felt independence marked "mine," which came with now seeing and feeling "me" in my movements.

It was tiring to move. One hour of moving with a me intact would require an hour of rest to recover. To push myself beyond this was to push myself into physical dissociation.

My disconnected fingers sat unfeeling on alien hands. These were the fingers that had played piano automatically, each movement playing the intervals heard in a mental audiotape. Ian picked each finger up and let it drop. The ballerina's fingers, flaccid, responded like heavy rubber. Some on one hand returned gradually to their starting point like slowly melting butter. Others staying exactly where he'd left them, in midair.

"Here," the snarl ordered, raising my six-year-old leg level with the back of my head in an arabesque. The leg stayed there without effort. "Now hold it there for thirty minutes," said the snarl, walking off to do other things, pleased with such talent. It never occurred to me to let it down. There was no alternative intention nor message to do otherwise until another cue happened. There was no tiredness or pain, no desire or thought to do something else. Five minutes, ten minutes, half an hour later, the snarl would enter and say, "You can put it down now." Off would go the videotape. The leg came down.

As all of this was happening to me, Ian was slowing all of his movements down to a snail's pace. Slowed down enough, he began to be able to keep up with his movements which, up until now, had happened at a pace too quick for him to process or feel any ownership of. Now, when he was following an intention that came from his self, it took Ian around five minutes to cross a room with mental, physical, and spacial awareness. Meanwhile, I was struggling with the bare mechanics of sitting up, getting to my feet, and walking.

I would have the idea to sit up, and either my body would do it as somebody else and then sit there waiting for further direction, or the idea didn't connect to my body. I became afraid of whether I was still intact with my body. I asked Ian to touch me and though he couldn't find his own movement to do so, what I felt told me these difficulties had nothing to do with tactile sensation because that was intact.

"Have you had a poo today?" asked the snarl. The answer was meant to be yes. It was almost always meant to be yes. "Yes," I said. "Bullshit, get to the toilet and have poo," it said impatiently.

When I hadn't been for a week, there were consequences; soap, laxatives, or a visit to the doctor's. I didn't mentally connect the consequences of vomiting and bile with my rear end because they came out of my mouth. Instead, I associated those consequences with eating and not with shitting, and the natural assumption was therefore that eating was the problem.

I went to the toilet and sat down on the seat waiting for this magical poo to happen but nobody was home. I had no visual copy to play out in dialogue with my rear end. Mentally knocking on the door didn't matter because my knocking was inaudible as far as my brain was concerned. Having someone expect something of you that you cannot make happen, and that you can see no purpose in, seemed like a kind of mental cruelty I could not escape. Though it didn't talk to me, my body did sometimes make me listen to its last-minute urges. I could put its urges or feelings on hold by refusing to relax or by tuning it out, but I couldn't tell my body parts what to do—we just weren't on speaking terms, body and I. Maybe I'd ignored it for so long that it figured I wasn't there and ignored me, too.

"Have you done it yet?" asked the snarl from the other side of the door. "Yes," was the answer as always as I got off the toilet and flushed the empty bowl.

When it seemed that things couldn't get worse, they did. What had happened to stored body movements and stored facial expression now extended to mimicked speech and further, to the interaction of diaphragm, lungs, voice box, tongue, jaws, and lips.

What began as an inability to stick to one pitch, pace, accent, or type of intonation now became even harder to keep consistent. Speech became a verbal mosaic with bigger and bigger gaps as intermittent stuttering and word-finding problems turned into stumbling over more and more sounds and how to make them. Finally, in the terror of helplessness, I found I had "forgotten" the natural sequence of connections needed to make consistently comprehensible language.

Articulation was happening without vocal connection. Vocal connection was happening without articulation. My lungs and diaphragm were responding to intention to speak but either my jaw, lips, and tongue weren't on speaking terms or my voice box walked out on the job.

The terror and the foreignness had me physically frozen, wide-eyed and unblinking with tremors from head to toe. Tears rolled out of the eyes that stared frozen straight ahead, and an animalistic, incomprehensible and ugly grunt came from deep inside of me from a feeling of horror and terror and frustration.

Ian held my rigid shaking body in front of him. "I'm going to help you," he reassured me with gentle urgency as he began to move my fingers for me and work my face, arms, and legs, each part responding like hard rubber. In the terror there was no feedback, the lines were disconnected.

"Just move one finger, that's all you have to do, just one single finger. Touch my hand with one finger and you'll be free," he told me. I put everything I had into moving one finger, but it wouldn't answer me. Then finally, as though the operator finally decided to put the call through after I'd hung up, one of my fingers jerked suddenly forward. Another grunt came from inside of me, but it was one of happiness and relief. It was only a finger, but it was a start.

Over the next hours we got my body and me on speaking terms again and though my physical connections weren't yet complex enough to sit up without help, I could move my arms and legs across the surface of the bed with the surface as a guide. My voice, however, was still AWOL.

"One for yes, two for no," said Ian, demonstrating the blinking we would use as communication for the next three days. In the meantime, the phone was disconnected, we lived on tinned soup, and the world outside our door ceased to exist.

My first words, as far as anyone could remember, were complex repetitions of whole sentences and whole conversations, replayed in the accents they were spoken in. What if the voice I had gone in search of, my own voice, had never spoken? What if all I had ever known as my true voice were patchwork copies of those of others? If this was so, then to do away with this database of stored copies was verbal suicide.

I searched for connection to the old automatic abilities, but since they had not been mine in the first place, the files had been thrown out. As my computer continued to self-abort, I found I had none of my own files to replace the old ones with. I used my knowledge of linguistics, of where to put my tongue and lips, to make sounds and tried to make speech.

My body parts were working in mono and I couldn't get my voice box and lungs to work together while my mouth was in gear. Ian sat before me, coaching me and coaxing me in an array of stored voices of his own to which my response was a mixture of vulnerability and fury—vulnerability in reaching out for help, fury that I was going through this and he still had stored skills to fall back on.

It took forever to get out a single word but I got some pronunciation going, spoken in breath rather than sound. With joy and relief, Ian understood me.

In the space of a week we had done miracles. Though we'd become virtual cripples, we had achieved an ownership of our actions and control of our intentions that had been missing all our lives. Though it took me forever to work out the physical mechanics of getting undressed, turning a tap, and stepping into a bath and took Ian almost as long to monitor his own moves, these were *our* baths that we took and we didn't see our bodies get into them, we *were* our bodies and *we* got in. Though it was too complicated to work out how to wash now that I wasn't using a replay of a shower commercial, I was glad just to lie here in the water, feeling the temperature change in my skin and knowing I owned this life.

"Have you washed? Get back in that bathroom and wash yourself. You stink," said the snarl outside of the bathroom door. I'd go back in, step into the bath and sit there for a few minutes, get back out again and come out. "Did you use soap?" the voice would say. "Yes," I'd reply, knowing that was the expected answer. "I bet you didn't. You still stink," the snarl would say and finally give up.

All day I exercised, moving each limb with intention as myself. Even opening an eye was a major effort, since it didn't listen easily to intention and had to be willed to open. I exercised the making of shapes with my mouth and the making of noises in my throat. I exercised getting my lungs and throat working together and then both of them at once with my mouth. Finally I heard the most beautiful sound in the world: my own whole connected voice, and the first word I said was "Ian."

"My voice," I said, crying uncontrollably, "Donna's voice." I sounded like a deaf person. The precise crispness and clarity of the voice I knew as Willie's voice, the slanglike and animated drawl of what I knew as Carol's voice were nowhere to be found. This was the voice of no one I'd ever known, and I felt an ownership of it that struck me with such a force that I felt it was overwhelmingly beautiful in spite of its aesthetic ugliness. To hear my own voice in my own ears, the foundations of a mental voice of my own that had been absent for twenty-eight years, was to give myself a key to escape the sense of deafness-to-self that had plagued me all my life.

That night, for the first time in my life, I heard myself speak in my dreams with my very own voice. I had a body, I had emotions, I had a voice, I had a belonging, I had a life.

Though I was proud, my defenses had been triggered with intense stored mock-disgust and mock-shame. I knew my defenses were at war with me and I tried not to attend to the self-hateful urges inside. It seemed my body was giving me stress signs as though the urges were mine. I told my mind that these urges were merely internalized mimicry of expected "the world" responses to apparent disability, impediment, and retardation.

Again and again the urge to hate myself struck in waves. I was washed over with a sense of intense ugliness. This hateful part of my mind played memories of my singing voice, so pure, so refined, so well articulated, nothing like my own poor articulation and lack of synchrony between lungs and voice box as I now emitted words with a hit-and-miss connection.

I was haunted by memories: memories of that singing voice and memories of others saying how seductive or attractive my phone voice was. All of it brought nausea. It was as if my past were my jury and I were the accused. It stood there with poking fingers interrogating me about whether I was guilty of being something unappealing, despised, worthy of being ignored or worse. It stood there waving a carrot to me as the donkey, showing me that all I had to do was to deny my self and continue with the by-products of my façades with their polished, impressive, voice baggage, so pleasant and appealing to hear, so worthy of life, so "normal."

In my head, I saw these bastard self-denying parts of me for what they were. Sure, they were "the world." I knew that. But my first and most influential microscopic view of "the world" had been where I'd grown up, in that mental-emotional, though impressively decorated, shithole where "spastics and retards deserved to die."

Though I'd never had the luxury of time to think through and gain conscious awareness of the actual meaning of such week-to-week, day-to-day statements of childhood, something deep in my guts clearly did.

Something deep in my guts knew that being one of these "spastics" and one of these "retards" had to do with the outward signs of retardation: the heard signs of a brain assumed to be slow in its connections, the memory of hearing the sentence, "deaf people are all retarded, listen to them. Listen to how they speak." Something in me must have known that my poorly connected voice mechanics sounded much like someone deaf and that equaled degradation, denial, and rejection.

The memory of someone mimicking me with odd movements, saying "look at the spastic," must have told something deep inside me that this word "spastic" had to do with moving in a way not considered "normal." When I was young, I had listened to this mindless arrogant, ignorant crap; and it had somehow got inside of me and walked around with me, haunting me, reminding me, as though following me about with some big, invisible stick.

This ashamed part had fluctuated between harassing me and bargaining with me, making me feel both abused and protected by it. This ashamed and abusive part had undermined my confidence in myself and justified its existence by virtue of my helplessness, which it itself cashed in upon and helped compound. It was time to exorcise that bastard.

Every time I felt this part of me raise that invisible stick, I now hit it back in my mind. When it hit me with feelings of mock-shame, mock-inadequacy, mock-fear, mock-intimidation, mock-rejection, and mock-denial, I hit back at its arrogance and its ignorance. When it hit out at me with examples of what I should be like, I hit back at its cheap sellouts and plastic bullshit. I hit out at its domination and put-downs, which it disguised as care and protection. When it made me feel ugly, I mentally said to myself, "I am beautiful." When it made me feel its stored voices were beautiful and replayed a voice-memory, I mentally said how false these were. When it made me feel awkward, I mentally said how brave and how real I was by comparison to its falsity and defensiveness. When it replayed memory of the delicacy of stored copied movement, I mentally said how pitifully acceptance-seeking and shallow it was.

After a week, lack of food in the house forced us to venture out of the front door. We made our way down the street feeling like a pair of fragile, elderly people, unsure of our movements and how they appeared and what the possible consequences might be.

Making our way down the street, I realized something else had changed—the way I used my eyes. Moving on automatic pilot, I had generally used my hands rather than my eyes to feel my way rather than look where I was going. I had always used my eyes to visually track where my body parts were moving, so the actual arrival at my destination was often the first time I had seen my destination in more than quick fleeting glimpses. What this meant was that my mind, my senses and perception had little time to prepare for where I was going. This total lack of forethought or preparation called for a compulsive stored response in the absence of any time for my own response, and so the vicious circle went. It also meant that upon arrival at a destination, I was vulnerable and either flighty or blindly compliant to anything that happened soon afterward.

I found that instead of watching where my feet were going or leaving my body on sleepwalking autopilot, while colors and patterns caught my vision, my eyes were focused ahead of me in the direction I was going. They would find a spot about fifteen feet ahead and walk to it, then find another spot and walk to that one. Legs that had always got there eventually on a set program now got there by meeting a visual intention. For the first time I had a sense of "from here to there."

Hands that knew objects by feel now went straight to the desired object like missiles on a projected course. My two-dimensional world was beginning to be experienced in a three-dimensional way and my brain was starting to listen to my eyes, rather than using them as scanning tools. What my eyes saw was becoming less irrelevant.

I looked up at Ian's face, no longer scanning it, but looking at its fragmented pieces. Then I looked from one eye to the other. Something was wrong.

One of Ian's eyes was looking at me, the other was looking at the side of my head. I focused on the eye looking at the side of my head. "Make it look at me," I ordered.

"It is," replied Ian.

"Not," I answered back, showing him where it was looking.

"Close one eye," he told me.

I did. The eye was now looking at me. "It moved," I told him. He reassured me that it didn't. Now that this eye was looking at me, his other eye was looking at the other side of my head. Ian moved my head until the eye looked like it was looking at me.

I wanted to know how this happened. "You only look with one eye at a time," Ian told me, "You look with both, but sometimes only one registers what it is seeing."

I knew that my senses worked in mono and that my limbs did, too. I knew that comprehension and expression worked in mono and so did sense of self and other. I knew that feelings and thought and words and pictures often worked in mono, but because I had always used my eyes to scan rather than look, I hadn't known that my eyes could work in mono as separate organs rather than in stereo.

I set about becoming aware when an eye stopped registering and which one it was. Then I'd focus my abilities on using that one and hope that it wouldn't be at the expense of the other one. If the other one switched off mentally, I focused on that one, until I could switch from one to the other at will. I would take control of these difficulties. They would not control me. They would not dictate my reality, nor have me walk into walls and doorways and think myself clumsy.

While shopping, we spoke in our own sign language. Ian had taught himself the alphabet in sign, but mostly we had our own private signs. They were more simplified, single-movement mime than abstract sign language. These connected with thought using much less physical strain, mental mechanics, and time than speaking did. They were also easier to monitor and maneuver than speech and left us less prone to flying off onto unintentional stored, triggered tangents.

I would convey my thoughts and Ian would speak them. I would get furious and throw a wobbly, hearing him lazily revert to using a stored voice. He understood my disgust for his weakness, in view of the consequences our pact had had for me. Very slowly he would repeat what he had to say, keeping track of the feeling of the sounds in his mouth, making sure that the choice of words and phrases was his own, not the tagalong, borrowed, irrelevant verbal baggage of others.

Finally, after several weeks, my speaking was roughly comprehensible to most people and I could now articulate fast enough to speak with my own voice in whole sentences rather than single words. The overpronounced *s* and deliberate *r* and *l* and *th* I had spat out as characters now showed why they had been so overstressed and deliberate—I found them the hardest and most time-consuming of all to pronounce and in the space and time I had (in fact, most were missing, especially in the middle of words). Vowels had been easiest and so had *t* and *m* and *p*.

It occurred to me how much of my processing time and energy had been diverted into articulating, in a presentable and impressive way, the sounds I could not easily connect with. It occurred to me how much of a backseat my selfhood had taken when "the world" applauded "my sexy voice," "my crisp clear voice," "my cheerful voice," "my bold sure voice," or "my interesting accent."

Just as there had had to come a time to relate without the masks of Carol or Willie, the time had come to dare to speak with my own voice to someone other than Ian. I had to prove in actions that I felt that I was nothing to be ashamed of.

Inside of me, my defenses ran a mental tape of impressions of what my monster might have said: "Your voice is so ugly," "That's not you," "You sound like a spastic." The mental mock-criticism had stung and I went to face Ian. My eyes full of tears

111

and defiance, I pointed at my open mouth. "Beautiful," I said, "my voice is beautiful. Donna's voice." "Yes," Ian replied, "Donna's voice is beautiful."

Mentally, I went through all the people who'd survived the derobing of Carol and Willie. Of all the people my defenses met, there had been no more than a handful I could trust with my real self. Of those, there were even fewer for whom aesthetics didn't matter. Any who had found my voice attractive were thrown out of my list. Any who found an ego trip in how "talented" I was for singing or dancing were thrown out because the body connections behind most of that "talent" were not mine. I wrote letters to most of the people I knew, telling them I wanted out. Finally, shaking from head to toe, I picked up the phone to call one of the few who I felt could handle it: Dr. Marek.

Dr. Marek was the educational psychologist who had diagnosed me, at the late age of twenty-five, as having the pervasive developmental disorder of autism. He was a hard-edged, strong, and yet gentle, wise old owl, someone who had understood the battle I'd waged all my life to "act normal" and maintain an impressive façade at the expense of experiencing a life. More than this, he had been enough of a human being to see what this had cost me and that, as useful as apparent abilities can be, there comes a time for all people to know acceptance as their flawed selves rather than the surface image they may have worked to refine.

My voice in my own ears sounded like a speech therapist's nightmare, even though it was more beautiful to me than the most beautiful bird's song. I didn't know if Dr. Marek would even be able to understand me.

From ten thousand miles away, in Australia, Dr. Marek answered the phone. When I realized that he could understand me and that Ian wasn't the only one in the world who could comprehend me as me, I started crying. Dr. Marek didn't laugh at me. He didn't tell me this wasn't me or that everything was in my head. He told me I was brave and that I sounded fine. He had kicked my defenses through the goalposts and I had scored the points. I felt the hopelessness subside. It would all be okay.

＊ ＊ ＊

As the weeks passed, Ian and I had got into a more manageable position with ourselves and our defenses. We'd cleaned up the mountain of mess with our dustpans and brushes, but debris still blew in every now and then.

We resolved to remain committed to not indulging automatic stored actions or stored voices in place of exercising and developing actions and voices that could come from ourselves if given the chance. But we also had to accept that there were some things which would, for the sake of functioning, convenience, and safety, have to be done on automatic pilot using stored repertoires.

One of these things was driving. Ian did almost all of the driving and agreed to monitor certain driving moves that were more obviously copied than others. Another of these activities was washing and dressing, which usually happened within time frames that were too narrow to fully manage the complex and rigorous movement of body parts and the management of the soap or clothing as well. For a while, Ian helped me wash and dress and then I did these things as a combination of him and me. It still felt better to be doing something partly as someone you liked and felt safe with, rather than as an array of someones you didn't like or feel safe with. We continued, however, to make sure that we tried to stand as ourselves, move as ourselves, speak as ourselves, eat as ourselves, and express or not express emotions as ourselves.

In a way, we had to accept that we hadn't won our battle. We had had a major war with our defenses over body mechanics and expression of emotions, and we had won back a lot of territory and overthrown a lot of alienation from our selves. There was still a long way to go. We had only begun to distinguish our own thoughts from the regurgitated and triggered stored ones—and thoughts were the most widespread and intangible bastion of all.

Ian went automatically for the cornflakes and I went automatically for the herbal tea. It occurred to us that although we'd reclaimed our bodies, we were still riddled with stored, theoretical assumptions about our true intentions and wants.

There had to be a way to check to see if we really liked or wanted something. Yet, there we stood facing the cupboard or the fridge with no internal feedback for anything we reached for. Plastic, compulsion-driven smiles would attempt to spread across our faces as we reached for things that were theoretically likable or delicious—according to our family members, people we'd known, or TV commercials and jingles.

None of the preempted outward expressions of emotion were connected to anything inside. We wondered if there were also feelings inside that were waiting for us to know what they belonged to. Each of these disconnected realms was like a person knocking on the doors of the same house from different sides but doing so in different dimensions. The questions were: How to get these two forces on speaking terms? How to bring those dimensions together and open the door for them, in order to show them who was on the other side?

Ian stood before the fridge facing a bag of green chili peppers left over from kebabs we'd bought. "Are you sure you want to eat those?" I asked.

"Yes," said Ian flippantly.

"How do you know that you know?"

"I like chili peppers," said Ian.

"How do you know you like them?" I asked.

"I've always eaten them."

"Would you check with yourself?" I asked.

Ian remained there looking at the peppers and asking himself mentally whether he wanted to eat some of these. "Nothing," said Ian. There had been no internal response beyond a flood of intellectual justifications as to why he must theoretically want them. He'd been eating them for years every time he had kebabs and he assumed he more than liked them from the frequency with which he ate them.

Ian tried again, this time asking himself out loud and getting a bit frustrated, "Do I want to eat these chili peppers?"

No response.

"I'll ask you," I said. "Do you want to eat these chili peppers?"

No response.

Then I thought about myself and how I might find out.

I'd never really seen the relevance of finding out whether I actually wanted or liked the things I assumed that I liked or wanted. As long as things were theoretically good for me or the commercials had said they were good for you or worked well, I had always assumed that was how other people knew what they wanted and liked, so that was good enough for me. Exceptions were only when something continually made me retch or made people laugh at me. Then, eventually, no matter what anyone said, that thing was no good. But I could remember internal feedback and the frustrating lack of it and I went into my mind to word-search the feeling and ran the film to see how it had worked.

"Do you like it?" asked the visitor who sat at the kitchen table. I looked at the string bag I'd been given as a present. I had no idea what I felt.

Another time, my father had handed me something. He didn't ask me if I liked it. He never asked, he stated. Maybe he'd learned there was no point in questions when you wouldn't get answers to them.

"No, she doesn't want it," he announced boldly to himself out loud, taking it back. I stood still, like a doll, looking at the object he had taken back. He looked at the object intently with mock-delight and fascination. "You don't want this," he said to himself. Without thinking, my hand grabbed for the object. "Yes, she likes that," he said out loud with an invisible and inaudible but present chuckle. My face had burned up and the feeling of eating lemons washed over me. He had seen the me in me. I had been there. I felt like I stood under stage lights, rawly exposed as my emotions ate me. I took the object and left the room.

I asked Ian again, this time indirectly, as a statement, "Ian wants to eat those chili peppers."

No response.

I figured that what worked for me didn't work for him. Then, another thought came to me and I said, "Ian does not want to eat those chili peppers."

Ian's face lit up like a house catching fire.

Ian figured maybe he wanted something else or maybe he wasn't hungry. "Wait," I said. "I want to check something first.

"Ian likes green chili peppers," I said.

No response.

"Ian doesn't like green chili peppers."

Ian lit up again, like some cheeky little boy caught out.

Ian was amazed at how this response had come about and I explained how I worked it out to check, even though I had never used it with anyone else, nor had I taught anyone to use it to help me.

Every new learning brings with it a temporary shake-up of old, albeit not so healthy, security tactics. Now that we had acknowledged that we had basically no idea of what we liked and wanted, the "ourness" of our things began to feel claustrophobic rather than secure. It was all potentially "other" now.

The worst part was food. Now, as our hands reached out assumingly, following deeply entrenched stored eating rules, we felt repelled by our own actions, as though we were somehow literally feeding our defenses and feeding compulsion. We watched each other eating, suspiciously looking for telltale signs in each other's unaware expression that would give away a dislike for the things we were ingesting.

Ian caught out some responses in me that I was unaware of.

"Do you like that?" he said, referring to the tahini covered rice cake I was eating.

"I think so," I said. All I knew was that what I was eating was "good for me" and that I probably wasn't allergic to it.

"Would you check?" asked Ian. I looked at the food and felt nothing. I looked from the food and back to Ian, but still felt nothing. "Ask," I said.

"Does Donna want that?" asked Ian.

There was no response. Inside of me, flat mental triggered responses of the expected choices of "the polite yes" and the "not so polite no" kept firing, and I tried not to let this mindless crap out of my mouth. "No idea," I replied. "My mind is just firing with possible answers. Say it instead of asking it."

"Donna wants that," said Ian, referring to the food.

There was no response. I wondered whether my defenses were so hyped up in there, so propped and ready to give their quiz-contestant responses that they wouldn't let my own responses through.

Ian tried another one: "Donna doesn't want that."

My feelings overtook me with a *whoosh,* like I'd just eaten a lemon. I looked at the food in my hand and threw it in the bin. Then I stood there sullenly. If I didn't want that, how the hell was I going to find out what I did want? I threw a wobbly and Ian said he would help me find out what I did want.

Ian and I went through the kitchen shelves packet by packet, jar by jar, bottle by bottle, and tin by tin. We checked for him and we checked for me. We found, to our surprise, that we didn't like and dislike the same things, and that we didn't like most of the things we thought we did and we did like a lot of the things we thought we didn't.

We got to a point where the rubbish bin was full of things neither of us liked. We were saying things about what was left on the shelf like, "Was it you or me that didn't like peanut butter?" We drew up columns on a piece of paper and wrote in them Ian's likes and Donna's likes.

The bin was full and the shelves were empty and we had a list of things we could use as a shopping list. It was a beautiful feeling to know that you knew what you liked to eat and could eat it. It was an empowering feeling to know that you no longer were ingesting foods you didn't like just because "the world" hoo-ha had somehow told you to.

What had began with the shelves now flowed into meal choices. While Ian stuck to eating things he at least had found out that he liked. I wanted to know not only whether I was eating something that I liked but whether I was having a want to eat a particular thing at a particular time.

Ian reached easily for the cornflakes day after day. Meanwhile, I would stand about the kitchen sulkily; finally, Ian agreed to forgo his breakfast and peaceful morning orientation and plunge instead into the plodding mental mechanics of helping me check all possible edible wants that our kitchen could hold until we had found me the unknown breakfast that I was unaware of wanting. When we stumbled upon it after the second, fifth, or tenth try, the effects were always the same—like being freed to actually enjoy my breakfast as my own choice, and a choice that came from want. It was the best way to enjoy a breakfast and improved upon the food itself in a way no amount of good cooking or so-called good food ever could. Breakfast was no longer "breakfast," it was "*my* breakfast"; and instead of being a chore that I forced myself through just to keep myself away from physicians, it was becoming an enjoyable event.

Checking extended into eating out. We found out that not only did Ian detest the Indian food which he had continually gorged himself on, but that neither of us liked eating out at all. We got ourselves a handful of takeout menus and sat about checking them with each other until we had an inventory to choose from. No longer would Ian have the waiters choose his meals for him. No longer would I eat according to the theory of what was good for me or meant to be delicious. We began to taste our food and all its textures. Food no longer felt like something forced on us.

The TV burbled most nights and Ian and I often sat watching whatever was on or flicking channels continually. At other times, Ian would pick up a book to read and I would do something I considered "useful." Late in the evening we would sleep, me using Ian's sleeping habits as a model to mirror.

We came to check about the want to watch certain programs, as well as our assumed interest. Ian found out that he didn't enjoy horror films after all and that Stephen King books weren't for him. I found out that I wasn't as interested in Oprah Winfrey and Sally Jessy Raphael as I thought I was. We both learned that we not only had unstoppable tiredness coincidentally come over us, but that we actually had wants to sleep.

Our defenses brewed and roared and stormed with each un-masked compulsion that was discarded. Their whole security had been wound up in these petty structures, which had provided a portable, though shallow and brittle, fragile sort of mock–identity which the defenses now defended fiercely. We weren't just dis-carding their symbols, we were discarding their structures and their memories—even though we had little or none of our own to put in their place. We were telling them that their presence was not only worthless but worse than having nothing at all.

There was another unforeseen consequence to checking. The specialship built between Ian and me was at least half built upon the appearance of what each of us was. Ian was the man who read Stephen King novels, loved Indian food, and ate green chili pep-pers. I was the person who watched Oprah Winfrey and Sally Jessy Raphael and ate tahini on rice cakes. Though half of our specialship was built on what we sensed of each other—the "be" of who each of us was beyond all appearances and transitory trim-mings—that other half could not sustain the earthquake it had been through.

As our checking stoked the fires under our defenses' cauldron of churning insecurity, Ian and I were more and more compelled to look at each other as strangers. Doors that were left open were now getting closed. Our defenses drove us to check each other's eyes, more for reasons to feel insecure than to build security; otherwise, we were avoiding each other's eyes altogether. In our claustrophic living space, we were winding ourselves further into our own spheres.

The unsayable was said. We admitted that we felt like strangers. My defenses cashed in with the logical follow-through. "What's going to happen about that?" came the verbalized thought that slipped straight out of my mouth. Surely, strangers do not sleep next to each other with pushed-together beds, came another logical follow-through. This undeniably made sense, even if it made no personal sense. We didn't bother checking for wants and just moved the beds apart to where they were "meant" to be.

In an all-or-nothing world, I knew where we were heading but I didn't have the strength to control or stop it. It was like part of my brain had locked me out.

The monster of compulsion is one that knocks upon your door in impulse or in thought. Once you've opened that door, he won't walk in, he'll barge in. It is a fool who thinks he can close the door on a ravenous giant. In our case, there were two fools.

When you feed the monster of compulsion, its hunger grows and it doesn't just ask for more, it asks for double. Separating the beds was the first step to where our defenses wanted us, rid of what they now knew was the potential source of their own destruction: our power to help each other.

I couldn't function properly without some of my defenses' structures, but they could act without mine. They didn't need emotion. They could get by fine without it and neither missed it nor apparently remembered it when it was gone. I could not entice them to listen to my anguish, even if they could entice me to listen to their logic.

Having compelled me to act upon their thought, I could feel my defenses grow in strength within me. No longer backed into a corner, they were winning this round. I could have tried to tell Ian what was going on, but logical, impersonal, defense-driven, stored thoughts were tumbling down on me like hail; my own connections to expression just couldn't compete with the barrage, the intensity, and the pace. It is wrong to say I wanted to stop thinking, because I wasn't thinking. I was having thoughts. I could feel these ravenous self-destructive urges almost glowing with vindication as they prompted Ian with the logical next step.

Getting Ian out of the door was the ultimate separation and it didn't matter a damn whether I wanted him out or not. Logic was logic was logic. My defenses had no empathy. It wouldn't have mattered if Ian had broken down in tears. They'd have dealt with the matter like tidying dust away with a brush and shovel.

Suggesting more than asking, Ian was given the option to leave. He did not break into tears. His defenses, glad to have an escape, seized the opportunity and had my defenses define their version of what I wanted. My defenses, unable to take the personal responsibility for what they were pushing him into, fired back, using our checking technique as a weapon.

Ian's face was not his own. It was riddled with poised anger and a competitive need to win that made him look scowling and sneering at the same time. The sight caused fear in me, and this fear fueled both my deeper retreat and the endurance of my defenses. "Go on," prompted my defenses in the style of a playground bully and hopeful that Ian would take up their offer, "check."

"Ian wants to stay living with you," came the words coldly from Ian's mouth, his icy, hard face unchanging. "Ian doesn't want to stay living with you," came more words, quickly and without prompt. His mouth sprang into a flick-of-the-switch smile, his eyes remained as cold as ice. Though I could see his expression was performed and that his defenses themselves had done an imitation of our own checking, it suited my defenses to accept it all without question. "You'd better arrange to move your things then," came a matronly gloat, careful to sound detached and not too triumphant.

My adrenaline level was sky-high. My heart raced. But none of my anxiety showed. I could feel my face, calm and cool. I was in there somewhere. I was terrified of my defenses' hatred of me and their frightening power to shatter my life ruthlessly. I was terrified of being out of control of my body and hearing the voice of my mother and other sharp-edged strangers coming out of my mouth. The takeover was so powerful that I was scared that my connections to expression were lost, perhaps for good. The dread of hopelessness compounded fear. I felt abused by an abuser in my own body and unable to fight back as it tore my life into shreds just because it was "on a roll."

Ian's body stormed triumphantly into the bedroom that was stacked from floor to ceiling with musical instruments and other salable things. His hands rifled the yellow pages like a sadistic dentist ripping out teeth. With Richard's crispness and professionalism his fingers forcefully began to dial the number of a moving van, but Ian's body was now shaking and his chiseled face was starting to crack.

Seeing him get real had coaxed me out of the shadows just a step. I could see that he was fighting and was just as scared as me.

I broke through and drove my body over to the phone and pressed the button down in the cradle, cutting off the call. Ian stood there frozen in midair. His defenses waited for the next trigger. Ian waited to be saved.

My body stood there expressionlessly. Willie buckled under the unexpected blow of my retaliation and sought to save face with a compromise. He changed his tactics saying, "Come on. Let's talk about this. You know it's silly to check when we're in a defensive state because it's only our defenses who will do the checking and perform the required responses."

"That's not you," said Ian's defenses sharply, recognizing Willie and not yet willing to surrender. I felt afraid they'd all take off again.

"Do you agree though? We should never use checking in a defensive state. We both know defenses can so easily call themselves 'I' or 'Donna' or 'Ian' and just respond to get what they want," said Willie, playing conciliator and attempting to win points with me now that I was pushing him back out of the door.

"Do you want me to go?" asked Ian.

I felt anxious about that question, unsure that I'd get to answer it and be able to tell him I was sad, scared, and afraid I'd lose my best friend, and that I didn't want him to go anywhere. "I don't know," replied my voice, with Willie's words, "I'd have to check some time but now's not a good time."

With great relief, we found ourselves again and did a postmortem on what had happened. Checking was like an herbal remedy. Just because it could be good for you didn't mean you could take it in all situations.

We pushed the beds back together and sat on them. Calmed down and back to being ourselves, we checked about wanting to live together and found out that we did want to stay living together. We also found out that we wanted to grow together and to learn together who each of us was, and we both admitted that we had a much better chance doing that together than apart.

I talked to Ian about the way my defenses made me feel that they struck bargains with me. Ian reminded me that they were not on my side. I told Ian how they made me fear that without them I'd be helpless in threatening situations. Ian told me that it was probably their interference that had stopped me from developing an ability to take care of and communicate for myself in threatening situations. He may have been right.

My defenses knocked at the door many times, sometimes filling me with the belief that I could say or do something so much more quickly as them. They made me hyperconscious of people's impatience and intolerance and they used this anxiety as justification to let them do "just this." This happened especially when dressing or asking for something was involved.

"Ian," I said. "I'm getting trouble."

"Tell me."

"My defenses make me feel you won't give me time to speak."

"Do you believe that?" asked Ian.

"No," I replied, "but that doesn't fix the pressure."

I explained that when my defenses created that anxiety in me they actually made it harder for me to connect and say and do things as myself. I told Ian how this made it very, very hard even to tell him that I needed time. "One word," Ian told me. "That's all you have to say. Just say 'time.' "

Though I could rarely connect to say "time" under the pressure of my compulsions, I was able to sign "wait." Then Ian would reassure me that I had time; if my anxiety made me unable to hear him with meaning, he would say it again and get me to clarify not what he had said but what he had meant. This external reassurance that I had what I needed and that my defenses were wrong was usually enough to disarm them.

Ian's body drove a classic twenty-three-year-old Volvo. His hand had paid more than £250 for it as it sat rotting in someone's backyard. Ian's mouth had named it Henry and his defenses were compulsively possessive about how anyone touched or even looked at it. His defenses would go about patting it and talking to it, saying sorry to it for driving it too fast or if bushes touched its paintwork.

If you slammed the door too hard for his defenses' impression of Henry's liking, you could see the disapproval. Ian's muscles would tense up and, like an old miser spending a penny, he'd get a rigid look about him. "Sorry," I'd say.

"Don't say sorry to me," his defenses would reply in what was always the same words, pace, and intonation. "Say sorry to Henry."

"Sorry, Henry," I'd say compliantly, feeling bullied.

I was not allowed to drive this car. Even Ian's body would rarely drive it if another car was available. The only exception was when it seemed a fitting trip that "Henry would enjoy." Ian's defenses dreamed of getting another Volvo of the same age as a "friend for Henry" and felt sorry for the car's loneliness in being so different and rare compared with the other cars on the road.

Ian felt guilty about his possessiveness of this car. He knew that it didn't seem fair that we shared just about everything else but he couldn't share this. He disliked what he saw in the way he behaved about the Volvo, and this drove his defenses to constantly justify why I couldn't be allowed to drive it and why "Henry wasn't up to it."

People would make a fuss over the car as it was parked in the street. Ian's defenses would scowl possessively at anyone who was looking at it, as if they'd somehow smeared the car's dignity. Yet, at the same time that one part of him made a big hoo-ha about its being noticed, another part of him compulsively dropped reminders that it *was* a "classic car."

Ian decided to challenge his compulsions. He would fight his compulsions to let me drive the car.

I drove it too fast. I changed the gears too roughly. I moved the turn-signal stick too harshly. I closed the driver door too brutally. Ian had been unable to stop his mouth as constant harshtoned criticisms poured out. I ended up so nervous, waiting for the next attack, that I could no longer think at all; I found myself unable to remember how to turn at a roundabout, or what gear I should be in, or that I should be indicating or changing lanes or checking the mirrors. I ended up asking for every possible instruction. My selfhood had found it all too personally dangerous and had gone AWOL.

Ian hated himself and progressively realized that he didn't love this car as he had believed that he did. He had been compelled to act like he loved it simply because he knew it to be a sought-after car, the kind of car a person would love.

We found an answer to the Henry problem. We would buy another car. We decided we would buy an old clunky Land Rover. The idea suited Willie, who thought of it as the ultimate rugged man's car. It suited Richard, because the need for something as clunky and rugged as an old Land Rover justified the need to preserve the delicacy of his classic touring Volvo. The justification they both gave was that, with the properties we intended to view, a Land Rover would stand up to the mud and blackberry bushes much better.

Without checking whether we actually wanted a Land Rover or whether it was just a theoretical possibility or something our defenses wanted; we were headed off to some backyard car dealer we'd found in the columns of a cheap car-trader's magazine.

We arrived at a private house with a long private driveway, locked gates, and a guard dog. The man put away the guard dog and we drove into a backyard filled with derelict Land Rovers, vehicles that Willie and Richard chose to consider restorable.

The man waffled on about how great and rare old Land Rovers were as he led us over to the one we'd come to see. It had been advertised in the paper at £750 with a newly issued Ministry of Transport certificate saying it was in good mechanical order. We'd taken £1000 out of the bank, which we'd brought there in our pockets.

The Land Rover had been hand-painted, but some of that was over sticky tape and the last few coats of paint, a few layers of rust, and a few holes showed through here and there. The man said, "You won't find a Land Rover of this age in better condition. This one has been taken good care of and has had a lot of work done to it. See this here, this is what you look for. See, this one's in good condition and this here has been recently redone." Ian and I looked at each other blankly.

Our mouths were just about to buy it when, probably as a last-minute diversion, we spotted another one on the other side of the yard and headed for it. "That one's a beauty," said the man.

This one was older. It was built in the fifties as a general's Land Rover, the man said. It had no engine in it, a few flat tires, and no license plates, was full of spiderwebs, and missing a few electricals. Wires dangled around the floor wrapped in painted insulation tape. It had no door locks or window winders and the doors themselves merely lifted out (the whole car was disassemblable, like Lego). "Can you start this one up?" my mouth asked, a replay of other car-yard scenes. Ian pointed out that it had no engine. The man told us he had the engine for it and was restoring it and that it would be ready soon.

I climbed into the back and looked at the interesting light fixture. Ian and I buzzed about the car looking at all its oddities. "Oh, you like this one then," said the man.

Ian and I looked at each other, assuming this man must have seen something in us that told him that. "How much is this one?" Ian asked.

"Well, this one's rarer than that one," said the man. "But I could do it for a thousand pounds with an M.O.T."

Well, we thought logically and impersonally, with a Ministry of Transport certificate, it would be ready and safe to drive—even if it didn't look capable at the moment. "When would it be ready?" asked Ian, following through on the same impersonal logical track.

"Oh, I could get it ready for you in a few weeks," said the man. We followed through to the next logical step and handed the man one thousand pounds in cash.

Four weeks later the man called to say it was ready and we arrived to pick up our Land Rover. We climbed into it and with a push of a button (it didn't start like other cars), we hobbled it away down the road doing its maximum speed of forty miles per hour with a *clunkety-clunkety-clunk, crunch, crunch.*

The Land Rover was the noisiest, smelliest, slowest car we'd ever been on the road in. I'd been in only one comparable, but that was just a shell of a truck that I'd driven around a farm field once.

The petrol fumes from the exhaust pipe were coming up through the holes in the floor under our feet—Ian was getting all muzzy headed, and I was clearing my throat constantly. The sound drowned out all other traffic as well as our voices; we couldn't hear each other speak and had to shout. Even then, we could hardly make each other out in the jumble of noises. The noise had one small benefit for me. My attention-span problem wasn't so bad because the noises kept me alert. I couldn't get lulled into doing everything in a dream state on autopilot because the sound was too loud and too inconsistent. Sure, I couldn't think about the driving because the noises distracted me too much, but at least I was aware that I was being distracted.

After several days of migraines, Ian decided we had to do something about those fumes. I climbed up into the attic and fetched down some old salvaged carpet scraps and went out to fit them to the Land Rover. I stuck tape over the holes and then laid the carpet over them—smells gone. We took cotton wool with us to put in our ears when we went out in Land Rover, so that solved the noise problem, too. I drifted back into driving on autopilot, but at least my subconscious mind could drive consistently well and without much distraction.

At home, we had hacked out a driveway where there was none; however, in the five-by-five-foot garden, there wasn't space for more than one car on our rubble driveway. With the Land Rover unlockable, "poor Henry" had to park out on the street. Henry sat there gathering dust and car emissions as we drove everywhere in the Land Rover instead without much criticism from Ian at all.

Ian's defenses went to visit the Volvo regularly. One week, it was one thing, another week, another thing. Vandals had run their keys down the side of its paintwork. There was a combination of indifference and resentment and silent rage within Ian. It was as though one part of him actually hated the car while the other part used it as some symbol of himself by which to test the worthiness of some people or respond to the unworthiness of others. Yet another part of him had just collected it as something socially valuable. I could see it was not so much a car as a wall, a symbol, and a prop.

We took the Land Rover out for a drive. It started to rattle and clunk even worse than before, like a pile of rusty old tin cans. It coughed and spluttered and then something hit the ground and dragged along with a scraping noise.

The muffler had fallen off. Oh well, we thought, we'll put it back on. It wasn't that easy. The whole thing was rusty, full of holes, and broken in too many places; it had been stuck together up until now only with a mechanic's version of chewing gum.

We tied the dangling old pipes out of the way with a few pieces of string and hobbled the car off to find a mechanic.

The mechanic we found at a shopping complex told us he couldn't do anything about it. The man who'd sold it to us had been right about one thing: it was rare. It was so rare the mechanic didn't have the parts, nor could he get them. We drove off again to find someone who would risk the operation on our vehicular geriatric.

The feeling that the whole vehicle was about to fall apart made it feel as though we carried that Land Rover to the next mechanic, a specialist in these vehicles. He took one look at it and told us we were wasting our money doing anything to it. We didn't understand. We'd paid good money for it. It was a good car. It was rare. It was a collector's car. It used to belong to a general. It had a Ministry of Transport certificate to say it was good and worthy of being on the road.

We asked the mechanic what he suggested we do. He suggested we return it and get our money back. He said that the Land Rover wasn't much good, and that it was made up of all sorts of other cars, and that he couldn't even fit the right exhaust pipe to it because the parts it was to join to were from two other different models. This mechanic had done the best he could with a bit of this and a bit of that and our car was just as unoriginal as ever. In fact, it probably was original and rare. There had probably never been another car with the same combination of odd and make-do parts as this one.

Next, we took the Land Rover to the testing station, which issued certificates of roadworthiness.

The Land Rover failed miserably. Its brakes were faulty, its lights were faulty, its steering was faulty, its wipers were faulty, its tires were faulty, its brackets and bolts and bits and bobs were all faulty, nonstandard, below standard, and every other polite but negative word that a mechanic at a testing station can say without gloating, "You got ripped off."

"How could it have failed?" we wanted to know when it had just recently been given a clean bill of health. Apparently, that M.O.T. certificate could have been nothing else but a fraud, written out by a friend of the owner who had probably never even seen the car.

Like a doctor writing a sick note, the tester wrote a piece of paper for the car. The car wasn't allowed back on the road until a car doctor had fixed it up—and that seemed likely to be never.

The Land Rover sat on the drive and we went back to using the Volvo.

Ian gritted his teeth against his compulsions and tried harder and harder not to let unmeant criticisms pour out when I drove, and hated himself more and more when they did. Then, he hated the Volvo more and more for being the object that compelled him to behave in such a despised way. He looked at the long scratch down the side. He looked at the snapped off aerial from another attack of vandalism. He looked at the rust coming through the paintwork. It was like the car itself was nagging and whining at him and making him feel guilty for not taking more responsibility for it, when it would have been so highly valued by others. Ian kicked it. Then he kicked it again. And he didn't say, "Sorry, Henry."

With the admission that we wanted to stay living together indefinitely came a threatening void that can only be called a "forever feeling." Nobody knows how wide or deep forever is, so it can't be described and I couldn't imagine it, even if I could feel it.

In each moment, forever does not exist. Only out of the moment does the perception of forever live as an experience. Without form, imagination, or description of this concept, it had an overwhelmingly free-floating feeling about it. If the emotional overload I called the Big Black Nothing was an express elevator with no bottom floor, then the forever feeling was an express elevator with no top floor. Partially hypnotic, "forever" beckons an impulse to free-fall. To that rigid defensive part of me that demands a map and book of guarantees. "Forever" meant lack of control and future-blindness. Ian and I, however, had seen what our defenses would do with their so-called protectiveness of us; we were forewarned and forearmed.

There had been an emotional admission of closeness and the winning of this new round against our defenses had had us both reaching out to that forever feeling, and with that came a daring to express it through touch.

Knowing touch with walls was the first step. To know touch through free-falling was to allow those steps to walk and that walk to run. Though my body seemed indecisive as to whether it would free-fall with me or desert me, Ian and I were now more able to explore touch freely with self-expression and without fear of emotion.

Instead of making us feel nauseated or deadened, touch between two free-fallers felt like we were swimming in a safe vastness without influence from the past or "the world." We freely explored each other's faces and hair with our fingers and noses and cheeks. We explored each other's outlines and curves, like a blind person feels a sculpture to internalize the experience of it.

Waves came over us and we spoke mentally to them, welcoming them and asking their names. When no answers came, we helped each other through checking.

Some of these waves were sadness in light of how shockingly different touch now felt by comparison with the past. Some of these waves had a shy and evasive face, which we called embarrassment. Some of these waves had an asking face, which we called the need for reassurance that it was okay to do something

131

when you didn't quite know why, what, or how. Some of these waves had a searching and eager look, which we called interest and curiosity.

We had stored ideas of how a person responds to the urge to be physically close and when a person is meant to feel urges to be physically close, but all of that felt alien and bullshit. Though our defenses prompted us with these stored databases, to use them would have been worse than self-defeating and futile—it would have been an insult to each other. Yet, every intention coming from ourselves didn't translate its way into physical actions easily, in the way it does on TV or in the bedroom-classrooms of "the worlders."

We felt our own bodies through contact with each other's bodies, each of us like a blanket we could wrap ourselves in. Where we had just developed touch as a social reassurance, we were now discovering touch as a physical and perceptual need. Instead of touch cutting us off from feeling where we were or who we were, touch was now doing the opposite. It told us who we were in relation to each other and what our physical boundaries, characteristics, likes, and dislikes were, all in a personal, nontheoretical, experiential way.

We lay against each other's body, smelling each other and tracing one another's outlines and exploring where the parts all came together. Though we had both been an ongoing part of the bedroom repertoires of a handful of "the worlders," we had always been too busy playing our scenes to notice how the other person's body was joined together, and we had never really seen the relevance in knowing.

All of the embarrassment we had never felt or been able to show we now felt and showed. The trust that had been irrelevant in our meeting of "the world" bedroom expectation we now felt and owned with its awesome presence and tentative balance. The variation of touch that comes from feedback from self had never been part of playing out a bedroom performance. The natural and spontaneous variation of touch now came through our fingers and hands and feet and toes and told us who we were, and we were embarrassed and vulnerable in the knowing.

Up until now we had had an "accidental-touching myth," whereby we would somehow find our bodies touching, say sorry, and ask if the other person had minded. The other person would usually casually reply that he or she didn't, and no one ever had to acknowledge intention or want. This was our safe way of relating as two people who had considered themselves strongly asexual.

Asexuality had been the only thing that had made sense of the total lack of personal connection to the sexual performances we'd each been through with "the worlders" as part of passing for "normal." When we'd found each other, we'd been so relieved to know that here, with one another, sexuality was not assumed to be the culmination of a closeness that we knew would never happen. We knew that kind of closeness could never happen to us because we were too autonomous. We lived in self-revolving worlds, where time spent with each other did not accumulate or build into anything greater. That had always been our experience of "me plus you." "Me plus you" never equaled "us."

We had no reason to assume that this equation would be different here between two albatrosses. We had no intention of breaking down our newfound self-understanding about asexuality. But, more and more, like an elbow wearing its way through an old sleeve, the accidental-touching myth was wearing a hole in our self-definitions as asexual.

Whether we felt asexual with regard to people who were "not like us" was showing itself to be irrelevant to what happens when two people "like us" got free enough of expectation and stored learning to know what they feel and to choose.

Self-definition can bring belonging, self-expression, pride, and self-assertion. That same self-definition, however, can wear out its time without anyone daring to notice or question that its time has passed. When that happens, self-definition can be the stifling of the same self-expression it once freed.

There had been a time when the label "asexual" had our names on it, a time when we stood in "the world" not as who it wanted or expected us to be but who we were and we'd felt free and equal and okay. Slowly, we'd grown beyond that label with each other. Though we were probably still asexual in relation to everyone else, our intimacy had outgrown this label—even if our defenses had found it a very warm cocoon.

Our minds were both shouting, you don't want this, you don't want this. Our emotions, however, were ready for this and were now on speaking terms with us. Our bodies both were shouting, yes, we *do* want this, we *do* want this. We'd reached the stage beyond having a body: the want to share it.

The performance of emotions, social interest, closeness, sensuality, intimacy, and sexuality were things that had been forced upon both of us before we had reached the developmental stage where these things could be experienced, not just complied with. Touch hadn't felt right before because it had always been the wrong time, with the wrong sort of person, with the wrong "motivations," and without half of the necessary developmental ingredients. We were like roses in poor soil that had been spray painted every so often to make us look good. We'd found each other, cleaned off the paint, given each other good soil to grow in, and we were more beautiful than we could ever have been under all of that suffocating paint.

For every strategy there is a counterstrategy. Our defenses were not our eyes and ears but their databases in our brains; these ever alert databases overheard and oversaw what we and anyone else did or said. To them, we were often just another form of threatening "other."

We discovered they had developed private jokes with the words "I" and "you" and even our own names.

Their trademarks of self-referral had been terms like "one," "a person," and "you." Though they used the word "I," they used it with the same give-away overemphasis with which they used words like "we" and "us." Those words sounded personal and intimate, but in reality they were distancing from the sense of responsibility or community in those words.

Now that the words "I," "Donna," and "Ian" were being used for checking, our defenses no longer had an aversion to these words. They'd learned that our checking usually resulted in a challenge to their ideas, accumulations, and rituals. Our defenses now took those words as cues to initiate a response to ward off a challenge.

I would ask to check something. I'd stand before Ian and say, "I want this." My defenses would identify with the word "I" and run a program of all the reasons why they theoretically did not want "this." My otherwise relaxed state would be disturbed, setting up instead a feeling of being pushed about. I would be blocked from any internal feedback responses to do with the want for what we were checking. I'd try again. "Donna wants this." The same barrage of their theoretical alternative wants would rain on me and I'd feel flustered and dead.

It was as though our defenses were thieves and we were banks that were constantly installing new thief-proof systems. The thieves were in our heads, though, and had access to everything we did. Like a computer playing chess with itself, they'd find a way to crack each new system.

We were disappointed to find that something that had set us free had led to a dead end. It seemed our defenses were trying to force us to live as them by frustrating all the alternatives we could find to living without them. We had been fools to think it would have been so easy.

We decided we would keep trying. Instead of relying on the same technique, we would keep discovering new techniques.

In order to stop the defenses from being cued by his name, we would emphasize each time that we were checking for Ian and not his defenses. If we used the word "I" we would say, "I—meaning me, Donna, and not my defenses—want a bath."

We would have to get very specific with our checking as our defenses would pounce on the slightest loophole. If we said, "Donna wants cake," my defenses would mentally prompt with the idea that the word "cake" meant cream cake, which I couldn't eat without reacting badly to it—even if the "cake" referred to was one I had made myself and could eat without any allergic reaction. Instead of being able to check simply, we would have to quantify which thing, when and where, so our defenses could not trick us.

It was not as though our defenses had wants of their own. They just had very rigid theoretical stored ideas of what a person wants, what a person likes, what a person eats with cooked meat, what a person wears with those shoes, and every other possible rule.

There was a rule about eating cold foods with cold foods and hot foods with hot foods, sweet foods with sweet foods, and savory foods with savory foods. There was a rule about wearing white shoes with white shirts and black shoes only with black stockings. There was a rule about only "proper" Rice Krispies being any good and a rule about only liking to sleep on sheets that were put on the bed with their seams down. Our defenses had rules for every occasion and they quickly called these rules wants. They considered themselves at war with us and their latest rule was to "win" at checking.

Our defenses interfered with our pronunciation of a key word, making it mentally meaningless, or they would replace an intended word with an unintended one that had an ambiguous meaning. We had to be very attentive to every syllable used.

Our defenses would resolve that a response to something was secret or not allowed and would block all natural body feedback to emotions. We developed a counterstrategy that went, "If Ian were allowed to show it, Ian would show that he didn't want this." They then created a "secret about a secret" strategy. So we had to say "Ian's defenses have a secret about keeping secret that Ian wants the black shoes."

We tried embarrassing them into departure by shouting out our checking in department stores. It worked for a while, but then our defenses started to do impressions of us.

When we would self-check by saying our own want out loud, they would sometimes preempt what we were going to check and speak the checking for us, cutting us off from our bodies and emotions so we could get no internal feedback. When this happened we would counterattack by not speaking, merely pointing to, touching, or signing the object or action of the want that we were checking. Our defenses then rallied by doing the speaking, signing, pointing, or touching. Then we had to get the other person to speak, point, touch, or sign our checking for us.

We developed a "one to ten" rating system for our wants, but our defenses countered with their own one to ten ratings. When they didn't interfere using their own stored "preferences," they developed standard responses to low, high, or medium numbers to try to portray their own wanted responses of "big want," "no want," or "indifference." In any one checking routine of one to ten, we'd find a combination of Ian's responses and those of his defenses.

We had to set up a system of checking the checking. We would check for our own wants and then we would contrast this with checking for our defenses' wants to be sure they hadn't answered for us. That our defenses had no actual wants was irrelevant. Our defenses considered their compulsions to be wants and had their own stored ways of responding to any checking of "wants" and "not wants" with their plastic imitations of our own smiles or expressions of indifference.

It was still possible for us to see the difference between a true emotional expression and a put-on one, but our defenses were constantly on the lookout for feedback as to how the other person had seen through their performances. At first we innocently gave this feedback to each other, not realizing that the question for the feedback had not come from genuine curiosity but from a compulsion to further build a defensive arsenal. Later, when we recognized this trick, for each other's own good, we simply had to refuse to tell how we had known. Yet the more successful our checking became, the more threatened our defenses became of it and the more wrenches they threw into our mechanics.

When Ian was checking a want that went against something that his defenses had stored as trendy and bringing approval, they would give him jubblies. Jubblies were unpleasant and happened in your stomach, like someone grabbing your insides in their fist and squeezing them. The emotional feedback of wants, however, also happened in your stomach, so it was sometimes hard to tell if the jubblies caused by defenses were a sign of personal want or not-want.

Ian and I looked around our kitchen, bathroom, living room, bedroom. We looked at all the things we assumed we liked, wanted, needed, or were attached to. We had some checking to do and our defenses weren't going to like it.

— —

Now that both of us were committed to doing things as ourselves and buying, eating, and doing only things we liked and wanted and not just assumed we liked, each of us became increasingly disturbed when the other appeared to be indulging in something that hadn't been checked. Finally, we decided to do a major exorcism and went around the house from room to room, checking everything.

We checked regarding linen and found that we disliked most of it and were indifferent about the rest. Our house was full of "what a person likes," "what a person needs," "what a person is interested in;" this was based on people we had lived with and TV, the reminders of which were anywhere and everywhere from incomprehensible and irritating to disturbing and traumatic.

We stripped the duvets of their covers and the pillows of their pillowcases. We filled a big black garbage bag with towels, sheets, and tea towels headed for the local Animal Welfare Shop.

We checked bars of soap, our toothbrushes, shampoo, and toothpaste. We checked combs and shaving cream, shavers and nail clippers. We found we hated the smell or taste of some of them; they made us dizzy or physically ill. Other things, we had copied from various people we had known or from the TV. The black garbage bag filled up even higher.

Into the living/bedroom. We checked the furniture, the curtains, the carpet. We checked the television and the video, the cassette player and the piano. We checked the contents of our drawers and wardrobes, knickers by knickers, shirt by shirt. We checked through personal papers and knickknack collections, through every shell and every lint sculpture, dried leaf, and stone. We checked our new wooden beds. If one of us was indifferent but the other had a dislike, it was going. If both of us were indifferent, it could stay.

The rattan living room suite was staying for the time being, out of indifference. The TV and video were staying out of want. The cassette player that I'd just bought was leaving, because it had checked out as my dislike. Ian's tapes of recorded music went and so did most of my collection of bits of rocks and shells and fluff and things. A pile of photos lay among other discarded ex-"treasures."

The new beds were going because we'd found out that neither of us wanted them. These were the first new beds I'd had ever bought myself and I'd slept on mine for only a few months. Now we were going to sell them cheaply and then sleep on the floor until we found some beds we did like.

All but one pair of Ian's boxer shorts were going, and just about everything else he wore. Ian's ex-girlfriend had thrown out most of his clothes about a year ago, because she felt they didn't suit him. Ian now found that he disliked—and felt uncomfortable in—almost all that was left. Ian's defenses were outraged because they'd bought most of these things.

Most of my knickers went. My "best" clothes were all going, too. Willie gritted my teeth disconnectedly from inside, with thoughts that people had said that a piece of clothing "suited" and that a person was meant to wear what "suited" her. Our defenses put up furious internal wobblies over the untrendiness of what was left. They gave us stomach-gnashing jubblies and hailed down upon us with thoughts of who wouldn't like us now and how people who wear something like that get bullied.

We were on the third black garbage bag as we embarked upon the floor-to-ceiling jumble of the bedroom, with its huge store of musical instruments, furniture, and other knickknacks, all bought with the intention that we'd do them up and sell them. We'd since discovered that we didn't want to sell at flea markets at all.

Ian had been involved with various groups and duos who had had a use for his keyboard-playing skills. Our shared "interest" in music had been the original basis upon which we had met but since living with me, Ian played progressively less and less.

Talk of music had led us onto a stored track about getting an electronic keyboard. This talk had been unquestioningly followed through and our legs had gone to a music shop and our hands had paid over the money for a keyboard that fitted an idea of "what a person should have." This, in turn, had been logically followed through with the purchase of recording equipment for this keyboard. The last of Ian's money, the fifteen-hundred-pound deposit he had had for the flat he was going to buy, had gone toward these items and I'd paid for the other half. We stood looking at each other with a mixture of dread and excitement. We checked on the new keyboard and the recording equipment. They were going, too.

There were only three categories of things left to check: the cars we drove, the people we knew, and the things Ian had at his father's house.

We checked about the cars. Our defenses wanted them and we definitely didn't. Both of them were going. We'd sell them and buy something we'd chosen in their place.

We checked about people and found out who our defenses wanted to know, who we wanted to know, and who we were indifferent about. We came to the decision that we would stop knowing anyone our defenses got fed from, we'd continue to know people we were indifferent to (provided that it didn't take too much from us to do so), and we would continue to know the very few people we actually had a want to know.

— ◄

We were out of toothpaste, soap, and shampoo. Ian's last pair of boxer shorts were ready to walk off on their own as he procrastinated over washing them while he considered what he'd wear if he did.

The beds got advertised and sold. We had bargained with the buyer to let us keep the mattresses until we got new beds, so we were sleeping on the floor on the mattresses that he now owned. We were running out of towels. We had only one set of sheets each, with no spares to change them with if we washed them and they didn't dry in time, and our now uncovered duvets were gathering dust. We had to do some shopping.

We went to a menswear shop and went to the rack full of boxer shorts. A shop assistant approached us, saying, "Can I help you?" We looked at each other and then said, "We're fine" and stood silently waiting for the shop assistant to go away. We spent about two hours checking for Ian's wants and likes in boxer shorts and then counterchecking with regards to his defenses. The shop assistant hovered about. "We're fine," I said firmly, trying to keep his annoying influence at bay, lest Ian walk out of the shop with the shop assistant's idea of "boxer shorts that a person would like." When we finally left the shop carrying a bag with boxer shorts in it, Ian looked pleased with himself and his achievement.

At the pharmacist we stood among tubes of toothpaste and toothbrushes. We checked every conceivable type and color of toothbrush and every brand of toothpaste. Staring at us were "Are your Maclean's showing?" and "the Colgate ring of confidence." Our heads were full of images of plaque tablet tests and

141

models licking their teeth, of toothbrushes that got into "those hard-to-reach places" and ideas about "choosing the right toothbrush." Wading through this mental mire was like standing in a rubbish dump and trying to get the smells out of your nose. These triggered thoughts were like TV static and all we wanted was to get a clear picture of our own wants.

It had taken forever, but having got our toothbrushes and toothpastes, we went on to the soap section. We smelled all of the soaps, checking each other's faces for some feedback. A triggered smile here, a triggered smile there. "No, that wasn't mine," one or the other would say. Then, a smell would make one of us light up from inside. "Check this one," we would then say hopefully.

Our soaps in hand, we went to find shampoo. Bottle by bottle, we went through the shampoos, smelling each one. I found some that smelled edible and had to hold myself back from tasting them. Ian held others up to the light to look through the colors.

Next, we went to a linen store. Shop assistants came after us with "Can I help you?" and "What would you like to see?" Before, we used to tell them what we'd come to look at. They'd bring out a collection of something or other and then stand there expectantly, asking, "Are there any here you like?" or "What about these?" There was no way in these situations that we could find any internal feedback at all. "We need to be left alone to choose," I said.

Our defenses led us to a whole range of towels they were "sure" a person would like. None of them checked out. We found two sets of towels that we liked very much after systematically checking through a few that our defenses had felt so indifferent about that they never even drew our attention to their presence. These were obviously towels that hadn't been seen in someone else's house or on a TV commercial.

We'd checked on beds and found to our surprise, shock, and

embarrassment that we didn't want single beds at all. We wanted one double one.

Among the linen were display beds. Our defenses looked for the most resalable, the cheapest, the most durable, the one most like X, Y and Z had had. They avoided the beds that didn't fit into these categories with the assumption that it wouldn't make sense to have one of those or that a person couldn't want them.

We were both strongly driven not to check on one bed in particular. It was a gaudy, white, metal display model with a prissy, dainty, floral duvet. When we came to it, our defenses drove us to think we were "sure" we didn't want it. "It looked like this," "it reminded us of that," "it would probably fall apart," "look at the price." Whatever the justifications our defenses gave for our not wanting it, the real reasons stood loud and clear: this bed itself was embarrassing and the longer they could put off purchasing a double bed, the better were the chances of their trying to redirect us into getting single beds.

We found ourselves wandering away from the bed, compulsively distracted by one thing after another. We realized what was going on and did something about it. We turned around and marched straight over to where the bed was. We found a shop assistant and took out a checkbook. Like a pair of cheeky little children, we bought our bed, defying our domineering inner monsters.

We checked in several stores for three hours through shelves of duvet covers, only to return to the first store. We went back to the bed we had bought. Our minds raced, compelling us to check again. Our defenses prompted us with the thought that we could still get our money back and that the bed hadn't been delivered yet. They compulsively scrutinized the new bed, picking faults with this nut and that bolt and, and, and . . .

The duvet on the bed had been staring at us. A person wouldn't want that, came the thought. It was so prissy, it would get dirty easily, it was too expensive. We checked and found we wanted it.

Our defenses seized an opportunity. They prompted that perhaps it wasn't the bed we'd wanted after all. Perhaps we only wanted the duvet. We checked. It was definitely both. Our stomachs were both in knots. "Jubblies?" said Ian.

"Jubblies," I replied. We both nodded.

— ◢

Just about everything in the bedroom was going to be advertised and sold. We had no garage and not enough backyard from which to have a garage sale. There was no way around the fact that, unless we gave the whole lot to the Animal Welfare Shop, we would have to have a pile of strangers tromp through the house.

All of Ian's savings were tied up in these things. He'd bought his way in and out of friendships and relationships most of his working life and other than this jumble of objects, he had just a few hundred pounds in the bank to show for the past eleven years of his working life. We didn't know how we'd manage, but we decided we'd sell these things from the house.

Our defenses fought harshly over the advertising of the cars. They harassed us with all the practical reasons we should keep one or the other, or that we could keep that one in case we changed our minds or keep this one as an investment for when it would be worth more. When we wouldn't credit this reasoning they gave us jubblies to pressure us into advertising them for what they considered them to be worth.

Ian's defenses were sure that the Volvo was worth a lot of money. After all, it was a classic car. After all, it was a car that "a person would love to have." My defenses were equally haughty. After all, we'd been told that the Land Rover was worth something and was rare and collectible.

The cars were both advertised in the paper for fifteen hundred pounds apiece. There were no replies.

The next week, we drove the cars to local car dealers. Our defenses had had the idea that a person who knew what they were looking at would pay what these cars were worth.

"Wouldn't touch it," said one car dealer, looking at the Volvo. "Fifty pounds," said another, explaining that it was old and rusty and that he was doing Ian a favor to give him even that much for it. As we drove away, I said nothing, but I could see that his defenses were shamed and appeared somehow wounded.

We drove the Land Rover around, telling people how old and rare it was. Most were uninterested. Others looked like they were holding themselves back from laughing. Others walked around it, putting it down like harsh judges at a cattle show.

Back at the cottage, we decided to use checking to find out how we felt about pricing the cars. The Land Rover was then advertised at seven hundred pounds, three hundred pounds less than we'd bought it for. The Volvo was advertised for seven hundred and fifty pounds or to swap.

Many people came and looked the cars over, putting them down and even laughing at the Land Rover. Like two gentle children in a playground of bullies, Ian and I stood silently holding hands in silent support. We ended up telling people right from the start everything they could possibly find wrong with the cars, before they told us.

We told one man who arrived to look at the Land Rover what crap it was and how he couldn't drive it on the road. He argued back at us how wonderful it was and how he'd do it up as a hobby. We sold it to him for six hundred fifty pounds as a project to work on.

Another man came around with his wife in a ten-year-old Ford Escort. It was smoky and sticky with lolly fingers and had bits of rubbish strewn everywhere. He got in the Volvo and we got in the Escort and we took the cars for a drive.

It was hard to breathe and the car felt irksome, but it drove smoothly and without much noise except for an hypnotic, lulling hum like so many other cars.

Back at the cottage, the man suggested a swap. We accepted and swapped keys and registration papers. Then we took the Escort off for a scrub at the carwash.

The Ford Escort lasted a long enough time before we found out that we hadn't swapped one car for another car at all. We'd swapped one car for two. The mechanic who told us this had the car up on a jack to look at its belly. He pointed out the red paint under the back of the car and the blue paint under the front of it. He pointed out the seam along the center of its belly. It was rusted and full of holes and you could see the interior through it. The seam looked like a badly stitched operation through which you could see the innards and through which guts threatened to spill. The Escort had been two different cars, welded together. "You can't drive it," said the mechanic. It would cost more to fix than the car itself was worth. We didn't know what to do. We couldn't drive it home, and we were basically being told that if they had a bin big enough, they'd toss it into it. "You could take it back to the person you bought it from," said the mechanic. The previous owner was long gone and we had another undrivable lemon.

━ ◢

We made a huge inventory of things to advertise and phoned the free classified section of the newspaper. As people arrived to look at things, we stood there like a pair of sparrows peeping every once in a while.

Some people came to buy one thing and left with five. Some came to spend twenty pounds and spent a hundred. At one point, we had three people in the tiny cottage along with us. Being mono and one-to-one, we were both about to throw wobblies as they all rambled senselessly over one another's noise and moved about us in all manner of directions. Occasionally, one would pop up unexpectedly in our faces, holding something and saying, "How much is this then?" We basically just stood near the door ready to take what money they were giving us. After that, we were determined to avoid that sort of chaos again.

We sat down and worked out how we could manage things better. We got sticky labels and put the prices on things. We got out the diary and made appointments for people, so that they'd come only one at a time. A few times, the sound of the people's voices on the phone scared us, so when they asked if what they were looking for was still there, we told them no.

More and more, the pile went down over the next three weeks of social and sensory chaos while our emotions were on hold. In the end, we surveyed what was left: a few bits and bobs and a pile of money that we'd banked. Ian looked like a freed man and I felt glad to have some space—mental, emotional, and physical. We were both freer to get on with the future. The loss of the vast array of symbols—so important to our defenses—had meant that, however they niggled and mentally bitched and connived, we could see through them more easily and were better able to shove them out of our way, instead of the other way around.

➤ ➤

The cottage had the word "ours" on it more than ever. We'd wiped off the fingerprints left all over that word by our defenses. Everywhere we looked, we knew that we had checked through our emotional, noncompulsive, nonmental feelings about everything around us. It was as if we'd spent our lives bathing in dirty bathwater and now we had a clean bath. It didn't have as much water in it, but the water was warmer and it would fill up as our lives went on.

It was time for bed. As we drew back the covers, there were two things that had escaped checking: Travel Dog and his friend Orsi Bear.

So many walls can be potential bridges. So many bridges can be hidden walls. Just as Travel Dog and Orsi Bear had been the go-betweens between Ian and I, we now considered their role as in-betweens.

Whenever we'd gone to sleep, though we remained primary to each other, our defenses used the symbols of Travel Dog and Orsi Bear to constantly reinforce that we were actually secondary, according to their definitions.

That I had feelings for the time spent with Orsi Bear and Travel Dog, or that I had worked through a lot with them, had little real relevance for my feelings for them as objects. Memories of a time are intangible and exist only in the marking that time has made upon one's soul (and markings upon one's ego are different to this and irrelevant to one's soul). One can symbolize those memories with objects, but that is to hold the experience frozen in time. Experiences frozen in time are good only for gathering strength to look anew at change and renew enough resources to continue up life's mountain.

Holding on to past moments through symbols that freeze time is saying, in effect, "I'm too scared to let this part of me take any more steps up the mountain" or "I'm too scared to lose sight of where I have come from, because too many parts of me are still back down there." There is a definite time and place for symbols beyond which it is a soul-crime to force someone before they are ready to go. But one must also be encouraged to recognize that time when it comes.

My time was staring me in the face and I'd ignored it for long enough. I looked at Ian and at Travel Dog and I knew I was ready now to take another step.

We checked on Travel Dog. My emotional response was undeniable. Travel Dog was going.

Tapping into an otherwise disconnected or hidden emotional response is one thing, acting upon that unburied or reconnected emotion is another.

My defenses swelled with mock-rage and they attempted to channel this into a mock-resentment aimed at Ian. While I could still think, I told him to disregard my face and told him what was going on inside of me and how I could see through it.

Overwhelming anxiety climbed within me. My stomach was gripped in jubblies. I was frozen and could think no longer. I didn't have any idea of what to do now. Ian helped me check about what to do, now that we knew that Travel Dog was going.

The part of my mind I called Willie wanted to give Travel Dog away to someone else "like me," so at least it would be useful, its whereabouts known, and its symbolic significance remembered and retained. The part I knew as Carol wanted to bury Travel Dog in a blame exercise against Ian and me for "killing" Travel Dog by denying his symbolic significance.

My defenses raged within me and I was compelled to throw uncontrollable wobblies; in between them, I told Ian to ignore them, because I wasn't really upset about getting rid of Travel Dog at all. It's a strange thing to watch yourself throw a tantrum you care nothing about.

I explained to Ian that I had a huge turmoil in me and was having a pressure to feel guilty because of hurting Travel Dog's feelings through rejection, abandonment, and denial. I told Ian that I knew none of it was true. I told him that I knew I couldn't hurt the feelings of this stuffed toy because it had none. I told him that I wasn't abandoning anything, because I would move forward more by what I was doing and that that was surely far from an abandonment of my self. I told him that I knew that this stuffed toy wouldn't miss me. I knew I had wounded no one and that there was a time for belief and a time to move on.

The more I told Ian about the pressure my defenses created within me, the more I disarmed them of their weapons and the more they were exposed for what they were really defending: a wall between closeness, a wall that made "being social" less important and relevant on the grounds that I still had closeness and "being social" with—and through—this object called Travel Dog. There would be no more "good night, Travel Dog," "good night, Orsi Bear." There would just be "good night, Donna," "good night, Ian."

There was only one real way forward. However I was to get rid of Travel Dog, I had to do it in a way that would make him cease to exist in his present form. I had to do it in a way that would directly challenge and disintegrate the guilt-ridden, bull-shit, mental pressure I was getting about Travel Dog's "feelings." My defenses didn't give a damn about people's feelings but they'd stored well how other people played on feelings to get things that they wanted. Damn them. I went and got the scissors.

As I dismantled Travel Dog, so did I dismantle the psycholog-ical weaponry of my defenses and their last bastion of refuge against closeness and social need.

"You can do it, Donna," said Ian gently. I blinked tears out of the way as I cut with a trembling hand along the length of each limb that could not walk, cut off each ear that could not hear, and cut out each eye that could not see. Finally, what lay before me was a tiny cut-out pattern of old acrylic fabric and a whole lot of lumps of chopped polyester stuffing where no feelings lived. I took the stuffing out and held it before Ian and stated, "No feel-ings," through my tears.

I looked to Ian and felt I needed him. I felt more alone than I ever had, not alone in being different, but socially alone: lonely.

Travel Dog, the last of the "my world" comrades to make "the world" secondary, was now "dead" as far as my defenses were concerned. This death called for an intense undercurrent of mock self-disgust and mock self-hatred and mock self-mistrust because there was a stored rule that people who killed things should feel bad. To them, I was a murderer. Though this "logic" made no personal sense and the feeling they compelled in me was illogical to me, I told Ian about it anyway and told him about the urges I was having to punish myself for what they made me feel was a crime. Ian explained that they were just doing that because we had taken one of their weapons away and that they didn't really give a damn otherwise. I knew he was right, and, after talking it through, was able to turn their psychological volume down.

Travel Dog had been the bridge away from the labyrinth of the Big Black Nothing—that place within the grip of my defenses where even I did not exist with any awareness, in a burial so deep that even "my world" could not be seen or reached from its depths.

Travel Dog had also been the bridge between "my world" and "the world." Travel Dog's tangibility and visibility were symbols that the defenses were wrong and that I could have closeness with "someone" external and tangible. Travel Dog had been the start of the means to cut the umbilical cord to my self-imprisonment, to deny it as being integral to my selfhood and damn its constraints to hell.

The bridges had been crossed to "the world," the war was over and a truce had been made but there were a few war-crazy diehards in the foothills. Now that I was safe on the other side, the bridges had to be burned. Defenses don't listen to changes in my belief. Travel Dog "died" in the line of duty.

Ian came with me as I put Travel Dog's bits in the bin. To fuss about it as though it were a burial would have suited the defenses better. Had I shown my compassion for the loss of what, to them, was the last symbol of the object world over the feeling world, it would have given them more of a way to hold a grudge. Travel Dog wound up in the garbage bin with eggshells and cereal packets.

Orsi Bear still sat on the bed. My defenses made the observation that Orsi was the relative of the murder victim. They played on the idea that Orsi had just witnessed the murder of his best friend and now had to live in the house with the horrid perpetrators of the crime. My defenses also made me feel that I was persecuted, since Ian had helped me destroy Travel Dog, but there sat Orsi Bear for Ian to still have company with.

I tried to rationalize this psychological melodramatic bullshit, but it didn't heed my thoughts with any significance. The compulsion-driven mock-feelings wouldn't go away and my stomach was still gripped in teeth-grinding jubbliedom. Half of my defenses aimed my fists at my head, ready to attack me for my crimes (I held my arms still and at bay). The other half looked at Ian like a threatened animal. I felt for neither of these things. I felt merely overwhelmed by all that had happened, uncertain about how things would be from now on, and insecure at the chaos that was going on in me.

I told Ian what was going on. For every challenge to my defenses, there was always a payback period. My defenses' payback period was usually more intense than that of Ian's defenses. Mine was more direct, less subtle, but also more short-lived. It was also usually more self-directed. That had some benefits and some disadvantages.

The benefits of this kind of payback were that, because the attacks were against myself, I could attempt in some way to ask for help or restraint if I needed it. The disadvantages were that there was no fear of consequences to hold me back from the intensity of such an attack (as there might be if one attacks someone else). Also, just as one feels guilt at unintentionally attacking someone else, self-attack always left an intense self-mistrust and physical dissociation.

Ian knew there was no more point in his reasoning with the melodrama of my defenses than in my trying to reason with them. They wouldn't listen to what he said, they'd use it.

Instead, he checked about Orsi Bear. He was indifferent to him, so we decided that Orsi Bear should go. This would get rid of one of the triggers that was making my defenses persist in giving me jubblies and making my mind race.

We took Orsi Bear to an antique shop that wanted him because he was an old German Steiff bear. My defenses compelled me to say good-bye to Orsi Bear and to feel sorry and repentant for everything I had done, as well as guilty at this abandonment. They tried to compel me to feel blame and resentment toward Ian, for who else could possibly have stopped them from keeping Orsi Bear?

— ⬤

It had been over a year now since most of my personal belongings had sailed ten thousand miles without me by accident. I'd been living in a London hotel then and had sent them back ahead of me to Australia before changing my mind about going at the last minute. They'd sailed for a long time before being met by an old friend, Tim, at the other end. Tim had been waiting for me to come back, him and Bryn both: a pair of albatrosses who'd found some belonging and understanding in finding me.

Instead of seeing me, Bryn had got the letter he already expected, saying what he already sensed: that I wasn't coming back to Australia ever. Tim waited for me but instead got a fax asking him to pick up my things and find somewhere for them to live until I worked out what to do.

That had been over a year ago. Since then, I'd met two other albatrosses on this side of the world. Olivier, whom I'd met at the London hotel, had been the reason I'd canceled my return to Australia. Ian, whom I met later, down in Essex, was part of the reason I decided not to travel at all. Another reason was that as much as I may have given some belonging to a handful of others there, there was no ongoing belonging waiting for me back in Australia. Any transient belonging that I might have found there would have been overshadowed by the monster hovering in the back of my mind to remind me I was not safe.

A letter arrived in the post saying that my old things had arrived at the dock and were ready for delivery to our cottage. It had cost £350 to ship them all in the first place, and now it was costing another £350 to ship them back again.

My defenses were excited at the thought of all those symbols and collections, which included a tea chest full of knickknacks, collections, photos, an old stuffed toy koala with the blue glass buttons I'd glued on for eyes, an old stuffed toy dog with velvet ears, and bits and bobs. I dreaded how much non-me I'd probably find among those once "treasured" objects. I was torn between being glad that Ian was there to see it all and my defenses "wishing" that he wasn't.

When they arrived, the things all stunk of damp and made me feel woozy from the smell and mold spores, which now crawled into every corner of the cottage. More dread rose inside of me, probably because my defenses knew that the opening of, and checking through of these things, would probably mean the end of most of them. There was also mock-embarrassment and shame, which were probably Carol's; this gave me some idea that a lot of what was in these cases and boxes was probably more a reflection of people past than it was of me.

I opened the boxes and took Ian on a guided tour of my past. My defenses were triggered in bursts and broke through with comments of mock-attachment, mock-excitement, and mock-entertainment, which didn't match my face at all. I looked through these things with a sense of alienation from much of what was in there. It was hard to feel safe among so much non-me.

There was a frilly lace evening dress, a tight black vinyl one, and a shiny skintight, low-cut, copper-colored one. All of them had been bought four years before, chosen by the shop assistant selling them to me. The lace one had never been worn and I could remember a compulsion to feel shame about owning "something like that." Ironically, it was the two more sleazy outfits that had been worn without defensive drama, as though it had been safe to wear these because they were so much further removed from who I was.

Looking at the lace one, there was a defensive compulsion to blurt out mock-embarrassment. Instead of letting it out my mouth, I told Ian about the pressure I was under to degrade the dress. It was too "prissy," mocked my defenses. Another description, much truer, might have been that it was a more innocent-looking and feminine dress. It was surprising that my defenses had even allowed it home with them back then, though I remembered the mock-contamination they had had about even having something like that hung in the wardrobe. The only reasons it had been kept were that Carol had been impressed by the shop assistant's unchallengeable authority and Willie was being a miser over throwing out something that had cost so much.

There were worn-out old socks and knickers held together with safety pins. There were shoes and boots with worn-out, lopsided heels and peeling, vinyl paint. There were old worn hand-me-down sheets and towels, a rusty bent potato masher, a not-so-well-washed nonstick fry pan with much of the nonstick surface scratched off, a thin duvet, and a bumpy foam pillow. There were shrunken tufty sweaters and others with the odd un-removable stain. There were oddly stretched T-shirts and clothes that had picked up the dye from other clothes. There were hair bands and hair ties and hair clips and two old cheap vinyl hand-bags. There were mittens and gloves, cheap earrings and hand-me-down brassieres, which were all either too big or too small. All of it stunk.

We checked through everything for my want to keep it. Though my defenses put up a battle and put on a show, almost all of it was going—except a scarf, one sweater, a pair of gloves, two pairs of socks, and the lacy dress. The rest of it was washed and dried and bagged for the Animal Welfare Shop, even though much of which was probably beyond selling and would be used as rags.

The sewing machine was staying and, though it no longer worked, so was the typewriter.

We opened up the tea chest and took out a collection of tins. We went through all of the photos, checking my want for keeping each one. We went through a button collection and, of more than one hundred buttons, I ended up keeping three. We went through a lace and ribbon collection and I ended up keeping about three things. We went through my record and tape collection and all of those were going. We went through my letter collection and most of those were going. We checked about the smelly old stuffed koala and dog. At the end of it all, I had kept very little. The Animal Welfare Shop was getting most of it. It had cost £700 to look through these "treasures" and the cottage was going to stink for weeks.

The bed we had bought had taken six weeks to arrive. Since everything was now sold, we now had a bedroom to sleep in. We'd checked about the bedroom and, despite our defenses' fury and excuses, we had wanted to use it, not as Donna's bedroom that Ian slept in or as Ian's bedroom in Donna's house, but as "our" bedroom.

My defenses were allergic to words like "we" and "us" and "together" and would grip my stomach whenever I said them. I would go to Ian and tell on my defenses, robbing them of their secret assault upon me. Ian would ask me about my feelings and I would tell him and they would rage about inside of me like trolls rumbling the bridge on which I stood.

They could go to hell. They'd kept me inside for most of my life, damning my discomfort to hell. I never caused them jubblies, I'd just shriveled under the impact of their daily assault, insult, and denial as they defied my very existence. If I gave them jubblies now by breaking their self-strangulating rules and snapping their compulsions like twigs, then they deserved it. I was going to run for real help and real security by running to a real person and not some dominating bastard part of my own brain that wasn't even a real whole person. All it had ever done was confuse me by painting its obsessional control as "caring" and its self-denial as "protection" and its self-abuse as "teaching."

Ten minutes away, Alex was starting to deal with his own rule book. He had gradually come to realize that he was understood and to trust and with this came the eventual realization that he had been the real loser in his war with "the World"; he had stifled his own development by putting all his energy into defensive strategies instead.

Alex asked us how he could get out of the cycle he had created. We wrote back, telling him that he had to expose to others what he had been doing and that once he did that, he'd be on the track to developing a whole new way of feeling safe. After spending a long time writing to us about whether he was safe to expose his own war strategies and disassemble them and what he would have in their place, he began challenging and disassembling his own rules. He wrote to someone at his school:

I had created so many "not" rules that I numbered 9483 rules not to be broken. I attempted to rule everyone because everyone attempted to rule me. I had, more or less, to turn the table round.

Please understand I was happy creating rules because it was great fun having the last laugh on you all. I created. You judged. I created. You judged. We went round and round in circles. It was, more or less, my revenge, laughing at last.

I know now, I see in retrospect, that I have nothing to gloat about.

I have been testing you all. I looked from my point of view that you were all treating me like I was retarded so I tested you all to see if you could pass my tests. You always failed.

I had code words for everything. If you did not find the word, you failed. I was satisfied then that, given tests that you were dreadful at understanding, you, too, failed.

I was good at reasoning but I had great difficulty trying to determine what I should do with my hands. I feel very angry that I dreaded looking because I could not see properly; I could not feel what I was doing, I could not talk to express my thoughts, I could not communicate my understanding in any way. Then, I perceived adverse noise that seemed so loud that I dreaded hearing.

Pediatricians never understood this. They just wrote me off as retarded.

I will try to mature the part of me that is scared to communicate. I understand. I have no more tests lined up for you to pass. The truth is, I was fed up with them interfering with my love of knowledge, fed up with counting them and fed up with remembering them.

Alex

It was four o'clock. We were still waiting for the bed to arrive. "The bed's not coming," I said to Ian.

"Yes it is," he replied. "I've done deliveries. They're just running late with their last delivery or something."

"No. I know it's not coming."

"You worry too much," said Ian, with a stored line.

It was five o'clock and the bed had not arrived. Mentally, Carol was delighted at this reprieve. Mentally, Willie was furious at the incompetence of the delivery company.

I could feel my defenses getting close to the surface, beating me into a corner within my body, mind, and emotions. I was weakening under their pressure and jubblies, the mind-racing they created with their adrenaline, the fading out of thought as it wafted away from my grasp. I didn't have the endurance to fight off the hypnotic switch to autopilot and was drifting away, leaving the seat empty for those bastards. I wanted that bed to magically appear *right now* before my defenses ate me up.

"Do you want to call the bed place?" I said to Ian, meaning that I wanted him to do it.

"No," replied Ian. "It'll be here."

"I know it's not coming," I said again. Carol punctuated my sentence with a humph and a flap and a bounce that broke through.

"This isn't you," said Ian, his defenses starting to eat him up, too.

"It is," I said, and this time Willie punctuated my sentence with a chiseled expression, putting sharp, forced edges on the end of each of my words.

"I'm not talking to Willie," said Ian.

"Listen to *me*," I said in frustration as Carol punctuated my request with amateur dramatics that were meant to depict desperation but made me look insincere. "The place will be closed soon," I added, hoping my words themselves would override Ian's negative reaction to the invasion I was having. "They finish work soon."

"Where's the number?" Ian asked as Richard punctuated his sentence with his "compliance to expectation" voice, stance, and facial expression.

I was disappointed to see Richard and reached out to touch Ian. "As you," I said gently.

"This *is* me," said Ian as Richard punctuated his reply with his "I'm being accused" routine. "Are you in there?" I asked Ian.

His eyes were soft and real against the backdrop of his chiseled face and stiff body as he spoke to the warehouse manager, who reassured him that everything was okay.

It was not okay. I knew the bed was not coming. I knew if it didn't arrive that my defenses would score huge points. This time, I picked up the phone and pressed the redial button. "The bed has *been* delivered," said the manager firmly.

"Where?" I replied in Willie's voice. Richard's eyes glared at me from across the room.

I realized what was happening and tried to take back control. "It hasn't been delivered here," I replied to the warehouse manager as Willie's voice gradually lost its stranglehold.

"The delivery man rang your doorbell. You weren't home so he left it around the side of the house in the driveway," said the manager abruptly.

"We don't have a doorbell," I replied as Willie punctuated my reply with an "up yours" attitude.

"Check around the side of the house, on the driveway," said the manager.

"We don't have a side of the house," fumed Willie, using my words.

"Well, it's there," said the manager, shrugging off the whole issue.

"Look! We don't have a doorbell, we don't have a driveway, and we have been here waiting for this bed *all day*! Now you find out where that bed is and you find out now," fumed Willie as I struggled to keep up with what words had burst out and what they'd said. Willie continued, "That bed is parked in someone else's driveway somewhere, who didn't pay for it and if something happens to that bed, if it is even scratched, you are taking it back. Do you hear me?"

"I'll see what we can do," replied the manager sheepishly. "We'll find out where it got delivered. I'm sorry about this."

Willie was pleased with himself. I was shaky. I'd been possessed and had words pour out from my mouth I had no idea about until I'd heard them spoken. I'd been used like a puppet for the issue of some robotic bundle of stored copied patchwork repertoires of "how people behave" and then I'd been discarded like a piece of used toilet paper. I felt exhausted, shocked, battered, alienated, and used. "The bed will get here," I said sheepishly, getting part of my own voice back and slowly finding my mouth, my body, and my face. "You could have done that as yourself," replied Ian. He was fed up with the theatricals of my defenses, just because they thought they could do things more easily, more forcefully, more efficiently. He was fed up with watching the person he loved, distorted, used, and discarded by a force that had no respect at all for my life and only for the playing out of its "cause" of the moment.

Another thought jumped into my mind. It prompted me that Ian didn't really give a damn about what I'd been through and that he was just "rubbing it in" about doing things for myself. "Arghh," I screamed back at the unwelcome and unbelieved thought in my head. My hands went out to the sides and came crashing in toward my face. I stopped them in midair as though an invisible wall had shot up just before impact. Was it not enough that I went through all this and then had to put up with being attacked from the inside with stored crap that belonged in some gossipy teenage conversation somewhere?

When the bed finally arrived, Willie went to answer the door as a follow-up to "his" phone conversation.

"No," said Ian, with Richard putting his intonation in. I got control over my body and answered the door as myself.

"It was across the road," said the deliveryman apologetically. "I delivered it to sixty-seven instead of seventy-six." Nigel smiled and Ian's body went into "salesman mode." "It goes in here," I said to the deliveryman without my voice.

"I know what it's like," Nigel reassured the deliveryman.

"Nigel," I said, pointing gently at him. Richard broke through and huffed. "This isn't the shop," I reminded, meaning that Ian was being invaded.

"I have done deliveries, I know what it's like," said Nigel.

"I'm sure you have," I said with Willie creeping into my intonation with the scent of sarcasm. Nigel strutted into the kitchen.

I felt angry and abandoned. Willie commandeered my feelings and channeled them to his own cause. "Are you going to set that bed up?" he challenged the deliveryman domineeringly.

"No, I just deliver the things," replied the deliveryman, continuing to unpack the components.

I went into the kitchen. Willie tried to take up his point with Ian that the bed should be put together.

Ian was having trouble. His face and stance were invaded. His eyes were changing from moment to moment, a mixture of crumbling sadness, raging anger, and a plea for help. His disembodied hand stirred the sauce for Nigel's favorite dish: spaghetti Bolognese.

"Come on," I said gently, taking his hand. "You can do it as yourself. Leave that and come and help me put the bed up." Ian seemed to soften as I headed for the bedroom with him in tow.

Suddenly, the hand tugged violently back from me and his eyes glared at me. The word "enemy" shouted so loudly through the expression possessing him that there was no need to speak it. Ian's body seemed frozen for a moment and his eyes went dead. His body turned toward the back door and his hands went up in surrender. "No," came a haunted yell from his body, like somebody falling over a cliff. His hands heaved forward, taking his head and body with it. Ian dived through the plate-glass window of the back door as glass smashed everywhere.

Her hand came crashing through the heavy, red, stained-glass window of the front door as I stood frozen watching. Blood and broken red glass merged on the red patterned carpet against a backdrop of red flocked wallpaper.

He raged about outside somewhere. It had been one of those parties. Very little motivated me to come out of my room when the house swarmed with noise and movement, but the sound of screaming and broken glass beckoned me like a sleepwalker compelled to face danger in a dream. In the face of real danger, my mind seemed to work so fluidly.

My eleven-year-old hand picked up the receiver to phone the police. The cord was ripped out. I left the house, went around the corner in my pajamas, and called emergency services from a pay phone. "Come to the house," I told them, "there are people trying to kill each other and glass is smashed and . . ."

Ian's hand was covered in blood and his head was bleeding. "Oh great," said Willie. "A lot of good that did."

"They had no right to make you do that," I said, with Willie's voice still intact. "Whose head is that?"

"My head," said Ian, bursting into tears.

"Yes, it's a beautiful head and no one should hurt it," I said, coming back to myself. I went quickly to the bathroom and got a washcloth and began to patch him up. A knock came at the door. "Hold on," I said.

A neighbor had heard the glass and came to check to see if burglars had broken in. They had, even though they weren't the sort of burglars he could help combat. "It's okay," I told him. "Just an accident."

The deliveryman had been silent for a long time; now he announced that he was going. Through the bedroom door, I could see he had put the bed together, put it into place, and put the mattress on it. He must have been scared.

— ◢

Since Ian had gotten rid of so many of the commercial foods and drinks that he assumed he liked but found out that he didn't, he seemed to have become calmer and had more energy. He'd known that I had a list of allergies that I had to manage, but though he had suffered from stomach ulcers, backache, migraines, joint trouble, tremors, bleeding gums, exhaustion, and fainting spells, he hadn't really considered that some of these and other difficulties might have been related to allergies, deficiencies, and metabolic problems in him, as they had in me, allergies which were also affecting his brain.

Ian was unable to keep weight on; his doctor had told him that his metabolism was too fast but either he hadn't told him much about what to do about it or Ian hadn't processed what had been said. From assessing the times in the day when Ian was getting tremors and fainting spells, his own condition sounded very much like my own—hypoglycemia, a diabetes-related condition stemming from pancreas dysfunction, otherwise known as low blood sugar. Like me, Ian fed his problem with the last thing it needed and the first thing it craved—sweets and soft drinks—and was probably making his condition progressively worse.

Since quitting his old job at the music shop, he no longer had chocolate bars for breakfast and a packet of sweet biscuits for lunch. Feeling too guilty to eat these sort of things in front of me when my own diet precluded them, he rarely let these items into the house. And because we went everywhere together, Ian rarely had such things elsewhere either.

Ian had been better since going off these sugary foods. His chronic fatigue and exhaustion weren't so much of a problem, nor was he having dramatic, almost manic, highs and his moods were more level. We considered what could have been the cause. Was it the sugar? Was it all the colorings, flavorings, preservatives, and additives crammed into those things?

Ian decided to go off all additives and added sugar. Nothing with MSG and nothing with artificial colorings, flavorings, or preservatives came into the house or went past his lips anymore. He felt better still. The migraines that plagued him every week became less severe and he dissociated less easily from his body, emotions, and self.

We visited a naturopath, who tested Ian for wheat allergies. It was like dark rain clouds came over him. Ian's whole personality changed and his insecurity and defensiveness surfaced. He was tested for yeast and became manic and got the same muzzy-headed, drunk feeling he'd had with fruit juice. He looked back on a life of sandwiches and biscuits, gravy, stuffing, and Yorkshire pudding. Like me, he had craved and often gorged upon the very things he was most allergic to. He was also tested for intolerance to Phenol and, like me, found to be allergic.

Some of his vitamin and mineral deficiencies were pointed out. He was also (as I had been) diagnosed with an opportunistic yeast infection called *Candida albicans,* associated with poor immunity; this was compounding and aggravating his blood sugar problems, food and chemical allergies, and vitamin-mineral deficiencies.

Ian was put on an antifungal, low-sugar diet and pointed in the direction of the vitamin-mineral supplements he lacked. His gums stopped bleeding once his vitamin C deficiency was sorted out. The spots on his fingernails disappeared once his zinc deficiency was addressed, as did his chronic anxiety once this was addressed with high dose multivitamin-mineral tablets. After he started taking Evening Primrose oil, the chronic backache for which he spent so much time and money at the chiropractor just disappeared, as did his painful and cracking joints, all of which he'd just accepted before as incurable bad "genetics."

Finally, we both got onto DMG, or dimethylglycine, a naturally occurring amino acid that had been used with some people with autism and epilepsy. (I don't know whether its use has been tested scientifically.) After the first week, Ian no longer had a personality like stormy weather. "Happy pills," he called the DMG capsules. They were happy pills for me, too; they significantly decreased both the frequency and severity of my episodes of the Big Black Nothing. Not only did DMG improve our mood and frustration tolerance of each other and stop my being "tuned out" so much, it was the first tool outside of mental application to stop my own urge to self-abuse.

＊＊＊

We had finally got our cottage back, reclaimed from the pile of accumulated non-us. We settled into it and enjoyed the luxury of having two separate livable rooms and were as stable as we'd ever be. We were ready now to go forward from the cottage with the confidence that the next place would be chosen by us and not our defenses.

We were off to look at another collection of country houses, this time up in North Wales. We drove through the vehicular bric-a-brac of outer London to the endless gray spaghetti of British motorway after motorway. Finally, we broke off from the conveyer belt of traffic to climb and dip over the lush green hills and valleys of mid-Wales and then wind this way and that around green furry mountain bends of North Wales as we climbed outward and upward to the coast. Past a castle here, a waterfall there, over a bridge here and onto an island there, we arrived at Anglesey.

Anglesey was a beautiful place, even in the mist and under a gray muddy sky full of dark clouds, which peed down on us relentlessly. Up here, you could not only breathe the air but taste it.

We drove along little country roads that were not even dots on our map and arrived at a secluded farm called Neuadd Wenn.

We'd driven up in light summer clothes and the wind had teeth and the rain poked at us with its wet fingers until we were wet right through in virtually no time as we walked from the car to the the front door of the long black and white bungalow.

The people answered the door. He was shy and retiring. She was bold and sharp edged. The blah-blah poured down on our ears like the rain had on our bodies. She spoke in a deafening shout that fired like bullets. Ian explained about sound: "Could you speak slowly, clearly, and very quietly please or we won't understand you."

She invited us in to look around. "Before we start," Ian said, "if there's any public footpaths or rights of way running through the property, we are not interested."

"Absolutely nothing like that," the woman replied.

We both had a change of clothes in the car and the woman said we could get changed in the house. She led the way along a corridor and up to one of the bedrooms, where she left us.

The bedroom looked out over the backyard. We were swept up in an awesome panorama of sweeping hills of all colors, peppered with wildflowers and shrubs for as far as we could see. It was like looking out of the window of a plane. It was like flying. Half dressed and half undressed, Ian and I knelt down by the big window like children at a TV screen and held hands. This was it. This was where we would live.

Alex had been faxing us for some time and occasionally we also got faxes from his mother, Mrs. Dawson.

It had been almost two years now since I'd first encountered Alex. Back then, he had been about fourteen, had very little communication, and had been mistakenly labeled as mentally retarded.

When I first visited the Dawsons' house, I noticed the way Alex moved about the rooms, each of which had different colored walls and lighting and different background noises and was crowded with different furnishings and objects. Just beyond my conscious mind, my brain ticked over like a computer, calculating the mathematics of behavior.

I could see how meaning dropped in and out for Alex because of the fluctuation in his surroundings. I could see how he used his eyes, or didn't use them, to cut down on the sensory bombardment. I could see how he navigated the room and its people, which spoke to me of a fragmented perception like my own. I could see how, under sensory overload, he—like me—was mono: switching from hearing without seeing, to seeing without hearing, to moving without body awareness, to speaking without hearing.

Finally, the triggers came when the Dawsons asked me a question here or made a statement there. Like a computer printout, my mouth spat out some of what it had calculated. I explained the variations in Alex's responsiveness, movement, and awareness under the various lighting conditions of the different rooms.

Somewhere in there, I mentioned the colored light bulbs I'd had in my bedroom as a child, how I'd been fascinated by looking through colored cellophane or colored glass.

My father had once brought home a string of colored light bulbs. My room had been purple and it had seemed that I could never get it dark enough. I often kept the curtains closed during the day, making the dark room even darker, as though it were always nighttime. Often, I'd sit in the built-in wardrobe out on the landing. In the darkness, it felt secure and less chaotic.

One at a time, various colored bulbs had been put in my lamp in my bedroom. The green one had had me in the cupboard much of the time. The blue one had had me staring into space, mesmerizing me as it threw a stark white-light effect into the room, making it "otherworldly." The yellow had been better than the green and blue, but didn't alter the room's lighting much at all. The orange had made me feel less chaotic inside and more alert. The red had had me alert and aware and I had started to look for things to do within the room, instead of staring hypnotically at the mirror or at the pattern in the wallpaper.

Once I was older, I knew that fluorescent lighting had a bad effect on me both mentally and physically—but I hadn't known why and assumed it was just psychological. It wasn't until I was in my twenties that an employer told me they'd seen a program about people who had trouble with fluorescent lights. The program had been about dyslexia and mentioned how these people had been helped with specially tinted lenses. At the time, it had made a lot of sense and I'd reflected how I had longed for a red world.

I was sure, though, that I didn't have dyslexia. I didn't jumble the letters of words up very much and even the printed lines on paper didn't jump too much anymore and the white background didn't swim up through the text as it had when I was small. Besides, I could read just fine and though I couldn't read with meaning when I read consciously, I'd trained myself to scan books peripherally and more meaning had sunk in, even if it had to be triggered by others to come out again. No, I had figured, I didn't have a reading disability.

Despite my certainty that I didn't have dyslexia, I did go to have my glasses tinted. I'd spent about an hour in a booth, trying out all the different shades of tints before finding the the best one to help me concentrate under fluorescent lights. I found that this did indeed help me cope with some of my hypersensitivity to bright light. I also wore polarized sunglasses for most situations when I couldn't cope.

Looking at Alex, I knew that he needed dimmer, softer lighting. He needed the visual chaos around him to be made more orderly and visually controllable. He needed movement to happen around him in an orderly fashion, on a one-at-a-time level. He needed sound to be slowed and softened, and the number of simultaneous sources of noise cut down. I explained all of these things to the Dawsons and suggested they investigate earmuffs and tinted glasses for Alex.

Mrs. Dawson had followed up on many of my suggestions. As his parents came to understand some of his sensory difficulties, Alex began his first complex communications with them. He explained to the parents whom he felt would now understand about his sensory hypersensitivities and about the unwittingly cruel treatment he had received at one of his previous schools from well-meaning but arrogant teachers who had had a bull-at-a-gate approach to Alex's sensory difficulties.

Ian and I looked at the latest fax from the Dawsons, which was full of information they'd uncovered on visual perceptual problems. Though Ian and I had sketchy childhood recollections of some of these things, we had both either outgrown them or developed strategies to get around the problems. The condition they were talking about in the fax was Scotopic Sensitivity Syndrome, or SSS. It was a condition that is often mistaken for dyslexia.

Headaches, backache, stomachache, migraine, inability to sit still while reading, and a tendency to read in dim light—the list of symptoms went on down the page. Some things described us; others definitely didn't. "Reads in short bursts," continued the list. That wasn't us. I hardly read at all, but when I did, I read compulsively, not able to remember much unless I swallowed the whole book in one gulp to be digested later without awareness. Ian read books just as compulsively. His rule of not putting the book down until he came to a "natural break" was a handcuff tying him to the arms of the chair.

"Trouble with stairs or stepping on and off escalators," the list continued. Obviously SSS had to do with more than just reading. But we had no trouble with stairs, even though we'd both had fascinations—even obsessions—with them and had both spent time dropping things down them repetitively. But the mention of escalators rang a bell. I could remember the inner panic in getting on and off the damned things. The lines on the escalators made me dizzy and unsure of where my body was and what was around me. It was almost as if the lines on the escalator made me disappear, just like the white of the page had made the print disappear when I was a child.

Slowly, all the pieces began to fall into place: the difficulty that I had in extracting meaning from what I saw, the inability Ian and I had perceiving faces as a whole or reading facial expressions from a whole face, the way Ian and I felt out the room or scanned it with our eyes to map it out fragment by memorized fragment, and the way that changing the position of one significant visual element could make it a different and unfamiliar room. I was having that "just around the corner" feeling.

What was just around the corner was a screener for the special tinted Irlen Lenses Mrs. Dawson had informed us about by fax.

I wanted to know what it was to read novels for pleasure. Ian wanted to help combat the fatigue, neck problems, and head-aches he experienced when he read for a long time. We made an appointment with the screener. It would cost us twenty pounds to find out if we had SSS.

We drove up to a little suburban house. Ian's defenses were giv-ing him hell and creating in him an "I don't need this crap" anx-iety. My defenses were open-minded about it all. If we didn't have SSS, the most we'd have lost was a little bit of time and twenty pounds.

The door was opened by a very round lady with a warm, gen-tle, but raspy voice in a larger-than-life floral dress. Margaret was a picture of roundness: a round body, a big round face, and big, round, tinted colored glasses. She showed Ian and me into the dining room.

Ian and I explained that we weren't sure that she could help us because our problems were not just to do with our eyes. Our hearing and sense of touch worked the same, switching like a broken switch from hyper- to hyposensitive and changing from getting no meaning to getting some but not enough to extract personal or relative significance from these experiences.

Margaret didn't seem at all surprised. As she saw it, 70 percent of incoming information comes in through the eyes. The similar effects we were having in our other senses were, according to her, because of the way that our other senses were compensating for our visual-perceptual troubles. It seemed impossible that it was all that easy.

When Margaret asked us a whole pile of questions, both of our defenses tried to answer for us. Bullying, exclusion, rejection, denial, and ridicule had been good training grounds for making excuses for being weird. Being rewarded, encouraged, included, and accepted for "acting normal" had stifled any free-flowing expression of abnormality.

"Read in the dark?"

"Yes, sure, but we just did that to be different."

"Get headaches or migraine or muscular troubles or restless legs when reading or doing things under bright lights?"

"Yeah, but we push ourselves too far. Most of it is just tiredness."

"Do your eyes get sore, ache, or get itchy when . . . ?"

"Yes, but that's hay fever."

"Blink a lot, squint, rub your eyes, press your eyes . . . ?"

"Yes, but I must have seen someone else doing it and picked it up."

"Could we close these curtains?" I asked, getting up to do so.

"Oh, that's better," said Ian. "The sunlight was really hurting my eyes."

Margaret's house was different. It was orderly, with little visual chaos. The furnishings were out to the peripheries of the room. This was how the furniture had been in the house I had once lived in with my parents: out to the peripheries and symmetrically placed. The lighting in Margaret's house was natural but fairly dim.

"You could see all right. You could find the loll-lols," (sweets) he said in his croaky old voice as he told me about when I was small, "but you kept walking into walls. We'd watch ya take off across the living room and, sure enough, every time, straight past the doorway and into the wall you'd go."

Margaret brought out some papers and sheets of colored plastic overlays of all colors. She asked us individually to look at each page and describe the background and the print. Ian told her about the patches of pastel color appearing and moving about in the white of the background. He told her about rivers of white swimming around the print. But trouble reading? No, he didn't have that. He could read just fine.

Like me, Ian had read the telephone book and the street directory and the dictionary. He could read novels with some consistent meaning. He knew what novels people liked and what they got out of them. By the end of the novel, armed with a few facts, Ian was sure he knew what he thought of the book. However, faced with a set of instructions or a document, it was his defenses who read it, not him.

Willie had scanned volumes of academic texts and books in foreign languages. Trouble with reading? Never.

The page Margaret gave us was covered in foreign language, one that I did not speak or read. I wondered if she wanted me to read it without meaning one language is as easy to read as another if the letters are able to be pronounced). She asked me to describe the print and the color of the page and the effect of the page upon the print. She asked me to look at one single word and describe what happened to the clarity of the print surrounding it.

She brought out some pages with puzzles with lines and crosses to count and a simple outline of a face. She had me count different things starting from various sides. She asked me to hold attention to certain parts of the page as other parts compelled me to look at them or my concentration waned and my mind went to sleep.

Margaret brought out yet another page of print and asked me to read it. "With or without meaning?" I asked. I had learned in school that you were meant to sound like you knew what you'd read, but there was no point playing games with this woman when we were here for her help.

I had several systems of reading. One was impressively fluent but without meaning, whereby the meaning would sink in well after the book was closed—hours, days, weeks, or months later. Another system was not so impressively fluent but was with meaning, albeit inconsistent and patchy. A third system involved silent scanning that would be too fast to speak out loud. Somehow all the unprocessed information from what got read got worked through somewhere in the back of my mind. Out of context and unable to be accessed deliberately, it would be understood nevertheless and could be triggered out of me.

"With meaning," said the woman.

"I can read much better without," I said pleasantly.

"With meaning is fine," she repeated.

I read the passage with confidence, trying to squeeze the meaning out of the words as best I could. Though getting the meaning of individual words or sentences, I struggled greatly to make combined meaning of paragraphs or of the whole thing as a story. I'd overlooked the periods and capital letters as reasons to change my emphasis. I realized I'd misread a few of the words and noticed that I'd skipped a line but I hadn't realized that I missed some words altogether. She asked me if I'd understood it. Mostly, I said, with a basic and sketchy idea of what the text had been about.

Margaret took the colored plastic overlays and covered the printed page with different colors, one at a time. She got me to read through each one. There was no real improvement. Then she tried various combinations of overlays together while getting me to read and describe the page.

Some colors and combinations of colors made the words jump out at me but still without meaning. Some colors made the words dance about, lines jump, or the print fade in bits and pieces. Some colors had no effect at all except to make the whole page colored. Then, suddenly, as I was reading through a combination of several colored overlays, I began to shake and cry. The feeling was so foreign and overwhelming. I was reading directly and consciously and effortlessly with whole meaning for the first time in my life. Pictures happened in my head and I actually could mentally see the story I was reading. I could see not just one character in the story, but all of them and what they were doing and the colors and look of the things described in the story.

I could hear my voice as I read. The trained-in unmatching meaningless intonation of the past was gone; so was my own truer monotone, which had always gone together with reading meaningless visual blah-blah when it hadn't mattered to pretend that you understood or found something interesting. What was there was a flow and intonation that came naturally from reading something that I could imagine and was entertained by.

"That's enough now," said Margaret.

"No," I said. "I want to read some more."

Margaret tested Ian. Ian held the colored overlay up to his eyes to look around the room. "They don't work like that," said Margaret. She explained that the color that works on the printed page is usually not the same color that works for lenses.

Margaret tried color after color with Ian. What had worked for me didn't help him at all (which was no surprise to Margaret, because every person's visual perception of light frequencies is different). The effect for Ian, when the right color was found, was also dramatic, but different from my experience. Suddenly, Ian's face became lighter, his muscles less tense as he read, his voice had more self in it. The animation in his voice as he read wasn't rehearsed or for show. It was for him and came from inside. He no longer had to consciously use his muscles and willpower to force his eyes to follow the words or ignore the colored spots that often danced about in the background of the printed page. It was the first time he could read without effort. "This one," he said with surety.

Margaret sat there smiling with her tinted glasses. The assessment, which usually took half an hour per person, had taken the two of us four hours. We wanted to get tinted lenses, which would do for our vision in general what the right colored overlays had done for our reading. We at least knew we were on the right track, even if we didn't quite know what track that was. We made an appointment to go to the Irlen Centre for Perceptual and Learning Development to be fitted out for the special lenses. The appointment itself was a number of weeks off and then the lenses would take six weeks to make up. Though we had both spent over two decades learning to ignore our visual perceptual problems, now that we had been pointed in the right direction to do something about them, a month or two sounded like an eternity.

—◣◢—

Back at the cottage, Ian and I had just come in from the garden. Ian stopped and stood at the bedroom door, looking at the bed. "What's wrong?" I asked.

"Nothing," replied Ian, affected. "I'm looking at our bed. This is *our* bed."

We sat on our new double bed, looking at each other and smiling and feeling very real. We were daring to be close. "I love you," said Ian.

I love you, I said silently in my head with depth and feeling. "I like this person very much," came the compromised words from my mouth.

I wanted to accept Ian's words and tried to stay looking at him and hold on to my own face. My defenses were compelled to deny even that my compromised words had ever happened, that my thought had ever happened, or that Ian had said anything at all. They were compelled to change or distort his words, or disembowel them of all emotional or special content, as though his "I love you" had nothing to do with me.

"I hate them," I said, with my head buried into the pillow. "I hate them so much."

"Why?" said Ian. "What are they trying to do now?"

I told him the word games going on in my mind, the way my defenses were mentally replaying and fracturing and reshaping what had happened to deny all feeling and closeness. "Damn them," I said out loud. "I know what's me. I know what you said. I know what you meant. I can accept that."

No, I thought, more than accept that: I liked it.

"Don't be so hard on yourself," said Ian. "Think of six months ago: you would never have been able to even acknowledge your own thoughts. You've come a long way. Look at all these big steps we've already taken to arm ourselves against our defenses, getting the bed, touch, moving into this room. . . . The only step left to take that would make us stronger would be to get married."

"Get married!" "Get married!" screeched Carol, going through the "I'm shocked" routine before I'd even had time to process my own feelings. One thing I did know was that *I* was not shocked at all. Ian's defenses went on guard. "I was only talking about it," he fumbled, scared by Carol's dramatics.

I looked at Ian and struggled to get Carol's manic grimace off my face. I was inside but my defenses had put my face in prison.

"That would be a good step to defeat the defenses," my words came out, filtered through Willie's clinical stranglehold. Ian agreed.

We decided to check. "I want to be married," I shouted in my own voice. The tide of my emotions came in and my face lit up like the breaking of a wave rushing to the shore. The truth was free.

Ian checked. "I want to be married," he shouted and his face burst alive like fireworks going off. His eyes looked as if they'd caught fire and his smile battled with invisible bars and broke free.

"My defenses want to be married," I shouted with equal conviction, and my eyes went dead and my face died.

"My defenses want to be married," shouted Ian, waiting for the impact that didn't happen.

"My defenses don't want to be married," I dared, and my own expression broke through, making it clear that even if my defenses didn't want to be exposed, it was true.

"My defenses don't want to be married," dared Ian, and his defenses maintained a calm chiseled façade for one second, two seconds, until Ian's face broke through like an explosion, his eyes laughing, his cheeks unable to maintain their composure. It was clear his defenses and mine were against us.

My defenses rumbled. This was my life, not theirs—they could go to hell.

We both fell silent. Compulsive displays of mock-embarrassment, mock-shame, mock-guilt, mock-fear, and mock-anger all fired at once as my defenses frantically rummaged through files of "what a person feels now." The turmoil of my defenses was so loud over my own emotions that mine were the barely audible, barely visible, barely tangible, barely knowable undercurrent to their torrent. But somewhere in the turmoil were two feelings that didn't explode the way a compulsion does. There were two feelings that rose like water in a well in spite of their subtlety. The gentleness and warmth of these two feelings made them stand out against the harsh background of defensive, triggered stored-emotional responses. Somewhere in the undercurrent flowed *relief* and *happiness*.

We were both committed to carrying out known wants, provided always they conformed to the rules of simply be and took from no one. My defenses were playing mental havoc with the words I'd spoken, replaying them repeatedly with less and less feeling and commitment until they sounded like a general, sterile, theoretical statement about "not minding the idea of marriage." Liars, I screamed in my own mind. I know what I said. I know what I meant.

"So how do we do this? How do people get married?" said Ian.

"I don't know," I replied honestly.

"When?" I asked a minute later. "When will we do this?"

"Soon," said Ian, aware of the havoc our defenses could cause in the interim, "as soon as possible."

We wouldn't want a big service in a church, we both agreed—we should just do it in a registry office.

We would need a witness. We decided we could get a stranger off the street to do that or an employee in the registry office.

We wouldn't get fancy clothes, we said. We'd just wear what we usually wear.

We didn't believe in tradition, that was all for "the worlders." We didn't want to be like them. We wanted it to be "just another day," we agreed. We'd go to the registry office, get married, come home, and get on with things as usual. We weren't even going to have rings. Rings were a sign of someone's ownership over someone else, and we believed in owning only ourselves. Even though we knew it all, we agreed nevertheless to check everything. We didn't want our defenses to get away with anything.

But none of it was real. It couldn't be real yet. All this said and done between Ian and me within the confines of the cottage suggested it was all still part of "my world." Ian was part of "my world," an extension of my own mind, my own feelings, my own body. The cottage was part of "my world," an extension of the physical space between me and my belongings. Nothing was made real until it was real in "the world." We would tell the Dawsons.

We could do it by fax, but that would be an impersonal reprieve to our defenses, who would accept that as the lesser evil. We could do it by phone, which would be easier than face to face. We didn't need "easy" and agreed our defenses could be damned. We'd go and tell the Dawsons in person.

Ian got on the phone. "We want to come over, there's something we want to tell you," he said to Mr. Dawson.

As we got into the car, a ladybug flew down onto Ian through the open window. "Ladybugs are for good luck," I told him.

Mr. Dawson answered the door. Alex hovered about and Mrs. Dawson stood back smiling. Alex sat down on the couch, and Ian and I approached him with some paper and a pencil.

Ian wrote a note and I handed it to Alex. He would be the first person to know. He took the note and read it. The note said, "Ian and Donna are getting married. We two will be stronger together as one."

Ian then took Mr. Dawson outside to tell him. I stood with Mrs. Dawson in the living room. I would tell her.

"We've decided to get married," I told Mrs. Dawson. Now it was out, it was real and undeniable. There would be no turning back.

All back together in the house, the Dawsons asked us where we were going to get married. Ian and I looked at each other. "We don't know yet how a person gets married," we explained. The Dawsons went to the yellow pages and got us a number for the registrar of marriages. It was a place to start. "If you need any help, any help whatsoever," said Mr. Dawson, "we'll be more than happy to oblige."

We phoned the number the next day and were asked whether the wedding would be in a registry office or in a church. "In a registry office," replied Ian, knowing we wanted something simple, nothing flash.

"I think we'd better check," I told Ian, when he'd got off the phone. We didn't want our defenses taking an inch.

"I want to get married in a registry office," shouted Ian, waiting for his face to light up as we went through our checking procedure. An impulse fought with his face for the place of a plastic expected smile but nothing happened. We looked at each other in dismay. "I want to get married in a church," shouted Ian, his face breaking into a real smile. Ian was embarrassed.

"Check about defenses," I prodded.

"My defenses want to get married in a registry office," shouted Ian, and his face lit up again. "I had no idea," he said. "I thought it was me who wanted to get married in a registry office.

"My defenses want to get married in a church," shouted Ian; this time, his face lost its aliveness and he looked more like he was discussing a funeral than a marriage.

Ian looked at me. I was next. "I want to get married in a church," I shouted, and my smile burst through uncontrollably.

"My defenses want to get married in a church," I shouted, and my face went suddenly solemn as my feelings died.

"I want to get married in a registry office," I shouted, and dread sat in my stomach despite a plastic smile wrestling with my face. "The smile's not mine," I told Ian. "It's not connected."

"My defenses want to get married in a registry office," I shouted, and my face lit up like an express elevator flying from the lower basement to the top floor. My defenses were shown up for the hypocritical, self-denying manipulators that they were.

"If we get married in a church, what would we wear?" I asked Ian. Ian thought about it and decided he would wear his black trousers. He'd worn them to work, had owned them for five years, and they had what looked like an old soup stain on the leg. He decided he would wear these and a casual shirt, nothing too dressy.

"What about you?" asked Ian.

I looked in the wardrobe at the dresses I had. "I think I want something new," I said. "I'll make something." I had in mind a casual dress, something that wouldn't go to waste after a wedding, something I could wear again.

"Let's check," I said to Ian.

"I want to wear a wedding suit," shouted Ian. His face lit up. He blushed and seemed to be overcome with embarrassment at his own hypocrisy.

"Check about defenses," I said.

"My defenses want to wear a wedding suit," he shouted with equal emphasis. His feelings died down.

"I want to wear my black trousers and shirt," shouted Ian, waiting for the response. Nothing happened. Then he shouted, "My defenses want me to wear my black trousers and a shirt"; his face remained staunch and expressionless, though his eyes seemed on fire until, one second, two seconds, three seconds, . . . and his expression broke free like someone trying not to laugh at a joke he'd found hilarious.

"Now you," said Ian. "A proper wedding dress."

I didn't mind checking. I knew I wanted a normal dress. But there was an anxiety. There was a feeling that my response might

make me do something I definitely didn't want. But this was illogical. Checking could not make me do anything I didn't want.
Checking would only make me true to my own true wants. If
there was a fear of checking, it was not mine. It was not I who
feared truth, it was my defenses, damn them.

"I want to wear a proper wedding dress," I shouted, my face
burning up as I blushed. My defenses exploded within and I was
left with a feeling that I'd look stupid and laughable, that such a
dress wouldn't suit me, that it was pretentious and wasteful and a
load of money better given to charity.

Ian was smiling but I was unsure whether it was his smile or
whether it was generated by his defenses as they now watched my
defenses "in the soup too."

By the end of the evening, we had found out that we wanted
wedding rings, we wanted to invite the Dawsons to be witnesses,
and we wanted to go on a honeymoon after the wedding. After
that evening, nothing could surprise us about the depth of our
defensive self-denial or the complexity of the justifications our
defenses found to back themselves up. We found out something
else. We found out that it was we ourselves—and not our defenses—who didn't want either of our biological families to
know or be invited.

We didn't know where to begin to find a church. It didn't occur
to me that I'd need a religion to be married in one. Though I
grew up without a religion or going to church services, I liked
churches. I liked their smells and their colored glass, their wood
and their marble. I liked their statues and their carvings, their
candles and their rows, and I liked their quietness.

Ian had been involved with the church when he was a boy, but
the church learning he'd had was so drummed into him that he
hadn't reached out for any of it. The only part of it that had
stayed with him had been the music. We'd found out that only
one of us needed a religion to get married in a church. Ian had
that, even if he didn't go to church anymore.

We'd found out that our defenses wanted the wedding over-seas. The reasoning for this was that we would return to a country detached from all that had happened. After this, we knew our marriage would have to be in the United Kingdom.

We thought of small churches in small villages, where we could get married without being seen, and found one on the top of a hill surrounded by countryside. "Who do we contact?" asked Ian. I read the sign on the old church door. It said the church was derelict. "We'll find somewhere," said Ian.

Back home, we passed the gateway to the church at the top of our street. Ian and I had walked through here the first night we'd got together. It was inside of these gates, in the churchyard, that Ian told me about his "faces" one and a half years ago. Ian and I looked at each other. "Let's check," said Ian. We checked. We had found our church.

We phoned the Dawsons. We told them we were getting married in a church and that we wanted all three of them to be there.

"Photos?" Mrs. Dawson asked. I didn't like having my photo taken. The best place for pictures is in your own memory, Ian had thought that he thought, photos were just something plastic for people to gawk at and comment on. "No," we both said. "We definitely don't want photos."

There were three weeks to the wedding and we'd done nothing about rings or clothes. The decision to have a honeymoon meant one thing to the defenses—a holiday—and all our energies were diverted into its arrangements. To us, the honeymoon was part of the wedding, the part that came at the end. To our defenses, it was the most immediate concern, a distraction, and a way out of looking at anything to do with weddings and marriage. A decision was made to buy an atlas and pick a place to go.

We drove to a department store to buy a big world atlas. The car drove straight past a quiet little wedding boutique on the corner. Each of us saw the other look at it peripherally. Neither of us said anything. Armed with the atlas, we went back home.

Nigel wanted to go to the Greek islands or to Spain—places he'd been with others in a long line of girlfriends. Carol wanted a visit to Australia and played out scenarios of "just happening to have run into people."

Carol kept saying "holiday" and Ian kept correcting.

"Holiday?" said Ian. "Honeymoon," I replied, as Carol gritted my teeth.

Richard and Willie weren't even in the race. They'd been knocked out in the first round. They'd been the ones wanting to come straight home after the wedding and "get on with life." Ian and I made a list of all the places chosen and checked on them all. None of them were our want. We looked for little islands that would have sunshine and not too many tourists and weren't too far from the U.K. We checked among these and found our want. We were going to Sardinia.

The honeymoon was organized and paid for; with no more excuses, we were able to go and look for a wedding dress. We found ourselves back at the same department store where we'd bought the atlas, as though buying a wedding dress was just part of our general shopping.

There was a small, open, quite public wedding boutique on the first floor and Ian drew me over to the gown rack. Carol rolled my eyes. Willie crossed my arms. I felt like I'd eaten lemons.

Ian held out one dress after another, waiting to see a response that wasn't stored and programmed. "Tell me you want this dress," he said as we checked through four racks of wedding dresses. He put up with Carol's melodramatic pouting and distraction with all things irrelevant. In between Carol's rubbish and Willie's "we've got better things to do" routine and pragmatic, "how to recycle a wedding dress" attitude, Ian tried to keep me keeping a hold on me. I was happy, but a stranger would never have known it. To all appearances, I looked like a lamb being dragged to the slaughter. Ian was being made to look more like a brother pushing his sister along in her unwanted arranged marriage rather than the man I wanted to marry.

Screaming children were running about the boutique playing hide-and-seek in the racks. Spoilt, pampered, daughters were there, displaying themselves like criticizing peacocks in front of mothers and mirrors. Haughty attendants were there, fussing about with veils and pleats and hemlines. But my wedding dress wasn't there. There was one we'd found that I had a like for, but a want is different from a like and there was none that I had wanted to take home.

On our way back to the car we passed the quiet little corner wedding boutique again. "Do you want to go in?" asked Ian. Willie had cashed in on my not having found the dress I wanted in the last store, playing on its theoretical relevance for whether I actually wanted a wedding dress at all. The logical follow-through for this was to put on an "expectations, expectations" attitude. Willie assumed this mock-attitude, attempting to make me feel pushed into going in.

I waited at the door to the shop, giving myself time and looking for my own reasons and what I felt. Ian waited patiently.

Willie's assumptions were wrong. "Pressured" feels heavy like dread. "Anxious" feels out of control, like nervous and scared. I felt anxious but not pressured.

Next, I had to work out the source of the anxiety. I focused on it. The anxiety I was combating was not because of pressure from the outside—from Ian or expectation. The anxiety was from battling the pressure and resistance I was facing from the inside. The anxiety was from the threat I felt from my defenses. Ian held my hand and we went in.

We walked straight over to the rack of wedding gowns and began to check again. A woman my own age came swooping down on us like a vulture with a polite smile. Her arm went out to the side as though she was going to scoop us up in her arms. Willie went to spin my body around with a scowl, a learned confrontation to scare off the vulture.

Ian stepped in. "Not Willie," he said softly but firmly. "Willie's not here to buy anything." Willie lost his grip and I broke through relieved.

"We're fine," said Ian to the shop assistant. "We need to be alone, we take a lot of time to choose. If you're there we'll just end up following what we think you think is good and we won't make any choice, so we'd rather do this alone."

We checked through dress after dress as I shook from head to toe and broke out in a sweat. Jubblies gripped my stomach. I was compelled to move past some of the dresses with the assumption that "a person could not possibly want something like that." Every time this happened Ian stopped me on those in particular, and he was right. Two out of these three dresses were definite likes in a sea of dislikes and indifference. It was not so much that my defenses believed in the assumptions they raised, as that they were quick to call justifications "reasons." The real reason to have me avoid the things I liked was their well-guarded rejection of my self-expression, self-exposure, and ability to be affected.

The shop assistant watched us from across the room and Willie shot quick sharp glances at her.

"Who are you here with?" Ian asked me gently but firmly.

"Ian," I answered, breaking through.

"She's not here," said Ian. We ignored her.

I came across a fairly simple satin dress with off-the-shoulder sleeves and a small sprinkling of sequins and flowers. I couldn't possibly want a dress like that, came the assumption. I passed it over. "Check," said Ian. I did and it *was* the dress. I had liked it. I had liked it more than any of the others I'd been found to like. But more than this, I had a want for it.

The assumption in me—that I didn't want to try the dress on—was so compulsion-driven that I confused it with knowing. We knew which dress it was. We could come back another day. "Tell me you want to try it on," said Ian calmly.

My face and body became a theater for second-long performances by the defenses. I felt out of control under the invasion, like my body was a puppet I couldn't get control of. Carol's manic grin danced across my face in one instant. She flounced about in the next, her eyes darting and looking, quite obviously, for other distractions. Willie's chiseled expression crept momentarily over my face and his "there'll be another day" look swept over me as he glared impatiently at Ian. I put my hands up to my face and covered the lot of them.

My lips trembled and my hands shook. "I want to try it on," I said and broke through in a gentle, trembling, real smile and tears of relief. "I want to try on the . . . my . . . wedding dress."

Willie was already running through ideas of how to cut this dress up and alter it later to make it "wearable" and not so wasteful in a world full of poverty. Carol was already playing stored mockery of how laughable and ridiculous I would look and what an ugly bride I'd make. Between these two overbearing social consciences I could hardly justify my right to breathe—let alone to buy a wedding dress I'd chosen.

The vulture approached again armed with pins and hands and eyes and blah-blah and a 3-D smile. Ian and I looked at each other. "We want to try this dress on," said Ian.

The shop assistant looked like she was about to launch into business. Yes, I said in my mind, tell her, Ian.

"We have trouble with communication, so you'll have to speak slowly and keep your voice down," said Ian.

"You both have the same problem?" asked the shop assistant, surprised. "Where did you meet each other?" Ian and I couldn't work out the relevance of the question, so we ignored it. "You're so lucky to have found each other," said the shop assistant, going on regardless. "You seem to understand each other so well." If there was one thing we were sure of, that was it. We were albatrosses. With no other albatross in sight, we wouldn't want to marry a pigeon.

"I'll pin the dress for her," began the shop assistant, moving toward me with the pins and hands and smile.

"We also have trouble with touch," explained Ian. "I'll help her."

"I'll have to help her put the dress on," said the shop assistant gently.

"No," said Ian firmly. "I'm going in with her. I'll help her into the dress."

"She'll need some shoes," added the woman, rushing away and coming straight back with some my size.

I saw the shoes and lit up. We checked. This response had been my own. Ian hung the dress up lovingly on the hook on the cubicle wall. I stood there shaking in a fluffy yellow sweater and jeans and sneakers.

Off came the jumper and the jeans and the sneakers. I stood there in patterned cotton knickers, a singlet, and socks, feeling like something the cat had dragged in. "Do you want to take this off?" said Ian, referring to the singlet. I looked down at the socks and singlet on my body and then up at Ian. I was scared and vulnerable and badly under attack from every piece of stored social shit my defenses could heap on me.

"I'm having trouble," I told him.

"What is it?" he asked.

As I told him, it was like I was a ball of tangled string inside of me. Together we gently laughed at the stupidity and arrogance of my defenses' thinking. Together we shared anger at these invisible abusers and Ian hugged me as I stood there in my underwear. Though closeness created anxiety and provoked the defenses, I felt safe hugging Ian. We were real people. They were stored mental crap. We were stronger than they. Together we cried and shared our understanding of the fear that had driven the whole mental explosion. My fear was a snowball but they made the avalanche. I wiped away the tears. Ian took the dress down from the wall. We smiled.

I stepped into the dress and put my back to Ian as he did up the zipper. I stepped into the white satin shoes like a Cinderella and turned to face him. His face trembled. His body trembled. His face had a gentle real smile and tears fell down his face. He was happy-sad. He was happy-sad bigly. "You are beautiful," said Ian in a whisper through the tears and, though I stood there in a wedding dress, I felt he would have meant it just as much had I been still standing there in jeans. I heard him with meaning and feeling. He was on my side. I didn't turn away.

We left the cubicle. Ian held my hand tightly and faced the shop assistant. "We want to take this dress," he said.

"It will take about two months," said the shop assistant.

Our hearts sank. The dress wouldn't be ready for two months and our wedding was only three weeks away.

Ha, ha, ha, went Carol's mental impression of some asshole's sarcasm. Willie used the opportunity to mentally replay the idea that "I" didn't want to get married anyway and that it was shameful to spend money for one dress that would never be worn again.

"But we want this dress," repeated Ian.

"Yes, it will take two months to be ordered and made. It's made in Italy, not here," the shop assistant said.

"No," said Ian. "You don't understand. How long for *this* actual dress?"

The shop assistant hemmed and hawed. "When's the wedding?" she asked.

"Three weeks," replied Ian.

The shop assistant was taken aback. "I'll see what we can do." She left the room. Ian stood there waiting in hope. I stood there trying not to crumble under the weight of my defenses.

She returned. "Three weeks will be fine," she said primly. Ha, ha, ha, I said in my head for the sake of my defenses.

"Do you want to pay for it now?" the assistant asked.

"Yes," said Ian and I in unison.

The assistant added it all up and waited for our response. Ian and I looked at the total and then looked at each other.

Our defenses were creating all the anxiety of chickens being chased and, for both of us, our minds were bursting with thoughts of why it was immoral, irrational, ridiculous, shameful, stupid, and wasteful to spend so much money on such things. Our minds compelled us to get something more practical, useful for later, not so expensive, to make it ourselves . . . *to at least hag-gle if a person was paying in cash!* Ian and I smiled. "That's fine," we said, again in unison. Ian paid the woman and she handed us a re-ceipt. Willie thought that we gave over all that money for that little piece of paper.

Ian's suit was still out there somewhere. We had to go for a spe-cial eye test the next day. We'd come back Thursday for Ian's suit.

━ ━

We got into the car for the two-hour drive to our appointment for the Irlen Centre.

The city gave way to country roads and thatched cottages, weepy trees and midsummer wildflowers. We pulled into an es-tate and up to one of several stone buildings that housed offices.

A woman named Meg showed us into the office. She ex-plained how the Irlen tints, or filters, worked. In its purest form, visual information comes in as a series of light waves and those light waves relate to colors. In some cases, people with informa-tion-processing problems take in more information at a time than they can process fully. In other cases, they take information in too slowly, not getting enough to make full sense of things. In each case, it is possible to assess which particular light waves are miss-ing or complicating the processing of visual information. At the Irlen Centre, they could manipulate the light waves received by the eyes through the use of various tints or combinations of tints to compensate for what was missing or filter out what one was getting too much of, until the processing of visual information is no longer a problem.

Meg opened up a box. Inside were a huge range of tinted lenses, or Irlen filters, in every possible slight variation of color and shade. She handed me a pair to try. I held the filters up in front of my glasses. The room looked less overwhelmingly bright but not much else. She handed me another pair, which made the fuzz of air particles in the air even more stark than usual: mesmerizing but not much help at all. A third pair just made the room look a different shade than before. Finally, she gave me a pair that made things improve slightly. These took out some of the visual distractions of shine and shadow that detracted from making sense of objects themselves.

Meg handed me a few more pairs of filters to try over this set that helped. Just as suddenly as the right combination of overlays had made all the difference to the printed page, the right combination of filters changed everything totally.

I looked through the window at the garden outside. Instead of looking from tree to tree and shrub to shrub, I saw one whole picture at once: one whole garden. More than this though, I saw the view through the window as no longer just a picture. It looked like a place—not just theoretically, but visually. It looked as if I could just walk straight out there, not "with" things, but "among" them. What I had had to learn in theory, I could now see in perception. I'd learned that the world had variable depth to be experienced in moving through it, but I'd never actually consistently or properly seen that variation. Now I had merely to look at something to know it as it was.

I was smiling and crying and shaking. "I see a whole picture," I said out loud. "I see a whole world."

Still holding the filters over my eyes, I looked at Ian. "Your face," I stuttered, "it's joined together." The face I had mapped out bit by bit to form a constructed mental impression was now perceived for the first time as a whole. Here lay the path to trust. In a perceptual world where my body-sense, my auditory comprehension, my personality, and my sense of surroundings were fragmented, I finally could do more than struggle to imagine an unfragmented whole. If only on one channel—that of vision—I no longer had to imagine. I could experience.

"Just a moment," said Meg. "I want you to read that overhead chart for me with your prescription glasses." I took the combination of filters away and looked at the chart. It was similar to an optician's chart.

As I read the letters, my prescription lenses made everything closer but they did nothing to take away the distortion and fragmentation.

At Meg's request, I read the chart again, this time without either my glasses or the combination of filters. The distortions caused by the bouncing light of the chart background and reverberating shadow of print made the letters vibrate.

"Now try the chart again through the filters only," Meg instructed. I held the Irlen filters up to my eyes and read the chart flawlessly. I couldn't understand why.

Next, I held the filters over my glasses, reading the chart through both at once. "Not as good as before," I stumbled, surprised that it had been harder to read with my prescription lenses than without them when using the filters.

"I thought so," said Meg. "You didn't need those prescription glasses." The optician, unaware and unknowledgeable about perceptual problems, had tried to compensate for my poor visual perception by making everything more close-up. There was nothing wrong with my sight. My eyes worked fine. The problem had been with my brain, not my eyes. Optometrists generally deal with sight problems, which are eye problems, not perceptual problems, which are brain problems (though some optometrists are now using the Colorimeter to treat visual perceptual problems). Looking through the right combination of colours, my vision was perfect.

It was Ian's turn. Because Ian lived in a world where he saw constant TV fuzz day and night, with his eyes opened or closed, it was easier to find the right filters for him. He just had to keep trying until something took the fuzz away. The ultimate effect on his depth perception and visual fragmentation was similar to that for me, even though we ended up with different colored lenses and Ian still needed his prescription glasses.

Although it was time to go home, we were leaving without the filters through which we had both finally seen each other. It was like being given the best present we'd ever had and then being told, "Sorry, but you can't take it home with you." We had to wait six weeks for these Irlen filters to be made up. By the time we would get them, we would be married and the only real glimpse we'd had of each other had been for a few short minutes here in this little office.

— ◄

On the way home from the Irlen Centre we stopped and ordered some chips and a kebab. It would take five minutes to cook.

From across the road, a shop was staring at us: a shop that sold men's clothing. In the corner of the window was a man's wedding suit with gray-and-black striped trousers.

Ian's defenses fired up quickly with excuses, saying, "Let's wait for the food. We won't come all the way back here again to pick a suit up."

"Check," I said crisply.

We checked and Ian wanted to go and look. He looked relieved but, as we got out of the car, Richard gave his "expectations, expectations" sigh. I hated that bastard. I felt so angry inside I could have hit him if he didn't happen to have Ian's body.

Richard stood next to me outside of the shop. The suit had black tails, a white frilly shirt, and gray-and-black striped trousers.

"I definitely want plain black trousers," said Nigel flashing an "am I passable as Ian?" grin. "I definitely don't want striped trousers," he went on.

"We'll see," I said. "Ian can check."

Nigel gave his "there isn't any point" eye roll.

"You can check," I said, referring to Ian. "Who is this?" I asked, pointing at him.

"Ian," said Ian.

"I want striped trousers," Ian declared loudly as his defenses again tried to hold his face, to no avail. Ian stood there embarrassed. His defenses made him look like a liar and a hypocrite.

We were going back to the first wedding boutique on Thursday. Ian suggested we wait till then, which, though it was potentially an excuse, sounded like a practical idea.

"Have you ever worn top hat and tails?" I asked him.

"No," said Ian, "only suits."

Ian had been in a wedding once. All the men had hired their suits. We checked for what Ian wanted. His defenses came through loud and clear; they wanted him to hire his wedding clothes. Ian, however, wanted something for himself. He wanted to buy them.

Thursday came around and we drove to the wedding shop. As we approached, Ian was shaking and scared but glad to be very much him. Inside the shop, he could hardly bear to look at the suits and shirts and ties and socks around him. When it finally came to asking, we were both disappointed. The shop only rented its suits.

Then the shop assistant from the adjoining wedding dress boutique who had helped me came in. We explained the situation. "I'm sure we can do something," she said. It would take about two weeks to get the suit in. It would be ready at the same time as the dress.

Ian was looking at something behind the counter. I followed his glance to a pair of shoes. They were black suede with gold colored buckles and cost sixty-five pounds. Without a word he looked away.

Behind us was a tall pile of shoe boxes with a sign saying, "Special Offer, £19.99." These now had his attention. The man behind the counter got out a few pairs of shoes. Ian's defenses were determined to find a cheap pair.

"I want these shoes," his mouth said, checking enthusiastically as his finger pointed at the £19.99 pile. His defenses plastered a plastic forced smile onto his face.

"The smile's not yours," I said.

"What smile?" asked Ian, unaware of the theatricals on his face. "Was I smiling?"

"I don't want these shoes," he checked again, his own smile breaking through.

"Can you pass those shoes?" I said to the man behind the counter, referring to the expensive shoes. He handed them to Ian. Tears welled up in Ian's eyes with what seemed like relief. He was smiling his own smile.

We looked at shirts. Ian was sure he didn't want a fancy shirt. We checked. His defenses wanted a business shirt. He wanted a frilled shirt.

We looked at gloves. Ian was sure he didn't want gloves. What would he use them for, he wondered. But wants have no logic. Ian, as it turned out, wanted gloves.

His defenses put up a battle about a top hat. He definitely didn't want one of those either. They were wrong. He did.

Finally, Ian asked, "Do you have striped trousers?"

"Do you want to try a suit on?" asked the man. Ian was definitely sure he didn't want to try one on today. He was tired and we'd been there long enough and it was getting late and we hadn't eaten and . . . We checked. Ian very much wanted to try the suit on.

The man got things together for Ian to try on and we went into the men's changing room together.

Ian shook as he put on the wedding suit. Finally, he stepped into his shoes. He looked up and the look on his face was one of a five-year-old boy who had slain his imaginary monsters.

Out of the cubicle Ian stepped in front of the mirror, afraid to look. It had always been Nigel posing in the mirror back at him, trying to look like something cool from a rock magazine, or Richard, examining spots and flaky skin but losing the face they belonged to.

Ian stood in front of the mirror, his hand trembling in the grasp of mine as he raised his head and adjusted his eyes to finally look from the suit to the man in the suit. He was crying. "That's me," he whispered, his voice breaking up. "That's me."

"Yes, that's you," I said, looking at the man I was marrying and forming a picture of him in my head.

The wedding was going ahead and both of our defenses tried to throw as many wrenches in the works as possible.

Ian's defenses tried to play the role of "going through the motions of a forced marriage." In a way they were right. They, like mine, had been forced into it by us. But they had no choice. We had chosen a life where we dared to have self-expression, wants, closeness, and emotions. It was none of their damned business. The problem for us, though, was that it was in their vested interests to play their subliminal advertising as often as possible, especially whenever we relaxed and weren't focused and aware. Defenses don't advertise, "This thought is brought to you by your defenses." Instead, half the time, we were lulled into wondering if it was we ourselves who were having the doubts.

My defenses mentally turned Ian into every slimeball I'd ever been with and kept noticing every possible physical resemblance they could to justify their angle. I had a fragmented perception of things at the best of times, seeing eyes or a nose or whiskers or a mouth but mostly putting the bits together in my head. When my defenses made a match between the color of Ian's eyes and some slime they had known, then Ian *did* look like that person.

Almost every night for the next two weeks I had dreams where Ian turned into other people, my father at his worst, or my mother. It was working. First my defenses made me scared. Then it went beyond scared and I began to feel defeated, complacent, detached, and indifferent.

Every morning I was compelled to jump out of bed as soon as I woke up. There was always something to do. Ian could see it but the excuses ran thick and fast. Besides, as long as the excuses were feasible and logical, the only grounds for possible justified opposition could be on the grounds that my behavior wasn't "me."

What is and isn't someone's true self is a hard thing to define and even harder to justify knowing. People and circumstances change all the time. Even feelings change. What doesn't change, though, is what you sense: a "feel" rather than a "feeling."

Ian's defenses were playing on my fear that my own marriage would be like that of my parents—a nightmare. Ian's defenses pushed him to ask me again and again whether I was prepared to marry someone with his difficulties. Then, they demonstrated "Ian's" difficulties in displays of amateur dramatics just to test out the theory in practice. Between his defenses and mine, they were doing a demolition job on us.

"You know what they want," said Ian in a good moment, referring to our defenses. "They want us apart. We've got to stick together." It seemed like something from the film *Poltergeist*. We had to stick together and keep these evil spirits out.

There was one week left before the wedding and our defenses seemed conspicuously absent. Compared with the last two weeks, it was as though they'd abandoned ship.

Ian and I had planned out everything for the day of the wedding, from what we were having for breakfast and lunch to what we were wearing after the wedding and what time we were leaving. Nothing was left to chance. Everything was checked. The defenses weren't going to get their hooks in anywhere.

"What if your defenses show up at the altar?" I asked Ian. "I don't want to marry Richard or Nigel."

"Well, what if Willie or Carol take over?" he replied.

We both knew that if our defenses thought they could play havoc that way, they surely would. We decided that if that happened we would go through the service anyway, knowing the person we were marrying was still in there, trapped. Besides, it was all about "for better or for worse" and "in sickness and in health." We weren't picking and choosing. Though we had no desire to marry each other's defenses and no intention of accepting or supporting each other's defenses, our acceptance of each other was a package deal, warts and all.

We had decided we were walking to the church. It was just up the hill and it seemed a silly waste of money to hire a car when we could easily walk the distance in five minutes. Besides, we decided, we didn't want to hide ourselves away.

We considered what we would do if it rained. We decided we would drive ourselves up there or catch a taxi. It was all beginning to sound a bit blasé again. We decided to check.

We did want to walk if it was a nice day. If it rained or was too windy, we didn't want a taxi and we didn't want to drive ourselves. What else was there though? Surely we wouldn't want a wedding car just to follow us up the street? But we did.

We decided to check about photos. We thought we were so sure about that too. We were wrong. Red-faced and embarrassed, we faced our hypocrisy and admitted we did want photos. We phoned Mrs. Dawson. "We found out that we wanted photos," we told her. "No, we didn't check about it before," we said. "But you are not allowed to make us pose, just take them when we're not looking."

We hung up and got out the yellow pages and looked under wedding cars. "Sure," said the man in a broad East London accent, "when's it for then?"

"Friday," Ian told him.

"Which Friday?" asked the man.

"This Friday," replied Ian.

"Oh God," said the man. But we got our car.

There were only a few days till the wedding. Though most of my usual problems with my defenses seemed nowhere around, other problems plagued me. In place of the troubles of the past two weeks, I had developed the old breath-holding, ear-clicking, sniffling, and coughing compulsions.

The problem with compulsive breath-holding is that as many times as you catch it happening, something inside fights all the more to mentally tune you out and do it even more. In the end you look a bit blue, your digestion and emotions are all over the place, and in the midst of all the light-headedness it causes, it is hard to think and stay aware enough to try to stop it through conscious effort.

In the end I was in tears and plonked down into the couch in despair. It felt like some bastard force within me wished me not to exist. "It's like they wish me dead," I said to Ian, referring to my defenses.

"Isn't there anything you can do?" he asked.

An idea came to me and I jumped up from the couch and went to the bathroom.

"This will fix them," I said, tearing some cotton wool balls into smaller pieces. "Let them put up with this," I said vengefully, laughing to myself and sticking cotton wool in my nose. My defenses went crazy inside, rebelling against the horrible invasive sensation of cotton wool in my nostrils with an urge to have me abuse myself. I don't care, I thought. I can handle it. If they can't handle it, then they can damned well stop holding my breath.

I had the upper hand. Not only could they not continually hold my breath with my nostrils blocked because of the suffocating feeling it created, but I had threatened them back. If they wanted me to listen to their phobia about the cotton wool, they could stop playing "I don't exist" games with my breathing.

The ear-clicking compulsion is where my ears "pop," just like most people's do with air pressure. But my defenses had long developed a control over this automatic mechanism, even using it to play rhythmic tunes while others went on and on in meaningless blah-blah or were likely to say something which, God forbid, might affect me emotionally, making me feel something. It was an irritating habit and made the muscles of my inner ear itch like a dog with a flea it can't reach. The monotony of the tunes they played in ear clicks would distract me and tune me out, making me swing between agitation and indifference.

The cotton wool had interfered with the ear clicking, too (which physically required little breathing), though it was still going intermittently. Defeated now on two battlefronts, they started up with compulsive coughing and sniffling. These were all part of a sort of suffocation theme.

In the bombardment, I felt so out of control. Someone would hiccup or sneeze or yawn on the TV and off my defenses would go in a compulsive fit of hiccups or sneezes or yawns. I did all but give up on the body I had fought so hard to connect with.

There was no real point stopping a compulsion, because it was like trying to zip a large person into a tiny dress: their body just popped out somewhere else. In my case, defeating one compulsion would give me a few minutes or an hour's rest but it only drove my defenses to start up another one somewhere else. They created compulsions as a kind of communication with the self they felt wouldn't listen to them. The only real solution was to kindly confront them in a personally detached and nonchallenging way with the basis for the compulsion. Sometimes, if the basis of their compulsion could be discovered and exposed with enough personal detachment, they'd disown it. Perhaps this was because it showed them that even if I wouldn't do their bidding, they knew they'd been listened to by "someone" who was not so obviously "against them." It was hard to think or communicate—let alone be impartial—when they had stirred up such anxiety and turmoil and caused such pain.

"Ignore it," I said calmly to Ian, with as much personal detachment from my feelings as I could find. "They want to believe that what they are doing is real. It's just because the wedding is coming up." Exposed, the bastards were caught. They dropped their weapons like the curtain on a theatrical flop and left for who knows where, defeated.

In the meantime, Ian's defenses were making him think about how to back out or make excuses, or even to manipulate circumstances to get a divorce if he did go through with it.

On the day before the wedding, I made the cake that we'd checked I wanted. We'd picked up the wedding clothes the day before, the car was booked, the church was booked, the honeymoon was booked.

I turned out a rather humble plain whole-meal cake from the small rectangular bread tin. After making a list of possibilities and checking them all, we'd found that for better or for worse we wanted a fruit salad cake. I cut the cake in half, opened and drained a tin of fruit salad and spooned it onto the base of the cake before replacing the top. We had checked and found we wanted wedding cake for breakfast and lamb chops for lunch before the wedding.

Ian and I woke up. It was Friday the thirteenth, the day of our wedding. The sky was blue and the sun was shining. We looked at each other and smiled in the first waking moments before the dawn of fear. Fear got us quick enough.

"How do you feel?" I asked.

"Jubblies," said Ian.

I pointed to myself and then held up two fingers: "me too," I had said in our own version of sign language.

Ian and I both had our piece of fruit salad wedding cake. Ian picked his up and started to eat it. I could see it was hard work. He looked like he was eating a lump of clay.

"Can you check whether you like the cake please?" I said to him.

"I like this cake," said Ian, wishing for a response but getting none.

"Defenses?" I asked.

"My defenses like this cake," said Ian, also getting no response from within. "My defenses don't like this cake," said Ian, again not getting much of a response. He looked at me with a mixture of apology and fear. "I don't like this cake," said Ian as an uncontrollable smile overcame him. "I'm sorry."

"It's okay. It's your 'not-like,' " I replied.

The hands of the clock on the living room wall ticked slowly around to quarter to one. The car was arriving at ten minutes to two. Ian was ready to serve up the lamb chops and roast vegetables that he'd cooked. I felt horribly ill and Ian had lost his appetite.

We sat outside on our lawn in our dressing gowns and under-wear, picking at our dinner with our fingers. "I can't eat this," I said.

"Me neither," said Ian. We went inside and washed all the grease off.

It was ten past one. "We'd better get our clothes on," said Ian. My stomach sank. I put on my wedding underwear and Ian put on his wedding socks and shirt.

Our clothes were laid out in the living room waiting for us. Ian unzipped my wedding dress from its bag, took it out, and helped me step into it. He did it up and I turned around. Ian burst out crying and couldn't stop. "You look so beautiful," he said over and over.

Ian put on his trousers, his waistcoat, and his shoes. He helped me with the flowers I had for my hair. We were both trembling and dizzy and overwhelmed.

I stood there looking at Ian as he put on tails, his cravat, and his cuff links. "Oh no," I said, heading for the bathroom. "I'm going to be sick."

The reality was too much for my defenses. That I was stand-ing there in my wedding dress on my wedding day about to marry Ian out of closeness and with real emotions and self was more than they could bear. They did somersaults with my stom-ach and I seemed to be burning up.

"Don't hold it back," said Ian, watching me about to throw up in my wedding dress. He went and got me some water and cut me a piece of apple. I chewed the juice from the apple and spat the rest out. "I have an idea," said Ian. "I think it would be a good idea to go out into the garden and get some fresh air and see what it's like to be out in the outside world in your wedding dress."

I squeezed through the narrow walkway of our kitchen in the flounce of the dress. At the doorstep, I felt terror. That was the outside world out there. If I stepped out there it would make it all real, undeniable, no turning back. Ian and I stepped out into the sunlight. I was gasping for air, like a newborn just come into the world. The fever broke, the knots let go. Ian and I held hands and let it all go, crying on each other.

The wedding car pulled up outside. We both stood at the front door knowing each other's fear from the inside. We were comrades against an inner war that would deny us life. We hugged each other.

"Are you ready to get married?" said Ian.

"Let's go and get married," I replied.

Ian opened the door and the sunlight of the day seemed to pour into the cottage, touching us and making us part of the day that we were stepping out into. We stood out on the sidewalk clasping each other's hands like a pair of lost children.

"We're walking to the church," said Ian to the driver. "Just follow us." We started walking hand in hand up the hill to our wedding, with the wedding car creeping along behind.

"Hey, your car's broken down," said the already predicted yahoo passing us in the street.

"You look just beautiful, love, just beautiful," said a lady with a cockney accent poking her head suddenly out of the doorway of an office on the way.

Ian and I walked up to the church door. We looked at each other and hugged.

"Are you ready?" asked Ian.

"Yes," I replied.

We entered the church as us. It felt right. We felt very free.

The deacon met us at the entrance and we followed her in. Her old, wrinkled, soft, puffy face and short, white curly hair made her look like a marshmallow. She had shown us all around the church just three weeks before.

We walked up to the altar, past Mr. and Mrs. Dawson and Alex. For a moment we looked at him as he sneaked a look at us. Then he buried his head into his father like a bird under a wing. Mrs. Dawson smiled.

"You both look very nice," said the fluffy deacon, opening her book. The service began. I shook through the whole thing. Ian cried through the rest. But we held hands through the whole thing and we looked at who we were marrying.

There were no music, no parishioners, no bouquets or best man. There were no parents, no flowers, no gifts, no wedding reception. There were no expectations, no falsity or fashion. There was no confusion of other people's egos or emotional baggage. There were no unwanted hugs or performed smiles or rehearsed tears or amateur dramatics. There were no drunks, seating arrangements, wedding telegrams, or gossip. There was friendship, realness, "belonging with" and self and that was more than enough.

The words "in sickness and in health" hit me. It seemed like the first time I could accept another someone and also be accepted for all my worth and difficulties. I no longer had to dissect myself into wantable and unwantable. I was marrying a whole person who was marrying me as a whole person, too.

Mrs. Dawson buzzed about in silence, snapping photos so unobtrusively we didn't need to avoid her.

We signed the register and the Dawsons witnessed it in turn. We walked past Alex and he reached out to us with both hands, taking one of mine and one of Ian's. We stood in a magic circle.

I was now with my husband and he was with his wife. We left the church and walked again out into the sunlight. Ian and I stopped and looked back at the church we got married in and gave ourselves the time to own our experience.

The wedding car drove us back to the cottage and we stepped out and back into our home as Mr. and Mrs. Another car would soon arrive to take us off for an overnight stay on the way to where we would spend our honeymoon. We got changed into the clothes we had bought for the occasion and reheated the lunch of lamb chops and roast veggies that we hadn't been able to eat before.

The taxi arrived. I felt awkward, scared, and happy all at once.

My defenses wondered how a person has a honeymoon. I tried to clear my mind.

It was a long drive. Ian sat smiling peacefully to himself, watching the countryside roll by. I was stretched out across the backseat and onto Ian's lap. Exhausted, I fell asleep.

We had booked an overnight stay at a poshy old lodge. They had sent us the booklet: four-poster beds, shower room, room service, and gardens.

The building was overwhelming and imposing. We couldn't see the whole building, only parts of it and we joined the rest together in our minds.

"Sir," "Madam," porters, pictures ten feet tall and six feet wide, crystal, velvet, marble, leather, polished silver and flower arrangements. The porter showed us to our room.

We couldn't wait for him to leave, and I couldn't understand a word he said. I just wanted him out. The porter gone, I felt like barricading the door from the oh so polite, "let me make you comfortable" people outside. Incomprehensible social conventions seemed to flow from their mouths, pour from their faces, and govern every stance, every move. They scared the hell out of me. Ian and I wanted to run away from this place.

We felt like prisoners in the room, afraid the porters would come knocking on the door again trying to be "helpful." We decided to go out for a walk.

The lodge was set in acres of fields and beautiful gardens. On our way back to the lodge, we passed a grassy entrance to a field. I knew I wanted to go and sit in there. "This field," I told Ian. "The way it just bursts open through that doorway in the bushes, it's like a dream I used to have. I used to go to a field like this in my mind and feel like dancing. This is like the field I draw all the time." Ian and I went through the parting of the hedges and into the open field on the other side.

The multicolored grass was dotted with tiny yellow wildflowers. Up in the sky was something really strange.

The blue sky had a few gray and white clouds. Among the clouds, there was what can only be called a sort of special rainbow cloud. It was not quite a cloud, but took up the same sort of space. It was made up of a multitude of colors that seemed to be tumbling over and over in place and changing from color to color, running through the entire rainbow. It was like a small swirling rainbow without the bow or the rain. It was a sky show, made especially for us on our wedding day, Friday the thirteenth. Ian and I sat down in the grass in that field and watched it for the ten spectacular minutes that it lasted before fading away. It had seemed like ages.

After a room-service dinner and TV, we ran a steaming hot bubble bath and sat in the bath together. When the water got cold, we got out and hopped into bed in the big, heavy, dark, wooden four-poster bed and took out our story book. We picked a story called "Queen of the Moon" and read the bedtime story out loud.

"Good night," I said sleepily at the end of it.

"Good night," said Ian, just as tired.

"What are we going to do for one week?" I had asked Ian when we were planning our honeymoon.

"We'll do nothing for a change," said Ian, meaning it quite literally.

We had booked a flight to a villa in Sardinia. Sardinia spelled sunshine, heat, and blue water. There would be no need to take anything with us to occupy our time.

Ian and I finally arrived at the villa, a big, stone, empty place, whitewashed wall to wall. It was like staying in a jelly mold rather than a house. You were meant to bring your personality here to fill in the blanks.

The villa overlooked a turquoise ocean, which stretched on into nothingness. Inside of the villa, Ian and I walked around trying to be happy but feeling utterly miserable.

"I don't know what to do," I told Ian after doing nothing all day and the next day.

"Good," said Ian, reeling off a stored attitude that on vacation people relaxed, did nothing, and enjoyed it.

Ian sat in the sunshine, sat in the lounge, sat on the balcony, sat at the table, and sat on the bed. I tried to make going to the toilet a major event of the day. I walked from room to room examining flaws and living and dead bugs and trying to abstain from becoming obsessive.

Night after night, we both looked forward to the major social event: a bedtime story that was read to the sound of hovering mosquitoes.

Ian's defenses moved about the villa with an air of stuffiness and the "I'm playing husband" role of a plastic, neutered Ken doll.

All physical closeness we had had before we were married had now fallen into the category of "sexual expectation between marrieds." Ian's defenses nonchalantly went about pretending nothing was happening about the nothing that was happening.

Every time any closeness came to the surface, Ian's defenses came to the fore to play it as a role. As they attempted to play a kind of snap-of-the-fingers, sit-com husband role, they killed off any self that had been in his initial feelings. The fact was that neither Ian nor I knew how to put our feelings of closeness into action within the context of having got married. The context of the cottage and accidental or incidental touch had put us back to square one.

My defenses stood back laughing to themselves as they watched Ian's defenses hang our marriage. At the same time, they also became more and more antagonized by the seemingly arrogant assumption of his defenses that "Donna was convinced" by their role playing. I was not convinced, but I did understand. When Ian realized what was happening, we decided to deliberately defy the lot of them.

The answer was for us to initiate unstored forms of touch with each other when our feelings to do so were absent. We both felt awkward as hell making moves with no known want. But even awkwardness was a feeling of some sort, so we knew we weren't feeling-dead.

Our touch was an open defiance and an assertion of freedom from the dictatorship of our defenses. They had, as always, an allergic reaction to our awkwardness. But, once discovered in their game playing, they could conjure up no convincing excuses to avoid what we had made them confront. They jumped ship like the infestation they were and we enjoyed our innocence and awkwardness and had our feelings without the anesthesia of role playing and its clinical and obsessional self-control.

We still didn't know how to be social. Our version of social had always been to take cues. Our version of "social" had simply been other people's and though we had simply be, simply be revolved around the sharing of something; in our new sterile little jelly mold, it was hard to find "share" within us.

"This is like a doctor's office waiting for the doctor to come," I told Ian.

Ian finally conceded that after the flights and the driving and the luxurious Sardinian villa, he wasn't happy either. "I don't know what to do either," said Ian. "What did we expect?"

Ian and I laughed and the honesty made us both feel less alone, even if it didn't teach us how to find something to do or share in anything.

The problem was that, at home, everything we did fitted into a routine. At home, the surroundings themselves dictated what to do. Mess told us to clean it up. Papers told us to file them. Letters told us to answer them. The time told us which TV programs to watch, when to eat, bathe, dress, and sleep. Sardinia was the jigsaw puzzle with no border or straight-edged pieces. We had no idea where to begin. We considered going out to try to buy the sort of things we had at home.

We got into the car we'd hired and drove around the tiny mountain roads for hours until we came to a city. We bought paper and pens, sketchbooks and pencils. We bought a badminton set, even though the villa had no yard and we didn't play sports. We looked for monoculars to watch birds and insects (as we only consistently used one eye at a time). We couldn't find them but bought a telescope instead.

We took the paper and pens, the sketchbook and pencils, the badminton set, and the telescope back to the villa. Ian spent time looking at the moon each night through the telescope. I spent time writing on paper. Ian spent time sketching our experiences in Sardinia. We got out the badminton rackets and tried to hit the shuttlecock back and forth across the long empty living room.

We had bought snorkels and goggles and the turquoise blue ocean that surrounded us everywhere called us to swim.

My fear found every reason and excuse for procrastination. Doing something I'd never been shown how to do with someone else was dangerously self-expressive. I wouldn't be able to pretend I was following, copying, or replaying the actions of someone else. I'd have to take responsibility for the want and the doing. I felt suffocated.

What about sharks? What about sunburn? What about something to eat before we go? What about packing some things to take? What about putting sunscreen on? What about not feeling well? About an hour later, my fear had run out of excuses. With snorkels and goggles, we left the jelly mold prison and went swimming in the turquoise blue ocean.

Under the water, fish appeared out of nowhere to swim with us in collections of blue and yellow and silver. They swam in and out of the sea plants and anemones that groped at the water with loads of little arms.

One minute the floor of the ocean was golden and sandy, the next minute silvery and shimmering with waves etched into the ocean floor. A few minutes later, it was a world of tiny rock caves and plant jungles or a drifting, shifting floor of bark and seaweed.

As the jumble drifted busily below us, my visual perception jolted fiercely in a medley of background-foreground shifts. One minute, I was a moving person watching an ocean bed below me.

The next minute, I'd lose track of the me in what was happening. The whole ocean floor was moving in huge overwhelming vastness, like an oceanic "landslide." I'd gasp in momentary terror and panic, treading the water as I lost control of the snorkle. I'd look to Ian, who looked composed. I'd regain awareness of myself and realize with relief that it was merely me moving over the ocean floor, not the ocean floor moving past me.

"Let's go snorkeling again," said Ian the next day. It hadn't mattered that I'd had a good time and found that underwater world fascinating and beautiful. The excuses were back.

My insides were in turmoil. It made no sense. I had enjoyed myself. "It's the salt," said my mouth. "It's the sun, I'm getting burned. What about this spot? It could be skin cancer. I don't feel well enough to go out. I don't want to go every day. I'll get bored with it." The feeble excuses and melodrama of my defenses just didn't fit.

Ian dug deeper. My defenses conjured up images of all sorts of potential accidents. The hook of a fishing rod could get stuck in a person. Someone swimming with a knife could cut another person.

Ian dug further and unburied what was driving these phobias. The real fear was that to go out again snorkeling had been a want that had come from self. A smile broke out from inside and I felt like Sleeping Beauty after the spell was broken. My defenses had been caught. We went out to do what we wanted freely.

As the last two days of our honeymoon approached, we were not disappointed to be leaving. It was one thing to be forced on the road by circumstances. It was another, far more threatening thing to venture away from the familiar by pure choice. We both wanted to go home. Italy was nice, but . . .

We were well packed by the time we were ready to drive to catch our flight. We piled our things into the car, along with lots and lots of cold water, and headed for the airport.

＿ ＿

The knock at the front door of the cottage was an unfamiliar one. Ian was still asleep and mumbled something incomprehensible. "I'm getting it," I mumbled in response, grabbing a dressing gown on the way to the door.

"Recorded delivery," said the postman, passing a padded envelope through the small opening in the doorway. Another piece of fan mail, I thought, having already been woken up by this kind of delivery once before.

I put it in a pile with all the other post, went back to bed, and snuggled up to Ian's warm back.

"Want to open the post?" I asked Ian's back.

"No," mumbled Ian sleepily. The padded envelope lay on the floor in a pile.

We got up, bathed, got dressed, brushed our teeth, and sat on the couch with the post: some properties from an estate agent, another property list, a receipt for paying poll tax, a checkbook. At last the recorded delivery: our lenses from the Irlen Centre!

It was like a birthday present. Ian had already told me that the Irlen filters wouldn't mean our troubles were over. "We could win a battle, a big battle, but we won't win the war just yet," he'd said. Nevertheless, we raced to phone an optician who could fit the lenses into frames right away.

While waiting for the glasses to be ready, we passed a charity shop. There was a book of short stories in the window: *Magic Stories, Myths and Legends from Around the World.*

I tugged Ian over to the window and pointed at the book. Ian walked inside. "There's a book in the window, magic stories," he said as the woman behind the counter looked at him.

"Oh, you want to look at it, do you, love . . . " she said as she fluffed about, climbing into the shop window to get the book. "Here you go," she said, handing it to Ian. He opened the cover to see how short the short stories were. He looked up at me for the go-ahead, took out a pound coin, and gave it to the woman.

"I must be feeling optimistic," I said to Ian—usually, even the thought of trying to read a book for pleasure would make my stomach knot.

The hour had passed and we returned for our new glasses. "Ladies first," said the optician, holding them up like a coat I was expected to step into as he held them.

I put them on and looked at the back cover of the book Ian was holding up in front of me. I could read it from a distance, from where I was sitting, without using a finger to trace each line. My eyes read each word in a line without flying off and scanning other words on the page. At first I said nothing but my face spoke for me. I read the line with meaning and with feeling. I read the line with pictures in my head. I looked at Ian and though I was smiling, nothing fought it: I could feel my face was relaxed.

Ian's face was joined together. His eyes and nose and mouth and chin were all held together with equal impact in a single context. Then I noticed that his neck and shoulders and torso and legs were also joined, not bit by bit as my eyes moved along, but as a whole picture, as if captured by a camera. Ian was joined together and he looked great. "Your face," I said. "It's joined together. Your head is joined to your body all at once. You look so beautiful, more beautiful than you've ever been."

I looked around the room and it didn't seem so crowded, overwhelming, or bombarding. The background noise I had always heard before—machine sounds in distant rooms, the hum of traffic, the mutter of people talking in the background—was not even apparent. I felt I was swimming with the tide and not against it.

Ian's glasses were next. He put them on and read something else on the desk. His face got softer. He looked up and looked around the room. His eyes filled with tears and his body began to shake. He was overwhelmed, not by visual bombardment and overload, but by the force of his own emotions. He looked at me and gasped like a small child filled with wonder. His arms went out and we hugged.

The optician looked on. "It's a wonderful moment," he said.

"It's like having sight for the first time," said Ian through the tears. He looked and sounded like someone who had been rescued.

We showered the optician with thank-yous. We wanted to see the world, to see it as others did.

We got two steps out of the door and stopped. The street was alive but not threatening. The people were getting on with their own lives and no longer looked like things thrown at me through the screen of a 3-D movie. I felt safe among them. They were everywhere and I felt safe. "The world is . . . so big," I said, tears falling uncontrollably.

"I know," said Ian, and I looked at him and knew he did.

We stood there in the middle of the sidewalk holding each other and crying. Like a pair of babies having just opened their eyes to the world around them for the first time, we were oblivious to anybody looking. Ian and I sneaked peeks at this new world, which no longer felt like an enemy waiting to invade or bombard us. Each time one of us took a look, we'd nuzzle back into the other like a child afraid to look. The change, the foreignness, being so intact, . . . it was all too much.

As we walked down the main street I realized that I now took in far more than I ever could before. Everything that was taken in peripherally before was now being taken in directly. But overload didn't happen; everything seemed more contained, more controlled, less invasive and frightening—it seemed in context.

"Milk crates," said Ian.

I looked where he was looking. "Yes," I said, not surprised.

"It's a dairy," said Ian, "that was just a dark alleyway before. I never saw what was down there. It was just a whole lot of shadow. Who could believe that a couple of tinted lenses could make such a difference?"

We passed a card shop we'd never been in. It had fluorescent strip lights, narrow aisles, and rows of colored illustrated cards.

From the door, the party of bouncing shadow, shine, and flicker in this shop had always made everything distracting and made the cards appear restless on their shelves and about to jump off. Ian stopped at the doorway as we passed. "Take a look in here," he said. We looked at each other in surprise. The shop that had intimidated us no longer gave us dread at the mere thought of entering. "Look," said Ian moved by the realization, "it's just a shop."

As we were looking, a car beeped as it drove past. We looked around in interest without panic. "That car beeped and I didn't jump," I said to Ian in surprise.

We walked a bit farther down the street. "I want to go in here," I said, referring to the local market. We had always both felt scared in there. Fluorescent lights ran from one end to the other, music blasted through overhead speakers, stalls seemed overcrowded with goods, and customers seemed to move unpredictably through the narrow aisles.

We walked in, waiting for the feeling that made us so defensive we'd almost claw our way out. We walked from one end to the other looking at the stalls. "The music," said Ian after a while. "I only just noticed it. I used to come in here and it seemed too bombarding to even think."

We got to the exit. "I haven't got that grip in my stomach making me want to get out of here," I said in surprise. "Me neither," said Ian, and we smiled from inside.

"I want to visit the Dawsons," said Ian. "I want to see them and their house."

"Me too," I said.

Back at the cottage, Ian went silently through the house in one direction and I went in the other. We met back in the middle. "The kitchen," I said. "It's not overwhelming."

"Come and take a look at the bedroom," said Ian. "We're messy." I stood at the bedroom door, looked in, and cried. I didn't see the cabinets, then the drawers, then things sitting on

them, then the shoes on the floor, then the T-shirt over the ra-
diator. Instead, I saw everything all at once, all in relation to one
another.

I had always seen bits of different mess in parts of a room. I had
never seen a messy room. All my life people had said things like
"Sorry about the mess" and I had known that somehow I had
never seen it. Now I understood. "This is *our* mess," I said to Ian.
"I can see who I am. I can see who we are." There had always
been yours and mine, but I could never see the different things
in the context of each other. "Look," I said, this is us."

It was too much for me and I crumbled. I threw my arms up
in despair. "Look how much I've lost," I cried, at last realizing
how much faulty perception had robbed from me.

Ian put his arms around me. "Live in the moment," he said.
"Think of what you've got now."

Ian called me into the garden. "Take off your glasses before you
come out," he told me. I took them off at the back door. At the
sight of the white brick wall, I pulled back like I'd been hit.
Shadow and light bounced off it wildly as always.

I stepped out of the doorway into the yard. "Look at the fluffy
pink flowers," said Ian. I looked at them, my eyes jumping as always from the green bits to the pink bits to the earth against a
background of color, shape, and pattern.

"Now put on your glasses," ordered Ian. I gasped. The flower
had come together. It had an overall impression and the finite detail of its component bits were now lost in the whole. It no
longer stood on its own like a miniature world in a swirl of peripheral universe. It now stood as part of a garden. I saw the other
plants directly and in relation to the flower I'd been looking at.
Things made sense. "My God," I said, "this must be what other
people see." This was "the world."

Ian and I sat on the couch, relaxed. I took off my glasses and
looked at a lace curtain. It was a mass of fragmented shadow and
light. My eyes moved unsystematically from one bit to another.

The rest of the room had "disappeared," becoming part of what I thought of as disconnected, peripheral vision.

I put the glasses back on and jumped. The whole room joined together in one big whole, as if by magic. The lace curtain became part of a wider context, which included everything along that wall and the wall belonged to the room. Ian did the same and we played with the shift in perception. We were in control of bringing the room back or making it perceptually "disappear."

Without our glasses we had seen everything. But all the light and shadow on and around that everything had registered equally and none of it had much significance or registered as context. It finally made sense why I could know so much in theory, impress people with stored knowledge, but seemed to either lose that knowledge, ignore it, or not use it in practice.

As evening approached, the sun shone golden through the windows. I looked over the rim of my glasses. The setting sun shone silver-white. Sure, there were lots of fine rainbow hues among the white but the color was still basically silver-white.

I looked out of the kitchen window. The sunset was gold and orange and red against a purplish background. I looked over the rims of the glasses and saw the gold as green-blue, the orange as yellow-green and the red as yellow-orange. All of it set against a dark gray, yet still daylight sky. Was this what other people saw? I could remember as a child being told to come inside because it was dark. It hadn't seemed like it. As far as I could see, the day had just become more comfortably darker.

Nighttime was different, as we discovered when we got into the car to visit the Dawsons. The headlights of oncoming cars, which had always been a bright distracting silver-white, were now pinkish orange. Driving was no longer a matter of finding the boundaries of the road and sticking to lines. "I wonder what pink streetlights look like now," I said.

Alex answered the door. He too had on Irlen glasses. "*We* look like a club," I said out loud.

Without much functional spoken language Alex, too, had chosen tinted glasses through a different technique, the Colorimeter. He had to look through changing tints from within a box and type his responses to perceptual changes on his Canon Communicator, indicating which tints he found best corrected his perception and improved his understanding of what he could see.

Ian's tints were reddish, mine were orangish and Alex's were purple. But what we all shared in common was that through these glasses we saw the full spectrum of color just as others did. The tints merely helped our perception make better sense of the spectrum of light.

We knew from Alex's letters that his tints had had a profound effect on his perception and anxiety level:

> . . . I had depended on mood totally. Eccentric I felt. I had learned how to see without tinted lenses. My prefered looking was in quick glances. Then I understood by piecing fragments. My different moods were governed by self-imposed dread of sometimes knowing I only could see vaguely. This made me miserable.
>
> Understanding that one's capability to see always ended, made one afraid.
>
> The people sounded as though they were so far away and asked questions so fast that I could no longer listen. Now, one hears without doubt, without trouble. I see, I hear, I learn.
>
> I understood not that there were some treatable visual conditions. I can see people and read clearly for the first time. I can see the world clearly for the first time.
>
> Before, I saw cracked children, cracked steps, print and writing. . . .
>
> Understand, had someone taken you to meet me, I saw one, heard one. However, the person, I did not see whole. I saw hair, I saw eyes, nose, mouth, chin, . . . not a face. Now I see the whole face, the whole person.
>
> I understand that people have not understood with regard to one having these different personal perception difficulties.

I have tried to explain, too, when reality seems to have gradually been lessened, diminished, until there is no longer awareness. I have had awareness, had sight and hearing and then too much input overloads my senses. Then, I have variation (fluctuation) in my perception.

Since having tinted lenses I have had the sight and hearing I very much wanted. I now have perception variation (fluctuation) no more. It is okay as long as I have my glasses on. I do, however, have preferences. I like the glasses, but then I pursue all knowledge. I need time to adjust to this new perception. I live as if I have sight and hearing for the first time.

Alex

My birthday was just two weeks away. I would be thirty. Birthdays and Christmas always set me thinking of my biological family, more out of dread I'd be contacted than out of sentiment.

It had been almost two years since I'd spoken to my younger brother, Tom. Part of me missed him but the him that I missed was the him I'd known when he was a three-year-old and I was ten and we had lived as comrades in a war zone. I had left him behind then, just as his communicative and social capacity was showing all the signs that it would exposingly and threateningly supersede my own. After that, I'd closed the door on him in all but glimpses and then he'd grown away from me. Before I knew it, we were strangers.

I'd seen him on the odd day here and there when, as an adult, I'd gone to work occasionally as my mother's paid housecleaner for a few dollars. He was a teenager then and my communication with him was limited to Willie's version of "good advice": a load of stored learned topic advice that made one seem "useful" and knowledgeable. Tom had found little in that worth knowing and I didn't blame him. Whenever I even began to speak as myself, my language was so obscure and so intangible that it wasn't easy to make out what I was on about or if I was actually on about anything at all. Other than this, there'd been nothing on offer.

I'd seen Tom only occasionally when he was an adult. I

changed a tire here, gave a lift there. I helped organize a surprise party thrown by his old girlfriend and disappeared less than five minutes after his arrival. I was a shadow with a title, someone called "sister" who wrote music and drew pictures and had a degree of some kind.

In my head, I daydreamed of a time and place where I'd be able to communicate with him as myself with acceptance and equality. That time and place never came. I wasn't capable of making it happen and, too busy handling his own life, it seemed he had no real idea of why it might have been worth it.

Ian had come to fulfill all those dreams of family. He was the brother with whom I could communicate as myself and feel I was being heard as an equal. I could take the risks with him that I couldn't find the courage to take with Tom. With Ian, there was no pressure to "act normal."

As I had dreaded, a package arrived in the post. I knew who it was from: my biological family in Australia. I put the uninvited package aside. Though my fear compelled me to touch it like flames, I had no want to open it. Ian could open it for me and decide whether it would upset me.

Inside was a big photo of Tom appearing to be riding on top of a huge mechanical fly that he'd painted on a huge wall. There was a newspaper article about a national painting award that he'd won. There were photos of my older brother's two young children, who I'd never get to know and who would never know me. There was a tape from Tom and a letter from my mother.

I looked at the photos of the children and hoped they were nothing like me, for their sakes. I looked at the photos of Tom. I looked not at where he was or what he was doing, but who he was. I looked to see how far removed or close he was to that "who" inside of him.

I picked up the tape but was too scared to play it. I feared it would have my mother's voice on it and though my defenses so often compelled me toward the things I feared, I knew I had no want in me to hear that voice. I had only to hear that voice and everything would freeze within me. Somehow, the very fact that her letter sat among these things contaminated them for me. Didn't she know she was irrelevant to me except as an object of intimidation, denial, and fear? Didn't she know that nothing on the surface could change what I sensed about her, her sharp and brittle, shifting edges?

To me, my mother was a handful of shards of glass. She was a ball of barbed wire. She was an explosion and implosion happening simultaneously, one that never ceased. She was a perpetually drowning man. She was a starving wild dog. She was a stray that had abandoned itself. She was fuel to the fire of my own defenses, a woman who fed on her weaknesses, her brokenness, her shame, her distortions, her jealousy, her obsession, and her rage. They fed on this and it made them strong.

It wouldn't matter if she rolled herself in honey or hoisted flags to the highest flagpole. It wouldn't matter if she advertised herself across envelopes with reeled-off public slogans of "I love Donna." It wouldn't matter if she sent a shop full of dollies or a shop full of frillies. She could not buy me, convince me, or even coerce me any longer. Even my fear could now hear me, so it was no longer free to compulsively take her side like a lamb, so compliant, on its way to the slaughter.

I did not blame her for my own broken mechanics. But when it came to her, I had no want.

There was a note in the package from Tom. It said that the letter from my mother didn't have anything bad in it. I looked over her letter. "Write to me, even if it's just to say you hate me," it said. Like hell I will, I thought, and put it to one side. It was a letter from someone to whom I was a stranger.

I put Tom's tape into the Walkman. A voice jumped out at me. The voice was so changed from that I associated with Tom. It was an educated voice with a cosmopolitan accent and intonations that rang of being "cool." He spoke in a way that on the surface fitted a stereotype of "laid-back," yet I could hear the voice was emotionally guarded. The inconsonance of the two made me uneasy and mistrustful.

Tom spoke on the tape as though he was talking to someone he knew. He said the word "sister" again and again, as though this title itself had more to do with the knowing than it had to do with the person who came with the incidental title. "I thought I'd visit my sister on her birthday," he said on the tape. He went on to say that he wanted us to travel about together. He'd pay for himself once he got here but he'd need a ticket.

The tape was finished. Tom had finally reached out to me as I had daydreamed in my theory world. He wanted to spend time with "his sister on her birthday." He wanted to be flown over to the U.K. He wanted us to travel and catch trains around Europe.

I looked back at the letter from my mother. Spending time with Tom would only be allowing her to spend time with me by proxy. If he visited, I felt she'd pick his brain for every crumblet of ownership she could grope, some tidbit of knowledge to wave about publicly and pretend I acknowledged her. Was Tom even asking to see me, or a title held by a body? If he was asking to see me, he wouldn't have included her letter in the package. He'd have known it would disturb me. He'd have known it would cast a shadow on any ability to feel free to be myself with him. If he'd known me, he'd have known that the only time I'd ever traveled was when I was lost and desperate and that I was lost and desperate no longer.

I wrote back telling him I didn't celebrate my birthday. I wrote that the best birthday present I could get would be that my birthday be forever forgotten.

—◂ ◂

The Christmas lights went up in the trees along the village's main street. Advertisements filled the shops; even a funeral parlor was advertising Christmas bargains. It didn't fit the rules of Christmas "cheer" and yet with everything else so "plastic" it didn't seem so strange.

Christmas seemed such a time of death. The death of so many

animals for the sake of overeating. The death of emotions and self in compliantly meeting expectations without thought or choice. The death of trees for cards that say "to" and "from" with names robotically filled in from address books. It meant arboreal corpses that stood in corners, draped in mass-produced sweatshop decorations that came from Taiwan and cost a few people their souls, even if it filled their bellies for a time.

Christmas meant the death of tradition under the guise that people were adhering to it. If Saint Nicholas was carrying a tree over his shoulder at Christmastime, it was probably for wood to warm the poor and destitute who might otherwise have been forgotten in the snowy winter of Europe. If Saint Nicholas carried food in his sack, it was probably for those who would have gone hungry at a time when people were supposed to remember their Christian spirit. If Saint Nicholas carried toys, it was probably not for children who had rooms full of them but still wanted the latest fad to update on what they got last year.

The advertisement of a funeral parlor among the Christmas hype didn't seem any more ludicrous than anything else. This was the time people were meant to think about the birth of a little Jewish boy thousands of years ago who was destined for torturous murder while nailed to big sticks for being too popular. That seemed less removed from an advertisement to buy a grave than shops that told you to stock up your freezer with hordes of dead animals, so that you and your friends could all eat more than your body could handle.

Ian and I pulled into a car park. In the small cabin space of the car, our defenses each threw a wobbly. Mine were point scoring by reminding Ian how crappy Christmas was last year. Their goal was not to make it any more real this year, but to strive to ensure that Christmas would again be Xmas. That way, it would be an emotionally and socially dead, nonthreatening replay of the year before.

Ian's defenses swung between humbugitis and feeling the bliss of self-denial that would come with complying with a stored

non-self role of how to meet "make it up to Donna" expectations. For our defenses there were two ways to spend Christmas:
at war or "dead."

Neither of us felt that way at all and finally, after a lot of crap
and fanfare from our defenses, we broke through. We went
through our checking procedure and found that we didn't understand Christmas, never had, and would rather spend the time
doing something we did enjoy and understand.

We'd just learned that our house at Neuadd Wen had fallen
through. All those months of waiting and lawyers' fees were
down the drain. We'd have to start the rounds all over again.
Looking through a newspaper full of houses for sale, we came
across a section for holiday houses to rent short term. That
seemed like the idea. We phoned a few.

Since it was Christmastime, this one was gone and that one was
gone. We eventually got through to one that was available. The
proprietor grilled us at lightning speed with loads of snipey intonation. How old were we? What did we do? What were our interests? Why did we want to go away from home at Christmas?
We fumbled and faltered as she tried to "make conversation" and
caved in to her demands for more money, payment in advance,
and references from our accountant and my literary agent.

We'd rented ourselves a little Welsh cottage in the snow with
no relatives, no Christmas tree, no decorations, no presents, and
no defensiveness or regret. With no rental prospects on the horizon and, in spite the depression of having to go through it all
again, we were heading off in search of another Our House.

As the date arrived, we packed our suitcases and food boxes,
books and paints and tools and shoes until the car was piled from
floor to ceiling. The house was about six hours drive away in
Wales, and because we were going for five weeks, we didn't
want to get panicky about anything we'd left behind.

Hours later we arrived at a little local post office and general
store to pick up the key and instructions to our house.

The woman who ran the post office was a tall, brassy, silver-
haired, larger-than-life character named Phyllis. She answered

the door speaking very fast and with obviously stored animation and intonation that never varied in response to anything. Her intonation reminded me of how I'd been told to put interest into my voice as I was reading (without meaning). Someone could have dropped dead right in front of us and Phyllis would have gone on smiling and sounding cheerful and interested. After more of her excited burbling, we collected our house key and left.

The road to the house was narrow, muddy, and full of potholes. Rain poured down like an omen. The uneven and rickety stone steps to the front door were covered with wet and rotten leaves. As we wobbled the rickety old door open, we were hit with a strongly musty smell.

Inside the smell was thick with dust and damp. We tried the lights. The place looked as bad as it smelled. Cracked windows in rickety frames, threadbare carpet, dripping wet soot, dirty settees with the handprints of too many holiday tenants and a clutter of the most unsalable, useless, decorative charity shop bits and bobs we had ever seen outside of a bad garage sale. The house made our skin crawl and made me wheezy.

Our options were few. The place had been paid for up front and a substantial deposit put down. Besides, this had been the great escape for Ian from traditional "happy families" Xmas expectation and it was probably the only place from which we could search for our dream house. We had no choice but to stay.

After unloading the car, we were sweaty and tired and needed food and a glass of water. We turned on the tap. There was nothing.

We tried to call someone to get it working, using the pay phone there. We had paid a deposit of fifty pounds for the luxury of using it as well as whatever the calls would cost us.

We got a dial tone and fed our money into the phone. The phone ate the money and then impolitely filled our ears with crackle so that the other person couldn't hear us nor could we hear them. We tried it again. "Thank you for the money," said the phone in crackle language once more.

Off we went walking down the muddy track in the dark. Back at the post office, Phyllis was there with a smile and the offer of something to drink. She had already figured that the personless crackle on the end of the line had been us trying to reach her and she had expected us. She called the water utility. We went back to the house to wait.

The lights of a van soon trundled down the muddy track. The water utility man told us there was nothing he could do. A pipe had burst somewhere between the house and the road somewhere down the hill. In the darkness and mud and trees and greenery and rain, looking for it would be like looking for a needle in a haystack.

We walked out in the darkness down to a stream at the bottom of the hill where a fast creek flowed and collected a bucket of water. Phyllis had sent us back with a few bottles and a kettle full just in case and they would have to do us till . . .

Well, we could at least cook dinner. We turned on the stove and nothing happened. We searched everywhere for another switch. There were signs here and signs there: "Don't cut on this side of the chopping board," "Don't burn this piece of wood," "Don't light this fire." Though the owner had left us signs about almost everything except how to pick our own noses, there was no sign to do with anything so practical as getting the cooker going to have a meal.

We moved the stove to check the connections. We checked for hidden switches and finally we checked the fuse box. The disconnected fuse for the cooker was sitting there on top. We put it back in and the cooker started up. There'd be dinner at least.

Though we were both tired, we dreaded bedtime. Filled with only the most unsalable of secondhand kitsch, the rooms were furnished with the kinds of common things we'd grown up around back in the seventies and eighties and for me that meant bad memories.

It was a nightmare to be surrounded helplessly by such a vast array of triggers of past places, faces, and feelings. These things didn't just remind me, they took me back. The bedroom here had my family's old living room carpet, the bedspread from an aunt's house I'd stayed at, the cot of my childhood, a light shade from an old flat I'd had, the wallpaper of my old family bedroom, and the bedboard of a business-minded slimeball who'd "taught me sex" when I was fifteen.

Ian and I moved a few things out of the way. "Can we please move this bed out?" I pleaded on the edge of phobia. Ian didn't know why it was that important and tried to reason with me. I threw a wobbly and he agreed to help. It was attached to the wall and wouldn't budge.

Ian climbed into the smelly bed in the smelly house and I stood there like a child being told to jump into the fire because it was safe. Inside, I was frantic, fighting the compulsion to run from the house, to run from myself, and to cut off from the body in this house. But Ian lay there looking equally lost and helpless. He looked like some symbol of my own potential abandonment. No, I wouldn't leave, physically or existentially. I climbed into that bed and told myself that just because it looked like another bed from another time did not mean that Ian was, therefore, the same person who had been in that other bed. I tossed and turned for hours, clearing my throat continually from the dust. Finally, I fell asleep with the fear of nightmares and the thought that we'd handle it together and it would all look better in the morning.

The next morning, the house looked just as depressing. The windows of the house were all on one side and even when the sunshine managed to find one to peek through, it didn't fill the house. In the daylight, the house had all the gaiety of an old prison cell.

I silently but manically moved furniture and bric-a-brac from room to room with a "get out of my way and don't say a word" look on my face.

I gathered everything that had bad associations for me and bundled it into buckets and bags. Then I dragged it all into one room.

I undid light shades and took down curtains. I stacked furniture on top of other furniture. When I had finished, the rest of the rooms in the house had nothing bad in them anymore, even if the house was as dusty and smelly as ever.

I went about cleaning and shaking out whatever I could. Furniture went out to air, windows were opened if they could be. The pane of glass in our bedroom jumped out when Ian closed it so that window was permanently open. This was the only room with a double bed and the other two bedrooms in the house were both very small. We tried to move two single beds together but they wouldn't fit. We resolved ourselves to spending the next five weeks sleeping together in a single bed. Though at some other time in my life I'd have felt better to sleep alone, in this dim, damp house of echoes past, I needed the security of proximity to Ian more than ever.

The water was fixed and the phone battery was charged and stopped crackling intermittently enough to speak and hear in short bursts. It made other annoying background noises instead and ate up coins at about double the usual amount.

The house stayed depressing but we didn't stay depressed. One of the fireplaces didn't work and all but one electric heater blew up, sparked, or hissed. We closed off the worst-smelling sooty room and the bad-echoes room and lived amid roughly the same number of rooms we had had in our own little cottage.

Without much heating and requiring fresh air every day, the house was almost always cold and we wore sweaters and thick, heavy socks, scarves, and hats most of the time. Though it was far from comfortable, we did manage to make this oversized cubbyhouse reasonably livable. When the snow did fall and cover the valley, the dim, dark, damp, cold, and yucky house didn't seem so bad there in the pretty white valley with the silvery creek running through it.

The cold of the house made the surrounding countryside more inviting to explore. We went on walks through ferny gullies and up through the trees to the top of the hill that overlooked the valley. We flew kites in a farmer's field and mooed to cows who mooed back, and we fed the birds.

Ian had been on the phone getting appointments to view houses. We would see two houses every day we were there except for Sundays.

By now we had a better idea of when we liked a house or didn't and we didn't trust anything that the owners said.

"No—no footpaths," said another owner. We went down to the village, bought a plan of the area, and found their farm on the map. There was the footpath marked out and advertised for every hiker to seek out and enjoy as they walked through the farm just twenty feet from the front door.

We dropped in to see Phyllis every day to collect our redirected post, and she'd become a point of familiarity and social safety. We invited her to the house.

Ian made cake and I made biscuits. Phyllis arrived as arranged, trailing her wiry little dog with her. She came into the sooty-smelling living room that we'd closed off. This was an impersonal room to let her into. We left the big sliding doors open, so we'd be half outside and half inside. In here there was nothing "ours" and we would feel less exposed and threatened.

She sat down and Ian and I fumbled about feeling clumsy and awkward. He offered her everything possible to eat and drink and then set about entertaining the dog with biscuits and milk. Eventually, he got down on the floor with the dog and ignored Phyllis and me as all but background noise.

Phyllis talked about the dog and talked about the village and talked about her neighbors and talked about the shop. She asked us about house hunting and we showed her the pile of houses we still had to view and she told us which ones she would like. She talked about wallpaper patterns and sweater patterns and tile patterns.

Phyllis sat and sat and talked and talked and we realized that she knew as little about when to leave and how to leave a social situation as we did. Though we had countless stored copied exits, they weren't always so easy to use in practice. This was especially true if you'd had enough realness to show the stored exits up as pretentious hoo-ha.

Carol sat in the living room of yet another person who'd picked her up socially and was, thereby, a "friend." It had been four hours now that she'd been here and about three and three-quarter hours since awareness had flown out the window and she rambled on triggered autopilot.

She flittered about this stranger's house making manic matches with the odd word heard or object seen and waiting to be told or made to go.

It had got dark since she'd been here and the other person had gone into the other room to cook something. Carol had followed. "I'm going to make myself something to eat now," said the person. "Okay," said Carol, noticing what the person was making and making conversational matches about having made something with that ingredient in it once and how that dish was meant to be nice with . . .

The person had finished cooking and returned to the living room with her meal. She sat down in front of the TV to eat as the volume blared. Carol sat watching the images on the screen, making conversational matches about programs she'd seen like this and what other programs that actress had been in and how she'd had a cat like that one once.

The hours ticked by as Carol still waited to be told or made to go. "I'm tired," said the person. Carol panicked. That meant the person didn't like her. She had learned that when people said "I'm tired," they were about to become insulting or agitated. The automatic verbal diarrhea escalated under the new anxiety.

"I'm going to bed soon," said the person. "You must be tired."

"Not really," said Carol, going on into a litany about not needing much sleep and what time she usually ended up going to bed and how she would sit up until . . .

"I'm going to bed now," said the person. Carol sat, not sure what to do but realizing she couldn't follow this person to bed and wasn't being asked to. Carol rambled on further for a while.

"I don't know what you're going to do but I'm going to bed now," said the person. "I'm going to go," said Carol, answering what to her had been a curious question about what she'd do while the person went to bed.

Leaving the house, Carol exploded with anxiety about whether she'd done the right thing and whether the person was still her friend.

"Tell me when you want me to go," Phyllis had said. We looked at each other. How the hell were we to know when we wanted Phyllis to go? Keeping up with all the blah-blah left little time to process anything so obscure and internal as a want. Still, we took comfort in knowing that Phyllis was as stuck here as we were and was no threat.

A publicity request came through on the phone. Could we do TV?

The publicity would be for the American edition of my second book, *Somebody Somewhere,* which was coming out in two months time. The program would go out to millions of viewers. The agent had left off the "such a privilege," "what an honor" stuff knowing that it just boggled and annoyed me, filling me with expectations to pretend to feel a whole pile of feelings that didn't happen for me.

The editor called. It would be a big favor to her. Ian sat there looking judgmental. "It's just business to them," he reminded me. "What do *you* want to do?" We checked. I wanted to do the show and Ian was curious about the experience, too, but they would have to come to us and it would have to be on my terms.

First, I wanted to see and hear the person who'd be interviewing me. The producers would send over a video of the host for us to view. Next, we wanted them to come to us in Wales so that the filming would be somewhere familiar without too much travel. That was okay with them. We wanted no harsh lighting and a minimal crew. They agreed that I'd only have to meet the interviewer and one sound and camera person.

Why, if I didn't want to do talks or be on TV, was I going to agree to this, Ian wanted to know.

We cast aside the guilt and responsibility angle, because it was only business to the publishers and it wouldn't hurt them personally if I didn't do it.

We cast aside the "what a privilege" angle, because the word "privilege" fell flat for me. Privilege was what you perceived it to be and what was a privilege for one person was not for another; what one person felt grateful for, another could feel indifferent about or burdened by.

We cast aside the "help others to understand autism" angle, because there were so many others who wanted the limelight and had as much to say. Besides, I was more than a bundle of walking autism and believed that no one person was necessarily a spokesperson for others just because they shared a label.

What was left was that I wanted to give people a chance to know about the second book, and this was certainly one way to do that—particularly in American society, where TV was like a fifth limb. Besides, the publisher had promised that if I did this, they'd stop bugging me about TV and there'd be less pressure to do so many interviews during the upcoming U.S. tour. There was another reason I wanted to do it: I wanted to do it to see if I could.

I had always turned down any offers to do current affairs shows; talk shows were out of the question. While a number of American people with autism were being fed to American viewers, who'd developed a taste of the month for them, I shunned the opportunities they'd jumped for. While others were going to brightly lit, noisy studios with live audiences and chat show hosts to talk about themselves, I had agreed to only two TV slots in four years, both on the news and lasting no more than a few minutes.

I'd found those bearable. My words had flowed easily as I'd walked around the path of a familiar park with the interviewer asking me questions I'd had a chance to see earlier and respond to on my computer. In the park there were no studio lights, no faces watching, and even the camera was hidden in the bushes where I could rarely see it, but for the occasional quick scamper across the grounds to another bush. In the park there were no microphones in your face, just a tiny clipped-on thing on my jacket, which sat in my pocket like a Walkman. Here there was no "with," just in front of. Walking in circles, I could forget that the interviewer was even there. The interviewer was just a voice without a person. The cameraperson was just a camera on legs.

Phyllis called us. "There's a parcel for you," she said, sounding more than curious. "Are you sure you're not diamond smugglers?" We picked it up and then, once back at the house, tore it open. It was the video of our host for the program.

We watched the pace of her movements and speech. The inconsistencies in the patterns of her intonation and facial expressions told us about her sincerity: her "appear" versus "be." The world of TV looked as infested with falsity as an old piece of untreated wood with woodworm. Still, this host, we decided, didn't seem too bad. We agreed that she was passable and told my literary agent. Arrangements were made: the TV people would arrive just after Christmas.

A redirected letter for us arrived down at Phyllis's post office. It was a Christmas card from someone called Gordon and in brackets were written the words "the postman." We laughed and put it up on the mantelpiece, not because we believed in the modern hoo-ha of Christmas, but because we'd rarely opened the door to the postman by more than a few inches and had never spoke to him in more than monosyllables. Yet he had still sent us a card.

On Christmas day we woke up, packed a lunch with soup, sandwiches, fruit cake, and boiled quail's eggs, and went to the beach for a picnic with the crows.

The ocean purred, the wind cooed, and the birds came to lunch. We played in rock caves and stood under the showering drops that waterfalled over the ocean cliff high above us. We played with the tide and the ocean froth and talked to the birds in bird. It was the most peaceful, real, and very simply be Christmas either of us had ever had.

— ◢

The phone rang. It was my agent. "Your older brother, James, phoned," he said. "I'm afraid he had some rather bad news. Your father has cancer. He's having an operation and after that he will have chemotherapy. . . ."

"Ian," I called with urgency as I felt nausea creep upon me. I handed him the phone.

I had nothing to say. All the theory was there of what a person should say: "Oh, that's awful," "Oh no," "Oh my God." But there was nothing.

I sat there trying to work out what I felt. Then I took the phone again. "Is it all right for a person to die?" I asked my agent. He reassured me that it was.

I thought about my older brother. I thought about my younger brother. I thought about shame and guilt and indifference and abandonment. I thought about myths and lies and priorities I didn't agree with. I thought about us all being so many more miles from one another than physical distance could ever measure. I thought about my mother outliving my father and about destiny. Finally, I wrote my father a letter

Hello,

The news was surprising but shouldn't have been. You knew. You just didn't have a name for it. Don't let a label scare you. They say, "Cancer is a word, not a sentence."

Chemotherapy works for some people. I also want to tell you though that some choose not to have it. If it takes away from the quality of your life and makes you feel sicker than the cancer does, it is *your choice* whether to continue with it or not. Nobody is a coward in making a choice—just, perhaps, in refusing to make one.

When people talk of dying, everyone gets scared to talk of death. They all talk of life. We all know about life, so I want to talk to you about death—in case you ever meet it.

As much as you may believe death is the enemy, death can also be a savior. I want to tell you something.

When I was younger I went unconscious I think. I experienced letting go of my body and of life. I felt lifted and the higher I got, the warmer I got. I felt a kind of tingling through my "body" (but my body was "down there"—I mean my floating non-body body). The tingling and the warmth made me feel an overwhelming sense of beauty and belonging and purity and honesty all at once. I felt part of everything around me and it was part of me. I felt like I was now part of a "knowing" without words or sight.

I was drawn into a light that was brighter than anything I have known but it didn't hurt. I felt so relieved. Then I began to come down again and the light slipped further and further away and I felt so sad that I couldn't stay. Then I "woke up" with a start in what, by comparison, was a flat and heavy world.

My word-picture for death is a beautiful huge bird that comes and sweeps you up and carries you away. (Don't fear the reaper— which I know you believe in. The reaper is just an omen; a warner to living people of the approach of something, not the thing itself that is approaching. If the reaper looked so beautiful and welcoming to living people, everyone would be committing suicide. So I think he just looks like that to people who are alive in order to keep the balance of things and keep the reality of what is beyond here a sort of secret.)

I want you to know that death is not scary. Dying is scary. Death is not. I want you to know that you will be okay in that place beyond here and beyond the place beyond the place beyond here. I want you to know that you would know belonging and self-acceptance in death. You struggled for these in life.

I also think it is important that you sort things out with people. I have sorted things out with you, but for the record, here it is in a nutshell.

I see you as a man I knew—in my past—a person I was destined to know who is my biological father. "Father" is a word of sentiment. Few biological fathers are truly experienced as fathers in the sentiment sense. That is destiny—some fathers and children feel like they "belong" and most don't but accept the relationship as a role.

As a person, you put a lot into proving your surface "strength" because you were so painfully aware of your inside weakness. But I have never admired the direction of this surface "strength" and effort—business and ego. This was always at the expense of self-honesty and acceptance of your emotions and acceptance of your own naïveté and vulnerability in not knowing how to "be you" or have deep ongoing unconditional friendships. The closest you came was with your girlfriend now and this is a credit to you and to her.

I have been angry and unforgiving. I can forgive you as a person and even as my biological father (but cannot within the confines of the word "father" [in the sentiment sense]). So, I forgive you for not meeting my standards while meeting your own. But I cannot use the word "Dad" and say this. This is not an attack. I want you to have my honesty.

I also want you to know that I observed the world and you in it. I know who you are beyond your images and your compulsive need to entertain. I want you to know that someone took the time to look for the "you" in you even if you found it so hard to live as yourself. I want you to know the real you was known by someone. I also want you to know that if you had lived as the real you in life, then you perhaps would have been my "Dad." But that was not your destiny nor mine—and that's okay.

I hope you resolve things with James and Tom. I think James has so much anger and unforgiveness and shame and if you died he would feel guilt and regret for some of these things. I know you can't say it in speaking—you always end up speaking to him about business. I know this is because you are trying to tell him things but can't. Write it to him. In writing, like me, you find your tongue in honesty so much more than face to face or in speaking.

I think Tom has become a world within himself. I think he, too, has shame, as you did over your own mother in life. His anger and unforgiveness run so deep they are probably even more beyond acknowledgment than these things are for James. Also, I think he lacks an internal belonging—what do you expect when he was always treated as "an afterthought"? Write to him. Write to him as you wrote to me. Write in honesty—in self-honesty. It'll free your soul—and that's been in chains for years.

I sent you my children's book. It is the new version. I did all the pictures. Ian helped me. Ian is my husband and family (in the sentiment sense). He is a beautiful and self-honest person and is "like me." We are happy and reclusive and that is how we like it. He has seen a photo of you. The only thing you share in common is a love of animals and nature.

Beyond telling you this, I have no wish to share my life. You belong to my past. I live in the warm nest of my present looking out over sunny horizons of my future.

Donna

After I wrote the letter, I read it out loud to Ian so my defenses could never deny it; then I buried my father in my mind.

— ◢

"Which houses do we have today?" I asked Ian. He looked in the diary. "The one I liked," he said, "and one of your number-ones" (the top rating on a one-to-three scale we used).

I was excited about viewing one of my number-ones but like so many bad books in glitzy covers, it was a flop.

Later in the afternoon, we drove in the rain down a long country lane to the house Ian had picked. This property was a plain Jane but, as Ian had sensed, though there was nothing exceptional about it, there was something special about it anyway.

We drove into a courtyard full of tired-looking farm buildings and went up to the door of a slapped-together front porch. The people showed us into the house. Boggledy wallpaper dominated the walls of the hall. An unusually friendly old Siamese cat purred and smooched around the kitchen walls. His claw marks were everywhere, since he had used the walls and doors for scratch-boards. An ugly little pug dog wiggled its body into the room like an excited hairy slug. The owner took him out.

There was a feeling about this place that hit you from the time you walked in. It was a cheerful place, as though nothing in or on the house could change the feel of it. It was a simple, happy house.

We went through the rooms and, though the carpets were worn and the wallpaper torn and the windows brittle-looking in rickety frames with more coats of paint than wood, the house seemed to wear everything well. This house had a smile that couldn't be wiped off or painted over.

We went for a walk around the property. It was surrounded by green, which in turn was surrounded by more green, rising gently all around as though the house were a pea in the bottom of a gently sloping soup bowl. Over the edges of distant hills the sun rose without effort. In the front yard, outside of the bedroom window, stood a poor bedraggled gum tree that, like me, had weathered the cold and foreignness of Britain in which he'd also, probably not so willingly, made his home.

By the time we left, we knew this was a house we would live happy in. Our defenses raged about all the money it would cost to fix up and how much nicer some of the other houses looked and how we could at least look at the others we had yet to see. Though we knew what we wanted we checked anyway. We had found Our House and we weren't interested in looking any further.

On the way back to the rented house in the hills, we pulled into a local village. I needed to use the toilet. Ian waited in the car.

There was graffiti on the door of the cubicle I was in: Nazi slogans referring to "English trash" and getting "contaminating English blood out of Wales." I felt frozen. I had heard of nationalists burning down houses and hounding people out. The graffiti was signed "the W.N.P."

I was afraid to leave the cubicle. What if someone came into the toilet and spoke to me and heard I wasn't Welsh? I imagined that I'd get bullied.

I went back to the car, sullen and haunted. "What is it?" asked Ian.

"What is W.N.P.?" I asked.

He didn't know.

We went into a shop. The man behind the counter was not Welsh. "Do you know what the W.N.P. is?" I asked him.

"The Welsh Nationalist Party," he told us.

Back in the car, I eventually told Ian what I'd read. We had been happy about moving up here. We'd bought some tapes to teach ourselves Welsh, because even though the population was bilingual, we wanted to fit in. The tapes now sat there on the backseat like a threat saying "learn me or get bashed up." We drove back to the rented house in silence.

Back at the house we both compulsively blurted out ideas of other countries to move to. We followed this through and made a list of all the possible countries. Then we checked for our wants from this list and narrowed the list down. Following this through, we went to the phone to make inquiries of anyone we thought might know about whether we would be able to live in these places. The only one that seemed possible was America.

Down at the post office, collecting our mail, Phyllis asked how the house hunting was going. We told her we'd found a house but had changed our minds. She wanted to know why. We told her about the Nazis. "Oh, don't worry about them," she said. "Some of my friends are Welsh nationalists."

We recoiled and felt like running from her place. I wanted to know what kind of people they were. I figured they had shaved heads and wore army boots.

"Oh, they're the nicest people," said Phyllis. "Teachers, farmers." It was hard to imagine that teachers and farmers would write intimidating hatred and violence on the doors of toilet cubicles. "No," Phyllis assured me, "they do do things like that but they're harmless." We told Phyllis that we wouldn't be coming to live in Wales. We'd live in America instead.

We had been sent some information about different states in the United States. We talked about how we would travel over there and rent a house and car and buy a place to live. Then we'd have our things sent over.

Someone wrote to us about riots and earthquakes and about trouble between people with dark skin and people with light skin. We started to see that we could find a reason to run from anywhere. If it was toilet door graffiti here, it would be natural disasters there or other problems somewhere else. We had let fear dictate the terms. It was time to put that wild and menacing thing back into its box and nail down the lid. We decided to live in the world, not on the run from it.

W e heard from the publisher. The TV host couldn't make it on the days we had suggested. Her assistant, Edie Magnus, would come if that was okay. They would send over a video of Edie so we could decide if we'd be okay with her and be able to get used to her before meeting her.

We had a look at Edie Magnus on the video that had arrived by post. She looked okay, even if her TV smile didn't match her eyes much of the time. We spoke to my literary agent. He could tell them yes.

We were sent a video camera. It was partly so that Ian could help me practice feeling okay about being filmed and looking into a camera. The producers had also thought it would be good to get me to use the camera to show them what I called "my world."

We unpacked the video camera and I walked about the house with it, making everything come to me by pressing the close-up button. I focused on my feet and pushed the close-up button. My feet came zooming at me and I ran away from them before hurriedly pushing the video camera toward Ian, so he could take the monster of a thing away.

They wanted me to show them "my world" with a video camera. How could I show them fragmented visual perception, auditory fragmentation, and words without interpretation? How could I show them the hypnotic nature of repetitive tunes and jingles and word patterns? How could I show them the Big Black Nothingness of undefined emotions? How could I show them the lack of meaning or sincerity I saw or heard in the inconsistencies of "the world" where people's "appear" was ripped away from their "be," distorted and deformed and handed back tied in ribbons, called "impressive" and said to be "real"? How could I show them a mind that used rules instead of context and that demanded guarantees in place of earned trust? How could I show them disembodiment or what it was to live mono in a stereo world or to lose self by virtue of experiencing other? How could I show them a mind where my own thoughts came out of my mouth only on pure trust that they made any sense? How could I show them speech that came out without tracking, without conscious grasp or experience of my own words, and robbed of the sense of ownership of them? How could I show them what it was to use a subconscious mind in place of a conscious one and yet have the conscious one monitor and interfere with dream states, when a mind should be free to dream and sleep? How could I show them a world where what was background to others had been foreground to me or where everything was taken in peripherally without judgment, filtration, or selection based on any sense of relative or personal significance? Handing me a video camera to show them "my world" seemed more of a statement than a request, a statement about their own limitations.

I opened the lid to the rubbish bin and shot a close-up of its contents. This was how I perceived so many meaningless concepts that were meant to have meaning but didn't.

I photographed a nut in a bowl of nuts and then put one into the rubbish bin. That was how I felt "the world" had perceived me and what it had done to me before I knew why I was "different."

I photographed the wall and then another wall and another. That was the inside of me.

I considered what the viewer would see in looking at all of this. Then I realized that it was not the lens looked through nor the image shown, but the eyes seeing it that gave things meaning in "the world." The eyes that would see this would never be my eyes. I erased all that I had filmed.

Ian and I did some mock filming. He pretended to be Edie Magnus and I tried to answer his questions. Erase.

I went for a walk down to the stream and filmed the running

water. I spoke poetry to the flow of the water. No, this was private and for me. Erase.

Ian took off his tints and filmed the world through them, so he could see how things looked through his tints to someone who didn't have Scotopic Sensitivity Syndrome. We erased everything else but we left this.

The TV people were going to arrive next week. After our pretend interviews it became obvious that the filming could not be done in the house, or we'd all be squashed in and claustrophobic. We arranged for the crew to meet us instead at a nearby manor house.

The journalist arrived at our tiny Welsh village. Phyllis gave us a call up at the house. "There's a visitor down here at the post office with me," she said. "Will I send her up?"

"We'll come down," we told her.

Standing outside of the post office was Edie Magnus, trying, as instructed, not to make us feel uncomfortable by looking too intensely at us.

She seemed cheerful but also nervous, quiet, and controlled, open-doored and not walled off.

We walked her back to the house and explained that we had found somewhere nearby to do the interview, a place that we felt better about. We asked how many people there'd be. She told us there would be her and a producer and a sound person . . .

"A producer?" I said to Ian, agitated that they were bringing along more people than we'd been expecting.

"How many are there all together?" asked Ian, to set my mind to rest.

"Seven," she replied.

My stomach was in a vise. "Too many people," I said to Ian in an anxious whisper.

"Who are they all?" Ian asked.

There was a driver and two sound men, two cameramen, the producer, and Edie Magnus. "They're all very nice people," said Edie Magnus gently.

We all walked back down the muddy road to the post office and then off down the street. We passed by some chickens and ducks and cows and sheep, all of whom I felt I'd rather be at an interview with.

Edie Magnus walked along with us quietly simply being. She was okay, more than passable. Ian spoke, getting Edie's name in a dyslexic muddle and calling her Meady Angus.

A picture flashed through my mind. I had pictured an Angus bull. Answering myself about how he became a Meady Angus, I had envisioned the bull drinking from a trough of thick beer that the Irish called mead. I looked at Edie Magnus and burst into uncontrollable giggles as my mind played with the words Meady Angus, Meady Angus, Meady Angus.

"What is it?" asked Ian. I told him quietly. From that point on, that was who she was as far as that childish and symbolic part of my mind was concerned: I was to be interviewed by a drunken bull named Meady Angus.

The next day, we had to head off to the manor house for the first of two days of filming. The two news slots I'd done had taken two hours, which had seemed a mammoth amount of time. So I had no idea how I'd go handling two days of cameras.

As we drove up to the manor house we felt roughly at ease, knowing we had already been there to get used to the room and feel familiar with the place. We figured we'd go early and settle in before the others arrived.

There was a van parked outside. A man in the driver's seat fumbled about and seemed to fall over himself a bit as we approached the big double doors.

We went through the next double doors, along the hall and pushed open the door of the room where we'd be filming, just as we became aware of laughter and voices. The door swung open onto a room full of wires and lights and TV cameras. Six pairs of eyes stared at me and Ian. The laughter and talking stopped dead in its tracks, making the sudden cold silence more scary than the noise.

The room that had earlier seemed so big was crowded with paraphernalia. Instead of looking like a comfortable oversized living room, it now looked like a TV studio.

A stranger stepped forward, hand over chest, looking directly at us and walking toward us like someone cornering a stray cat. "Sorry about that," she said. "Someone was telling a joke."

I was frozen to the spot. I couldn't move and couldn't leave. I trembled from head to toe as I stood like a scared bird with half a dozen cats watching me. Finally, I explained to the room, "I don't want to be scared of you lot.

"I want to make a noise. Is that okay?" I asked Ian.

"Yes," said Ian.

"It's okay," I said out loud to myself, "I can make a noise." Then I made a loud "arghh" in front of the room full of strangers.

There was nervous laughter from one of the men. I explained that I didn't want to be scared of them and that I needed each of them to make a noise, too.

I needed to see them lose control. I needed to see who they were. "You, make a noise," I ordered, pointing at one of them.

He glanced pleadingly at Edie Magnus, who simply nodded. "Ahhhh," he bellowed.

"You," I ordered, pointing at another.

He roared.

"You," I ordered, pointing at Edie Magnus.

She made her noise.

"You," I ordered, pointing at the man with the nervous laugh.

This man's noise was not his own. It was performed and I could feel it. It hadn't come from himself.

"As yourself," I ordered. "That wasn't yours." He was a sound technician and was shaking, but made another noise equally not his own. I looked in his eyes: "Why can't you make a noise as yourself? You frighten me because you're hiding. How can I show you myself if you can't show yourself?" This man looked nervously about his body and he looked disarmed and vulnerable. I felt sorry for him.

The others had made their noises. I had heard who they were.

It was like reading their souls, like the blind reading braille. I could feel their gentleness and sharp edges, their strength and weakness, their integrity, and their relative trust and mistrust of themselves and of others. It only took one sound that came from self to know the feel of a person, and that was all you needed to know whether you could be safe for them to get anywhere near to knowing the feel of who you were.

The two lighting people also operated the cameras. They were staying and we felt safe with both of them. The two sound technicians were going to be outside of the room. The producer was a strong but emotional person and she was staying, and so was Edie Magnus who was vulnerable but courageous enough to live with her vulnerability.

There would be four of them and two of us but since two of them were going to be cameras with legs, it was pretty much two on each team, and we'd all agreed to play by my rules.

After everything was set up, they all left us for a while surrounded by wires, monitors, cameras, and stands. Ian and I sat quietly in front of the crackling fire and turned our backs on it all.

The interview took two days to film and filming was done in short twenty-minute bursts. The manager of the manor came in every so often with good nonallergenic, home-cooked, rubbish-free food. His young daughter followed him quietly, peering shyly at these people being filmed, as though it made us some other breed of human being she'd never seen.

Though I'd seen all the questions in advance and I'd seen all my thinking through writing, it didn't look that way to the cameras until Edie Magnus attempted to spring some questions on me that she hadn't sent before.

In front of everybody, my self-expression was still there but my mind had closed me out, giving me nothing to express. I grabbed my computer and typed in her question. My fingers started to talk to the keyboard, firing back with whatever the mentally constipated me inside had to say in response, but to which I was otherwise allowed no mental access. I read her the answer that had come from me.

We did some of the big long interview walking around outside and some of it in the big room, and they'd even gradually included Ian in the interview. We'd had them crying and laughing and they'd had us crying and laughing. We allowed them to see who we were and they allowed us to see who they were. They watched us when we weren't aware they were watching and we watched and listened to them peripherally when they didn't notice that we noticed them at all. It was an intense time and a time of real team effort. There was some wobbly throwing and there were real personal efforts on all sides to comprehend things and make things easier.

Though Ian and I had worked in the presence of other people many times, we had always taken over, taken no part at all, or set up a kind of workplace of our own within the workplace. Neither Ian nor I had ever worked well on a team together before we'd worked with each other, and it was really nice to finally do successfully something we knew we'd always failed so miserably at. By the second day, we had grown accustomed to the people and the conditions and it had felt nice to feel we had coped with working as a team with these people, all of whom we'd probably never see again.

We ate all our meals in the big room away from them as they sat all together around one big table out by the bar. At the end of the second day, we went out to their table and watched them all together. They were social and friendly, spontaneous and un-stored with one another. They would have been like this with us too, if we had included ourselves and been able to keep up, or even had enough personal interest in them to keep a nonstored conversation going.

They would have had us join them even if we couldn't have conversed as ourselves. It was we who couldn't join them. To sit among them, watching them being social so easily as themselves, and be unable to do the same (except as some cheap regurgitated performance), would have taken all the enjoyment out of what should be enjoyable.

I wished that I'd been able to let down my guard enough to call Edie by her first name, instead of addressing her indirectly through Ian by referring to her formally as Edie Magnus. I looked at her peripherally and tried to say something to her in my head, addressing her directly by name. But it got no further than a thought and even saying it in my mind had given me the sensory-emotional feeling of eating a bag full of lemons.

The two cameramen had also never been addressed directly or informally. The producer had been addressed by her first name, though only indirectly through everyone else but her. It was sad that the want was there but these few days wouldn't be enough for me to get the mechanics going.

It was time to go. The filming was over. We felt proud of ourselves and felt like together we had achieved something really good. The success of the filming had taken work on everyone's part and, seeing them together, we knew they had put in a lot of effort in relating on our terms. We appreciated that. We knew it took real people to keep up that amount of personal adjustment and empathy, without the insult of sympathy, for two whole days. We didn't know what to say to them to say good-bye as ourselves as others do, so we just waved and left like we were leaving work. We went home.

The next afternoon we eventually realized how much more than just a job it had been and that we would miss seeing those people. We wished we'd said something more to them. We phoned their hotel to say something to them. They'd left a few hours before.

It was time to leave the village and go back to the cottage in Essex. We'd achieved what we'd come for and more. We piled the car up again and put all the furniture, light shades, and paraphernalia back exactly where they had been when we'd arrived. We'd grown used to the house in the way that we'd had it, and now it looked as depressing as when we'd arrived and worthy of leaving.

We handed the key back to Phyllis. She said she would miss us and that she didn't know anyone else like us. We thought we made her feel "normal" and not so different.

It is one thing to be accepted as different. That is acceptance. It is another to be accepted as "normal" by virtue of being among others like yourself. That is belonging.

"We'll be back," we said to Phyllis. The house we were going to buy was not so far from where she lived.

— ⬛

We arrived back at the cottage the next day. The cottage looked and smelled like home and like us. We went around rediscovering everything, as if we were visiting old friends we hadn't seen for ages.

We went out into the little garden we had made in what was once a pile of concrete rubble. We went walking in the village's main street. Even in the five weeks we'd been away, some shops had closed down and new ones had opened.

Snow fell on the village, making the entire street cushiony and white. The trees hung with icicles and little flowers peeked out occasionally through the snow. The birds found whatever branches they could. Bright, redbreasted robins perched on twigs, looking like orphans against a white snowy backdrop of everything in pastel shades.

Children played in the snow and adults pulled small children on sleds. Snowpeople of all descriptions were built in front yards. Cars slid about and people pushed the ones that wouldn't go. Other people were digging cars out of driveways and drivers were cursing.

We walked through a park where ice covered the pond and

there were little snowy hills that invited you to roll down them. We went past a football field covered in a blanket of snow. We went in and rolled a huge snowball and then sat on it, looking at the beauty around us.

By night, lights peeked out through windows like candles glowing in a dim room. Ian and I went out walking in the snow, sliding every so often upon the sidewalk where the snow had turned to ice. We walked two miles to the Dawson house to visit Alex.

Alex busied himself with his noise machines and his pictures of noise machines. A school he had once gone to had ignorantly believed they could rid Alex of his overwhelming auditory hypersensitivity by treating his troubles as a phobia. Instead of offering him headphones to cope with the particular noises that pained him and avoiding any that were unnecessary, they'd intentionally and deliberately dragged him repeatedly up to the sources of these overwhelming and terrifying noises. In return, Alex's mistrust of people had heightened. He had retreated further into his own world and his hypersensitivities remained as bad as ever.

Just as I was drawn compulsively to the things that scared me, Alex had developed obsessions with things that made noise. He collected toy washing machines and tumble dryers and toy fans. He compulsively took them apart, looking for how they worked and where the noise came from. He became obsessed with the corresponding real appliances in his own and other people's houses, as well as with vacuum cleaners, electric drills, and hair dryers. He knew all the different types of each and would have his father draw them over and over again in detail down to the plinths and seals, cords and plug ends. These he collected in a booklet that he took with him daily to his new school.

Alex's obsessions with noise gave him an "interest" in "the world" where he otherwise showed or shared none. His obsessions were a bridge to interaction and communication. They were also a wall.

Whenever someone spoke to him or came over, Alex seemed compelled to reach right away for the nearest thing that made noise or stood for something that made noise. During one visit, he raced straight for the washing machine that was going; on another he picked up his cassette player and put it up to his ear at a deafening volume. Another time, he grabbed for his talking bear, which played repetitive lines of blah-blah. Sometimes he turned up the TV so loud that we could hardly hear ourselves.

The way in which Alex did this was both excluding and expressive at the same time. One could use it to join in with Alex by capitalizing on his observed "interest" or one could acknowledge that the main point of many of his sudden "interests" was merely to tune you out and use against you the weapon that Alex had found had always been used against him: noise.

Trust had been built with Alex by acknowledging his "need" for his machines and other surrogate noise machines and noise-related pictures. There had to come a time, though, for building real security in place of defensive security. Like Ronald Reagan, Alex had built a huge arsenal of defensive security but it was transient and only lasted until the next slight perceived threat. Then, only adding a new piece of weaponry to an already futile and overflowing arsenal would make the defensive security feel stable.

The path from defensive security to internal security is not one that a person can be dragged down. Always, there is the memory of a time of no security at all, and this reminder of limbo will always undermine attempts to drag someone to a place he isn't yet ready to go.

Internal security cannot be handed over on a plate like a ready-made dinner. It cannot be given by someone else, like dishing out the peas and the mashed potatoes and the broccoli. Internal security is built up tiny piece by tiny piece, and each tiny piece cannot be taken without being reached for.

To force-feed what is not being reached for to someone who lives in a world where all rules conform to the goal of defensive security is to attack. The very giving you think will save a person will be perceived as a weapon used against him, and treated as such.

Internal security is not something that is given, it is a direction shown. When you live in the world of defensive insecurity, all you can see from your ammunition factory is a ludicrous and petty offer of tidbits.

It is like offering a piece of clay to a rich king in place of his ruby collection. For the king to find that piece of clay worth giving up his ruby collection, his ruby collection has to lose a lot of its shine and interest. If you try to take his ruby collection away so he will see the worth of the piece of clay, he will always remember the wonderful ruby collection that he had, and the clay on offer will never be valued or turned into something great.

Alex was a king with a ruby collection. We never tried to take his rubies away. We did, however, throw ours away and let him see that we had. Then—when others who'd had ruby collections had discarded them—the king's rubies no longer looked so valuable. Alex looked for what we'd discarded them for. All we had was clay. Yet each time we saw Alex, our clay was being slowly formed into something greater, more beautiful, and more real than those rubies ever could be. Alex began to fear being left behind. But Alex wasn't free to walk down life's path from behind the walls where he guarded and built up his arsenal. Slowly, he came to see this. His rubies were losing their shine but he didn't know where to go from here.

We told Alex that he had to make friends with the different parts of him and parent them and encourage them through things if he could get them to listen to and trust him. We told him that, this way, he could begin to build a consensus within himself about what he wanted and didn't want to do, to tell compulsion from want, and to plan how to get to where he intended to go in life. We talked to him about how we'd done this with the parts of us, telling him about Willie and Carol and about Richard and Nigel. Alex had written back about his own characters, Jumping Jack and Dawg.

Donna and Ian, my friends,

I have looked to see how Jumping Jack can be creating while the parts of me that are undeveloped catch up.

I will be a parent to Dawg, we will communicate together. I, Alex, will give only love to Jumping Jack. I will give only love to Dawg. I will give myself love. I will see if I, Alex, can race ahead letting Jumping Jack and Dawg race with me.

I write to friends but dread stopped me from having conversation. Now, I have found out that Dawg has courage too. I never knew that. I have told him that he has to believe in himself. I know he can.

I know I have you to thank. I had no idea that you had characters too. I have wanted to ask you if you have been pained by nonautistic reality as I have.

I love you both, my friends. I know you dread, but I write in the knowledge that I have, no longer, fear in telling you this. Dawg has courage. He was bottled out. Now, he has tuned in to himself. In prayer, he has asked God to bless you both.

I feel I owe you so much. I never had the wits to see you communicate in writing because you cannot communicate face to face. I can understand how you feel. I began asking you a question and you were frightened just like Jumping Jack. Ian came and answered when he could. I was frightened too.

We have more to learn but we have come this far. I understand how to *be*. I verified this when you came. You dread communicating, but you *be*.

I know now I have to jump higher. I will fly like a bird to places I have never been. I look to see you there too! I fly in words, now I will fly in full flight, giving action as well as words. *You be there!* I cannot go without you.

Remember this. No freedom is worth having if you have no one to share it with. You know this, but have to learn for yourselves.

I begin living today. You will understand this too.

Good-bye for now,
Alex

PS: Donna. I want the book you wrote. I will read it now. I was trying to free Dawg first.

"Get rid of your weapons," we told Alex. "We are seeing you without our weapons."

We weren't giving him the same old "the world" crap about stopping people from indulging in obsessions. Obsessions had their time and place—even a constructive time and place—but this time and place was past. Like a person who could walk but still used his old wheelchair, Alex couldn't bring himself to walk until he discarded his wheelchair. That discarding was the job of no one else but Alex. If anyone else threw out his wheelchair, his fear would have had him sit on the floor like a man with no legs *and* no wheelchair. He'd get rid of his wheelchair when he was strong enough to admit he'd grown beyond needing it. We were just reminding him.

We talked to his father about Alex's pictures. We told him that if Alex asked him to draw a fan he could draw a fan, but a hand-held, noiseless one. We told him that if Alex wanted him to draw a washing machine, he could draw a noiseless one: a person doing endless reams of washing. We told him that if Alex wanted him to draw a dryer, he could draw a noiseless one: a towel. We told him he could compromise with Alex by doing literally what Alex asked him for but slowly showing Alex that drawing didn't have to be the constant confirmation of defensive security. He could show his son, through the very things that Alex asked him for, that drawing could be a form of sharing and communication that had nothing to do with defensive arsenals.

We'd stayed for ten minutes at the Dawsons and then walked home.

Walking home in the snow in this so very foreign environment. I felt strangely at home. I was an Australian, from a country with almost no snow. Though I felt in self-imposed exile here in England, mine was a gilded cage that could, at times, be as

252

beautiful as any forest of towering gum trees with its warbling birds and the smell of sunshine baking the clay earth.

— ▬

The U.S. and Canadian publication of *Somebody Somewhere* was coming up and Ian and I were going to do a publicity tour. In writing, I'd told the publishers that Ian was my new personal assistant and that he would be helping me during tours. He would be looking out for my safety when I couldn't, cooking when I was too busy or overloaded to get the mechanics together to cook for myself, and negotiating with journalists and publishers when I might otherwise mindlessly say too many unintended yeses, with little thought for context or consequences.

The tour dates were all in a muddle until the last minute. The German, Australian, Canadian, British, and American publishers had all wanted publicity at roughly the same time; I was one person wanted in too many places all at once.

We did a bit of publicity for the British edition, but insisted on at least one free week before embarking on the American and Canadian tours. The Germans had wanted time during this free week. They were told they could have some time when we got back from North America in five weeks. That would be too late for their publication date. They would go ahead without publicity.

The Australians got in touch, assuming that time had been made for them where there was none. We agreed to slot interviews with them in London into a few available days in our only free week before we left for the United States and Canada. They took those few days but needed more. We told them they had to wait until after we got back. They said that would probably be too long to wait and asked if they could arrange some publicity during the American and Canadian tours. Groan groan . . . yes.

We had arranged one week free between the American and Canadian tours. Publicity tours would involve meeting and speaking to journalists almost every day and writing everything I had to say to them in between interviews. There was no time for a slow brain to catch up on any feelings or thought about the experiences of the week. By the end of a week of interviews, I would be getting fairly disoriented and on automatic pilot and much more prone to wobbly throwing and shutdowns. The spare week in between New York and the plane trip to Toronto would be enough time for my mind to adjust to everything that had happened. It was the only way that I was going to arrive in Toronto without waking up in a Toronto hotel apartment and walking into walls that hadn't been in those places back in New York.

Ian and I arrived at the New York apartment that had been arranged for us. It was like being eaten up by a biscuit. The walls were beige. The floors were beige. The furniture was beige.

The traffic outside beeped continually in Manhattan gridlock and the streets were filled with snow and slush and piled onto the sidewalk in a mixture of crisp, fluffy white and messy, ash gray. Chimneys bellowed smoke up into the sky through the narrow slits between tower blocks. A few winter birds flew in and out of these cracks of sky as though they were valley gorges.

Hungry pigeons walked about the snow-covered pavements. Hungry cold people walked about, too, with a look that said they weren't going to anywhere in particular, just going. Trendy well-dressed people sat in the windows of cafés sipping hot frothy coffee and people in business suits headed for somewhere with apparent, though impersonal purpose and cold eyes.

Journalists came to the apartment building and met us in one of the spare apartments. Jean, who'd been so nice to me during the *Nobody Nowhere* tour, was the first of them. I handed her my interview. On paper, I'd spoken to her through writing about everything she'd asked me when she, like the other journalists, submitted her questions in advance. She pocketed the ten or so typed pages with not much else to say about them. It seemed she just wanted to get on with spending time with us as people.

———

Others journalists were a taxi ride away to a radio station where I spoke to them through wires as faceless voices never seen.

A radio interview was my last interview before we had our first day off on the American tour. I had been feeling sicker and sicker. The whole room seemed to sway with my nausea. The interview was ready to start. I needed some water, or I was going to be sick.

Once I'd started talking, I had changed channels and I'd lost awareness of how sick my body was. The interviewer said thank you through my headphones and it was over. I took the headphones off and stood up. Fever and nausea overtook me again. I looked at the fuzzy carpet on the floor. If I vomited on it, they wouldn't be able to clean it up properly. I needed to lie down. I needed to lie down fast.

I lay down on the floor in the little studio. "Are you okay?" asked Ian. If I'd said no, he'd only have fussed about and made things more chaotic than they already felt. "Yes," I replied.

My editor came to the studio door to collect us to leave. Out into the lights of reception, my head was swimming and I hoped that no one would say anything or make me speak. "Could you sign the visitors book?" asked somebody from the station. My hand signed me out of there.

Down the hall and into the elevator, my stomach seemed to be moving independently of me. We left the radio station and walked up the street on our way to the publishing house.

It was sad that I was too sick to give a damn who was around me. I had liked the editor and she was glad to see me and to meet Ian, and it would have been nice to have seen her and given a damn that I had.

Off the street and into the lobby of the publishing house, I couldn't cope anymore. I just managed to get a paper bag to my face when my stomach tried to climb into it. The bag broke and vomit splattered my feet.

We had been invited to dinner at the apartment of my American literary agent that night. She was a nice person, and Ian and I were looking forward to getting out of the biscuit with its loud humming fridge and its dial-a-lawyer TV set.

The taxi arrived to pick us up as arranged and I lounged about in the back feeling toxic. After the taxi dropped us off at the agent's building, we were shown into a rather posh lobby where a man spoke on the phone up to the agent's apartment to tell them we were there.

The elevator opened out onto a little hallway with a door that belonged to the agent's apartment. The door was open and we walked in.

The agent's apartment was a whole house inside of that one little door off the hall. There were proper house carpets and wallpaper and a cat and the whole place didn't look at all like the sort of apartments I had rented. Her apartment looked like she and her husband had lives and they lived them there.

I felt woozy, as if I was going to be sick again. I looked around this lovely apartment and felt really bad that I was likely to throw up here.

Food was dished up. Ian and I both ate a bit of this and that. I looked desperately in Ian's direction. My whole body was sweating and I felt like I was going to fall off the chair. I felt bad that I hadn't given a damn about being there when I might otherwise have been glad to see the agent and her husband. "We have to go," I told Ian quietly but urgently.

The agent called a taxi and got me a cold towel. I felt like I was on fire. We got back to the biscuit and the meal I'd had reintroduced itself like an expected guest.

The following days were more of the same—interviews in between vomiting. By the time I recovered, Ian had caught it. It was the sickest that we'd ever been since knowing each other. It was just as well we had each other.

The flu left us both and we were about to leave New York. We had booked a house to stay in outside of the city.

Ian and I were flat and lifeless as we got through the crowds of baggage claim and customs, afraid of questions about passports and purpose of trip, or to be felt up and down for something we weren't meant to have. Airports were sweaty, noisy, smoky places of hustle and bustle, bureaucracy, and intrusion.

We arrived at the Toronto apartment. It was a modern and clinical apartment up so high that it made you feel like a bird. Inside, there were flowers for us, which made the place a little more alive and reminded us that although we hadn't met anyone yet, we were here to work together with people.

It was snowy here, too, and the wind had fangs that bit at your face. The Canada of Toronto seemed neither American nor English yet had influences from both. It was a subtle evolving culture that seemed a bit dominated by the shadows of its overexposed cousins. Had Australia not have been so stuck out in the middle of Asia or its climate so different, perhaps it too might have had a Toronto feel about it.

The publicist here intrigued me. She was always so businesslike with me. This was easier to follow and cope with than dealing with someone who you could see felt personally, but I wondered why she too hadn't seemed to want to "win me over." I asked her. It was simple, she had told me, she was a private person. I understood that and respected it.

At one radio interview, the journalist asked us about our tinted lenses. I took them off and described the room. The relatedness of things disappeared and everything was now conceptually a separate and unrelated entity. The "on" and "next to" and "in front of" didn't mean much anymore, because whatever something was "on," "next to," or "in front of" no longer had a reality until it itself was focused upon directly. The interviewer's face was again in unrelated bits. A toy bear that had been sitting on a table next to a lamp now became cognitively disconnected from its surroundings, which were no longer processed or taken account of. Everything became sort of free-floating in the cognitive disconnectedness that resulted from renewed visual overload. The words for things failed me and were defined instead by their size, shape, textures, sounds, and materials—or by their use or relationship to other things or people around them. The glasses on the interviewer became shiny, metal, round, "ping-ping" things. The pen became a long thin thing for writing. The shadow and shine on every object in the room cut the room and its objects and people up into angles and shapes. The interviewer's hand was now conceptually disconnected from his body in all but theory and seemed merely tacked onto the end of his sleeve, rather than protruding from it. His head and neck looked plonked onto his shirt collar in the same way, as though he were a statue, disassembled and reassembled again into some bizarre work of art. Visually Ian didn't mean so much now. In his place was a bundle of associated, but only vaguely connected, bits that I knew theoretically was him. The lights were too bright and the rainbows reflecting in the light fittings themselves were starting to sensorily hurt. I had had enough and was starting to shake. I was feeling alienated from my surroundings again.

I put my tints back on. My body relaxed and I sighed. Ian was back and looking at him made me feel secure. I looked at the interviewer and he didn't look so bizarre and unreal. I looked at one of the objects I had been staring at and knew now what it was, what it was called, and what it was sitting on. I even had a rough idea of why it might have been there.

On our day off we went to the Toronto Science Centre. It was an amazing place with lots of things to look at and touch and listen to. There were loads of things to experience, experiment with, and learn from without having to interact with anyone. In "the world," things didn't present themselves to me with questions to be asked. Here, the covert questions inherent in things were presented overtly. Here, you weren't expected to have curiosity, you were challenged to.

There was a section about the environment and you could see all the different layers of earth under the surface. I'd looked at the ground all my life and never wondered about what was underneath or how it went together.

There was a section about food and you could see how much food you would eat in a year all stacked high to the roof in shopping carts. Without seeing this, my mind could never have accumulated the collection of simultaneous mental pictures necessary to have any idea how much food went through me.

In a communication center was a computer programmed to talk back to whatever you wrote into it. It sounded just like the psychiatrist that I'd seen as a teenager and it talked just like I had as Willie.

"How do you feel about that?" the computer asked.

"You aren't even real so why should I tell you?" I replied.

"What makes you think I'm not real?" it prompted.

"I'm not speaking to you," I argued.

"Why not?" it prompted again.

"Because you're just a machine," I replied. "You don't even know I'm here."

"What gives you that idea?" the computer went on.

There was a display to do with something called the principle of interference. It was just a pile of color-words written in colors that were different from the word spelled out. The word "blue," for example, was written in red letters. The word "yellow" was written in blue. You had to read the word that the letters spelled out without being influenced by the color of the letters it was spelled out in. It was impossible. We stumbled and fumbled, stuttered and spluttered and figured we'd failed miserably. We read what was meant to happen. This interference was perfectly normal and expected. We wondered what it would be like without our tints so we took them off and did the exercise again.

Without the tints, there was no interference. Without them, we had read the list without pause or fault. What then, we wondered, had the tints done for the way we processed visual information? If it had been so easy to read the list without our tints, then there had been no interference of the two systems of the color of the letters and the word that they'd spelled out. If that were so, then, without the tints, could it have been that we processed only one system at a time? Could it have been that without the tints, our visual perception was mono and that we had spent most of our lives dropping out entire whole aspects of

259

visual information that was meant to be processed simultaneously? Was that where our proper development of understanding
visual social cues had come to a standstill and left us? Was this
why, instead, we'd come to rely totally on a handful of simplistic
stored formulas that we applied mechanically to all situations?

Before leaving Toronto, there was an interview I had been both
nervous and excited about. I was to be interviewed by a journalist who herself had autism.

Bette was a very well known author of fiction who had been
given the job of interviewing me for a major Toronto newspaper. She had sent a copy of her book in advance for me to get
some idea of who she was. I had only to read a few pages to see
that she wrote with a similar structure to my own, with a strikingly similar use of symbolism and image. We even used some of
the same "special" words. I had also been given copies of interviews with her and reviews of her work. She had, like so many
other high-functioning people with autism, been previously mis-
diagnosed as crazy but knew that she was autistic. She referred to
my first book, *Nobody Nowhere,* as "her bible" and had found belonging and confirmation in it.

I was anxious about meeting her. I didn't like to be made so
important. Also, what if I didn't see her as being "like me"? What
if I didn't recognize her as sharing the same things (in common
with me and others) that made up what people called being
"autistic"? If she were looking for confirmation and all that I had
was denial, would I share it with her? Would I let her see it?

Ian and I pulled up in a taxi to the publishing house, where the
interview would be. Bette stood there on the pavement looking
like a small and skinny stray cat and not nearly so hard and cold
as her photos had made her.

We entered the building. She was kept out of the room until
we had settled in. I felt both guilty and grateful, feeling as if I was
excluding someone who saw herself as being "like me" and who
needed belonging. But I also felt like no journalist had the right

to break the rules just because she shared developmental problems with me.

Bette entered. Her staring eyes didn't scare me because her eyes were not looking for me at all, but for herself. Still, I didn't have any want in me to know who she was and I felt shame over that. To me, she was a journalist here to ask me a pile of journalistic questions and that was all.

She sat down burbling at a hundred miles an hour on so many tangents that she was like a spider running around and around her own web. She was falling all over herself with compliments and gratefulness and my stomach was churning with every one of them. Her directness was shattering and reckless and without any awareness of how uncomfortable it was making me or any interpretation of my near allergic-looking body language. In short, she was as oblivious as any high-functioning autie I'd ever met.

The publicist had noticed I was totally boggled by the bombardment, so she leaned over to tell Bette to speak slowly and succinctly so that we could get on with the interview. Bette fell over herself with apologies, making ever more elaborate new ones with no apparent awareness that she'd just made a few already. It was as though she had no ability to perceive that her apologies had been understood and had had any effect. Her ears and eyes were under glass. It was becoming painfully apparent that she'd come here looking for confirmation but was so overloaded that she could neither see nor hear feedback.

Bette had meant to ask a question but it had been framed in such an overuse of context that I couldn't separate one from the other and had no idea what to respond to. I sat looking helpless and curling in on myself. I tried to speak to her. Without bad intentions, she spoke over me just like my father so often did and—like him—she seemed to have no idea that she had.

I handed her my typed responses to the questions she had submitted in advance. She said thank you, took them, and put them aside without reading them—as though she had little idea of what they were. Then she started firing paragraph-long questions at me again, the same ones I'd answered for her on paper.

I asked Ian to ask her to read my answers first and then ask me her questions. Bette compliantly took my pages and skimmed through them very briefly, scanning the pages instead of reading them. Then, after flicking through a few pages, she began the same questions again.

It was clear that she fluctuated sharply between having a sense of self with no sense of other and having a sense of other but no sense of self. She approached things externally, unable to make use of assistance by integrating that assistance back into her own track. She could ask questions but couldn't take in the answers. She could hear answers but lost the context that had been the question.

We talked about what made someone "autistic" and we talked about simply be. I told her that I thought she was different from me but had some very similar difficulties. Her background, as she described it, seemed to fit the picture of someone with Asperger syndrome, a more mild form of high-functioning autism. As a child, she'd had very highly developed language and had talked to herself all the time. Her communication problems, as with so many other people with Asperger syndrome, were to do with social communication, not the mechanics of spoken language in its broader sense.

I asked her if she'd ever been diagnosed as autistic. She said that though she felt sure she was autistic, she'd been told she couldn't be on the grounds that she stared at people and that autistic people had trouble with eye contact. She'd obviously asked an ostrich with its head in a bucket of stereotypes. I had seen just as many people with autism who stared too much at people as I had seen those who hardly looked at people at all.

I'd heard these things from other people, too. Adults and children who had pervasive developmental difficulties had been seen by unqualified or inexperienced people and been said not to have autism because they could smile or cry or could speak or were friendly. These backyard experts would have made great bigots.

If they'd been making such sweeping and uninformed statements about race, gender, age, or sexuality instead of disability, they'd probably have been sued or laughed out of their profession.

"I think that's enough now," said the publicist, realizing that among the three of us, nobody was giving or getting cues properly enough to know when the interview was over or how to end it. Bette looked as alone and empty as when she'd walked in, perhaps even more so. "So that's it," she said out loud to herself with an air of finality or futility or both. It was as though she'd come looking for belonging but, in her world under glass, it couldn't reach her, even from the person "like her" whom she'd so admired. Perhaps, processed out of context, it would sink in over time as things did with me. Then perhaps she'd feel some belonging that came out of nowhere but never know where it came from.

We boarded the plane back to London and slept in the taxi on the way back to the cottage in Essex.

———

Our moving date had arrived. We would be moving to live in the country in a way that looked permanent. Though we'd both lived most of our lives in the city, we didn't think we'd miss it at all. At home with trees and bugs and birds, we'd fit in just fine in the beautiful Welsh countryside. We'd learn Welsh and not worry too much about Nazis.

An invitation had come through the fax machine. Alex, the young man who professionals had wrongly assessed as mentally retarded, had won a major literary award for a short account of his life with autism which would be included in a compilation of children's writing soon to be published. He was the most beautiful writer and poet I had ever read. He had an incredible depth of soul well beyond what were now his mere seventeen years of life in that body. His private writings were the few writings beyond my own that could make me cry. His were the few writings that left me other than indifferent enough to say I was impressed. There would be a ceremony at a major bookstore with photographers and journalists. We were Alex's friends. Could we be there?

We had told Alex months ago that we were moving. We had seemed to be two in a long string of people who'd come into his life and affected him and then moved out again. That was the stuff of disability, where specialists are 'friends' and non-professional friends are hard to find and too often just passing through. We assured him we were not passing through. We'd come through the last two years daring each other forward up an invisible mountain, consoling one another as we surveyed the next peak, and hoping and pleading not to be left behind. We assured him we would be just a fax away.

The movers arrived and packed our things for the six-hour drive to the other side of the U.K. We had rented out the cottage until we could sell it. We took our last look around at the spring flowers that had blossomed here as we had. In this little house, we'd gone from brother and sister to best friends, to specialship and to marriage. Then, we got into our car and drove ourselves out of life in the city.

We arrived at our new house in Wales. The movers had already put everything inside. Everywhere inside of the house was space. Everywhere outside of the house was more space. There were outbuildings in which we'd house a workshop for which we had one toolbox of things. There was a garden shed for which we had one small box of recycled plant pots, a fork, and a pair of accidentally well-painted garden gloves.

The garden was overgrown with weeds and the fields we would be responsible for were full of nettles and thistles as high as my chest.

Big, chunky bumblebees buzzed about the trees. Little, chattery acrobatic birds zipped about over the house, climbing up under the eaves and nestling into holes left in the walls where the concrete rendering had fallen away. For the first two weeks, birds flew in through the small openings we could make in the few rickety windows that did still open. It was as though they weren't accustomed to the house being open like this. It was like we all lived in one big nest collection and we were living in their house as much as they were living in ours. Maybe we were just all living in House and House put up with all of us.

Every day, Ian would go outside into the fields, flying a kite or just sitting out on the grass. I would watch him through the windows and sometimes he would look up to see me watching and just smile as if to say that I was invited, too.

Though it was quiet and peaceful, it was hard for me here. It was yet another move in a life full of too many moves. It was also physical permanence in the making in a life that almost never imagined that as a possibility. It was as though, if I went outside and accumulated experiences of our surroundings, I would be building the permanence that was so foreign to me. I would be building our future here and that would be confirmation that the temporary, just-passing-through past of the cottage was truly left behind. If I went out there and experienced where I was through reaching out to it, it would map itself into me through my own body movements.

Already, all the walls were in the wrong places, the furniture on foreign sides of the room, the doors not where they should be. Inside of the house, I still had some vague semblance of the now fragmented rituals that had made up daily life at the cottage. Outside, with Ian, there was no familiarity yet formed here and I wasn't ready for it.

It took me a week to get out of the "moving house blues." Gradually, I went from watching Ian through the window to watching him from the back door, and then I hovered around as he went about doing whatever interested him. Gradually, I joined him in a few things here and there, following his lead.

My emotions, too, were breaking free. My happiness burst out through my body and I danced and skipped and leaped about making all sorts of happy sounds. These were probably the very things that my environment had tried to extinguish in me as a child in its "well-intentioned" attempts to make me appear normal. In doing so, it had probably expected that connected and natural facial expressions would flow without having gone down the developmental path to get there. I hadn't got to where I was expected to, and there seemed nothing at all abnormal to me that my emotions would connect so much more easily through movement and sound than through a bundle of facial muscles.

"The world" had only succeeded in teaching me age-appropriate ways to portray emotions that I was expected to feel but usually didn't because I didn't necessarily share "the world" priorities. When I did feel emotions, they'd been extinguished at the point where they connected with my body—either because I was having them in non-age-appropriate circumstances or because the way that they were expressed didn't look "normal" or "intelligible" to other people. If they'd seen the same connections in a baby or an infant, they'd never have questioned its inability to understand it. Seeing the same things in a child of ten or an adult of thirty not only made no sense to people, but it also scared them by threatening their ideas of "reality" and "normal."

Although the main cause of my aversion to emotion had been my attempt to control overload and shutdown (and the Big Black Nothing), I had come to realize that it probably hadn't been a "my world" law that had taught me that emotions were against the law. When "the world" was impatient with and embarrassed by my underdeveloped and infantile emotional expression, it had incidently reinforced within me that these already problematic and troublesome connections were not allowed.

With Ian, emotions—and their expression—were allowed; with Ian, I grew. My emotions would progressively connect more and more with my body and thoughts and become gradually refined in those connections. All I needed was to be somewhere where I was free to be myself in the company of someone who showed me I was safe to grow with acceptance and belonging and evolve not in a way or at a pace that someone else ex-

pected me to, but in whichever way and whatever pace that came
naturally to me.

One day, Ian looked out of the window. I was outside laughing
and laughing as I *boing*ed about on a pogo stick. I hadn't waited
to be asked to try something. I had felt feelings and they had connected with a want and the want had connected with the thought
of how to satisfy it and my body had listened to the thought and
helped it get realized. My actions were not intended to entertain
or impress. They did not spring from evasiveness or the compulsion to run, hide, or deny true self-expression. I was breaking
loose and letting go, knowing I was not on my own and knowing that that didn't matter and that I was safe and free nevertheless. Ian came out and silently joined me on another pogo stick
and we *boing*ed about together in the courtyard, laughing like a
pair of mad hares.

We hired a builder, a quiet and gentle man, to help us fix up
the house. The builder went about his work, getting to know us
very slowly through teaching us new Welsh words here and
there. One day, I passed by where the gum tree had stood. The
builder had cut him down.

He lay upon the ground dismembered. His stringy bark and
silvery trunk, his olive green leaves, all lay sadly on the ground. I
went to where he lay in bits and knelt on the grass next to him.
I stroked his trunk like he was an old cat I'd known. I smelled his
leaves, the eucalyptus smell, half blown away by the Welsh wind
into which his life too had dissipated. My eyes were full of tears.
I wanted to put him back together. I wanted to keep him whole.
I gathered his parts and then laid them across one another, hugging them like he was my dead friend. There we lay, two Australians, far away in a foreign place that wasn't ours, where we'd
made the best of things.

I picked his parts up and carried them to the woodshed. His
wood seemed too unique, too alive, to burn along with the waste
timber we had gathered here for recycling. Old floorboards and
fence posts contrasted with him as sharply as a living cow does

with packaged meat in a supermarket. I gathered some of his big branches and took them to one of the outbuildings.

I had painted up that outbuilding to use for crafts. I had painted it yellow and white, like a sunshiny sky full of puffy, fluffy clouds. I placed his branches around the room. His silver and olive green looked somehow at home here in the sunny room. Outside, the sky was gray and cloudy, the grass was rich and green, and the dusty dry land of scratchy grass from which he'd come was ten thousand miles away.

— —

Though I'd written to my father, it had been about two years since I'd spoken to him or to my brother Tom. The thought of speaking directly to either of them had always been countered with the thought of hearing my mother's name spoken or their being later needled into telling her everything I'd said. It had felt better not to speak to them at all, than to speak to them in a war zone. Even if they did their best to stay neutral, they would inevitably be made to take sides or convey messages. Exposed, any links that we had with one another would be used as weapons in the wrong hands.

Since settling into the house, I'd come to terms with permanence. The security I'd found in having a self, having a body, having a voice, having belonging, and having a specialship with someone like myself was now bolstered by the first physical place I knew could be forever. The thought of contacting my father or brother and the implications it might have for indirectly reminding my mother that I existed didn't seem so hard now. I wasn't teetering from where I stood. I was on solid ground.

I called my father. He was out of hospital and was on the road to getting better. It was nice to hear his weathered raspy voice, each sentence alive with image and sounding like it danced on the edge of a chuckle. It was as familiar as the gum tree. There was something different about him, though. He had rarely been able to listen to me for any length of time. His mind had been constantly booming ahead like an express train that never stopped at any station long enough to let off passengers—unless they dared to jump out while it was moving. He was always rambling off down his own multitude of tracks, usually making only the most flimsy of connections to anything I had said. Though he took me seriously and never ignored, fobbed off, or laughed off my own monologues, he had always seemed like a manic puppy, unable to take much account of anyone else.

There was a definitely social person inside of my father and an equally definite recluse. I think he hid behind the same strategies I'd used for years when he didn't know what to do with what people said. He made matches with words said or topics spoken, told stories of his past, gave out accumulated information, or clowned about. With the effects of his condition and the chemotherapy, he had been slowed down. It was like when my food and chemical allergies, yeast problem, and hypoglycemia had been sorted out. After that, I had begun not just to hear others with more consistent meaning but also to keep some track of my own ramblings and actually have some time to occasionally do something with what others had said.

It was a really strange feeling to talk to my father in dialogue instead of as two people talking in monologue. We were now equals.

There had always been a kind of security in my father's being unable to really "hear" me. I had felt free and unrestricted, able to say anything I wanted on any track. With him, it was like when I was a child and would phone strangers from the phone book just to do a monologue at them. I didn't have to make sense. I didn't have to know what I was saying or why, as long as the patterns sounded like language. Now that he was actually taking account of things I said and responding in a way that showed he'd actually thought or felt something about these things, it was surprising and exposing; I found myself stumbling about more, aware that I was being heard with meaning and significance. Though I'd drilled him for information before, and we'd talked in the obscure language I'd called "talking in poetry," we were now conversing out of the closet like two people free to be ourselves. I was glad he was alive and that I'd been there to share not just my ability to converse, but his, too.

Ian was listening in on the phone. I signed to him with surprise that my father could "hear" me. Ian was smiling. I could tell he thought my father was an okay person. He'd never met him, but he could tell that he wasn't damaging to me. I told my father how Ian and I had got married and how Ian was listening. "That's nice," he said and then said hi to Ian. As always for my father, as for me, it was as if no time had passed at all.

I decided to call Tom. My father had told me Tom had moved and didn't live with my mother anymore.

I wanted Ian with me while I called. I'd never been able to speak with Tom socially and always just lectured him, reeling off stored "this is good for yous" and "shoulds" that I'd accumulated and which passed for conversation. We'd never been on safe territory long enough for me to dare try anything nonstored, and Tom was far more attentive than my father. He didn't have much trouble taking account of the meaning of what you said, even if he missed some of the significance.

I held Ian's hand. Ian listened in, signing emphatically, "As you." I didn't know what to say. "Yes," "yes," "I don't know," tumbled out of my mouth in mousy response to Tom's attempts to get conversation going. I was shaking and it got too much for me and made me cry. "Talk to him," Ian signed gently, silently mouthing the words.

"I'm scared to speak to you," I told Tom.

"Scared of me?" he replied. "Don't be scared of me."

"I can't help it," I told him. "I'm afraid to show you who I am. I'm afraid for you to know me." I had told him how I felt about him. It would be easier next time—if there was a next time.

Ian and I talked about whether or not I wanted a brother. There was no doubt that I had no need for one even if biologically I had two. My older brother, James, was so estranged from me and strange to me that there was no way I had the energy and motivation to try to build anything with him any more than I did with any other stranger. Though he was as human as anybody, all my memories of James were either flat or negative. My memories of Tom were not so flat and, though he felt like a stranger, we two strangers were not so estranged. I felt that I would never know if I wanted him to be my brother unless I attempted to know him as myself. I would also never be able to lay to rest those theory-dreams of "my brother Tom" unless I had some experience to measure them against.

Over the next few months, I called Tom again a few times, progressively talking to him more. I knew my version of social conversation was simplistic and stilted. I felt scared to hear the signs I was being ignored or steered or covered for with mock-humor. I knew this "oddity" made some people feel awkward or embarrassed. I asked Tom if he thought I was mad. "Only as mad as I am," he replied.

When I spoke to Tom in an unstored way, he hadn't pretended that I hadn't said anything. He didn't act as if what I'd said was odd, out of place, or backward. He didn't act like he was putting up with me or try to lead me into "proper conversation." He didn't lecture me, advise me, or pretend I'd been joking. He just spoke to me like I was an equal human being and it was nice.

"Say hello to Ian for me," Tom said.

Instead of feeling threatened at what would, at another time, have been perceived as an attempt to invade my life, I felt good about that. Tom's attempt at inclusion in not just my life but the "our lives" that me and Ian shared, felt warm, not sharp. "Okay," I said to Tom, turning to Ian, standing near me. "Tom says hi."

▸ ◀

Alex had written. He had been in touch since we'd moved. He'd achieved a lot in the last year: and was now going to college part-time. He had gradually weaned himself more and more off his obsessions and had come to relate more broadly and express broader interests. He had managed to channel his obsessions with noisy electrical objects into a general curiosity about sound and energy and, later, physics in general. He was developing an interest in understanding other people and was studying physics and art history and reading literary classics.

He was developing an understanding of himself, discussing his past, his present, his mind, and his feelings with his family and people working with him. He was comparing notes with people like me and Ian to gain what he could from our self-understanding and share with us some of his own. Beyond typing, Alex was getting real with the world, starting to speak with more people and in a way comprehensible to "the worlders."

For some time Alex had referred, in his letters, to being unable to speak. But in the last two years, I'd heard him speak fluent "waffle," stored comprehensible phrases that he used again and again to ask for food or to go somewhere. We pointed out to him that the only times he couldn't speak was for the pure purpose of being social in an emotionally and personally expressive non-stored way, and that maybe he had to look at the question of blocked motivation rather than blocked ability.

Alex had written back furiously, attacking the idea. Of course he was motivated to speak. He had written that he had all the words in his head and could think-talk fluently.

We wrote back from the other side of the battle line, pointing out that the want to speak is not motivation enough to have the social curiosity to drive "conversation" and that motivation can work in more than one direction at once. We told him that as big as his want and interest were in one direction, his fears could counter the want.

He replied:

I understand how one pulls backwards. . . . Today, if your "parts" went, with inner wanting, their separate roads, would you push them together?

I depended on want to know. If one could not try when one wanted to, how could one try if one did not want to?

I saw really the dread would not understand that to free the words one was happy creating, writing, but then feared there was not time to try speaking. I speak the words in my thoughts but they dread the realization that they will take too long to get out. I am slow in attempting the interaction in talking. Were you ever slow to get the interaction of speech?

You terrified me when you came here. I was trying my utmost not to react, to form questions from written words. You are free, try to understand. I hope, Ian, you hear the *be* that has tested freedom but is not ready to have freedom always.

Alex wrote of the fear of not knowing how someone would respond or judge what he said and the fear of not getting the time to form the words in the way he intended. He wrote about fear of other people asking him questions. He wrote about fear of not knowing if he'd be understood or whether people would find him to be an "interesting person." We wrote back to him, explaining that these things might fuel a kind of countermotivation, perhaps what he called "dread," that canceled out what would otherwise drive him to converse.

Alex had written that the logical part of him, Jumping Jack, had nagged him to speak his word-thoughts out loud; but the emotional and fear-driven part of him, Dawg, had fought this, convincing him that he couldn't speak. In his next letter, he'd realized that one of the things holding him back from speaking his words fluently with others was his own fear, and he asked whether he was right and that he could follow logic and actually dare to "do."

We wrote back:

Hello Alex,

Thinking in speech is called subvocalizing. That part of you is right, you can let those words out of your mouth (if you have the ability to form words, which you do). Just try letting them out as an exercise on a regular basis for the next few weeks. You will have to trust their effect upon others. No one can ever guarantee the effect of communication on others. You will have to take a risk. The greatest risk in life is taking no risks at all (because you achieve nothing and lose life).

Yesterday we had visitors. I could not join in a game with them. They all played with a ball I like, Ian and Steven. Then, I knew I wanted to join but part of me couldn't *let* me so I defied that part that wouldn't let me and proved I could. I ran to where Ian was catching the ball from Steven. I took it and then I threw it. That part that wouldn't let me play *with* others threw the ball over my head away from everyone. I defied it and went and got the ball. I was so scared. That part of me created total "I can't" against the idea to throw the ball to Steven (a stranger), conceiving of such an action as potential symbolic "joining."

Marie joined in with us and I went to throw to Steven but couldn't (let myself) so threw to Ian. Then I threw the ball to Marie next time (as a compromise with the fear that was otherwise stopping me). Then, finally, I tried to throw to Steven. Fear drove my body to be against me, making my head refuse to look and making my body reject my intention to throw. I fought the bastard and did it.

I lasted for about ten minutes playing together this way, then I broke down as I was very shattered at the reality that I had managed. One of those word-thoughts had said the line "hours of family fun" and that had made me see that I was doing in reality what I had always believed only possible for me to do as myself in dreams (or daydreams). Then, terror set in with the thought that if I could do in reality what I thought I knew was only possible for me in dreams, then where were the boundaries of possibility? That thought threatened to tumble all boundaries down on me with no time to adjust and it filled me with terror. Marie had asked me, "Why, Donna, can you share verbal communication but find it so hard to do an activity with others?" I replied, "Because doing the activity with others involves their impact upon my body" (by making me move in response).

Perhaps for you, there exists such a boundary for speech, but not an undefiable and uncrossable one. For me, such a boundary exists also to thought, as that part of me that knows I will defy it often uses the master strategy of cutting me off at the thought level, so I cannot access in order to be motivated to defy. That, too, is illusion and it is up to you to prove such illusions to yourself for what they are. Yes, you have autism *but* the adaptations you make to your autism are in your hands. You *can* be verbal. Your connection to thought, verbalized thought, and body (as in lungs, voicebox, tongue, etc.) are all there and you also often have the motivation to speak (curiosity). Now there is nothing stopping you but your own self-defining within the very defiable words "I can't." *Thaw out!*

From Us

The phone rang. The answering machine picked it up and we listened to who was calling. Alex was speaking on the phone. "Hello, Donna. Hello, little boy," he said, referring to me and Ian. We picked up the phone. Hello, Alex, we replied.

—◂ ◂

It was evening and I sat about in the living room thinking about our prospective trip to Australia. We were taking a trip there so that Ian could see where I was from. I wanted him to know what the smell of sunshine in the air was like, the thud of clay earth under his feet, the beauty of a flock of rosellas, cockatiels, galahs, or cockatoos. I wanted him to have the chance to view kangaroos and koalas, wombats and possums, goannas, echidnas, and platypuses. I wanted him to see wattle and bottlebrush and forests of tall gum trees. I wanted him to visit the Australian bush and coastline, which were dotted with natural wonders that remind a person that human beings don't run the place and aren't the only things capable of creativity. I wanted him to meet Dr. Marek, the educational psychologist who diagnosed me as autistic, and his family, so he could put faces to their names.

I also needed to go visit my father. It had been three years since I'd last been there and I knew it would be many more years before I'd go again. Perhaps there wouldn't be a chance to see him when that next time came up.

I would visit Tom, too. He was using words like "sister" and "love ya" on the phone and I had gone from believing these were empty words to realizing that, even though I didn't have feeling concepts for these words in relation to him, maybe he was capable of feeling them even if I couldn't make the connections between such words and feelings.

In the film *Rain Man,* Raymond, who was autistic, had taken care of his younger brother, Charlie, as a child and had sung to him when he was scared. Perhaps Charlie had thought this meant that Raymond—Rain Man—knew him and loved him.

For me, the word "knew" could be exchanged for the terms "accumulated information about" and "sensed." In this sense, I had "known" Tom. The word "love" could be exchanged for "took care of" and "had responsibility for." Particularly in the absence of other close family relationships, perhaps Charlie felt his brother had shown him love and Charlie loved Rain Man back— even if Rain Man hadn't felt the same love in the first place.

Rain Man put up with Charlie's feelings, maybe knowing— like me—that it really shouldn't matter if you had them back or not. Love is the baggage each person carries for himself. If I didn't have any baggage, then that should have been okay.

I used to think that nobody else really felt love because I didn't (or, if I did, then constant system shutdowns made it a highly inconsistent and fragmented, almost unintelligible experience). I had learned how to pretend its existence, so I assumed that that was what others did. To me, the illusion of love as a real thing was a sort of agreed-upon, mass social conspiracy to self-delude.

Now that I had been able to recognize my out-of-context, overwhelming sad as "missing someone," I knew that I, too, had become capable of love. But love involves more than just being able to "miss." It also involves having shared your self with someone and having shared in theirs. This arises from trust, and trust arises from comprehension. By the time Tom had come along into the world, I was just beginning to get inconsistent meaning through what I saw and heard. By the time he was three, he'd outgrown me. What I'd felt then was close to love, but it was frozen in time because I closed him out once I could no longer keep up. Now that I could keep up, the him I had loved was back there somewhere, twenty years ago. When he said things like "love ya, sis," it didn't feel nice. It felt alienating, because I didn't feel anything from the words and the silence that followed was a nauseating and heavy invisible pressure and nagging reminder that I was supposed to. I had decided that I wouldn't see James while we were there. As far as I was concerned, James was a scratchy surfaced person who confused me and was embarassed by me whenever my "differentness" showed.

The entire basis for interaction between James and I, back then, had been his ability to provoke me into responding in some way. He was the provoker and I was the provoked and that was our relationship and one I was glad to be rid of. My difficulties had set me up for that and he had merely slotted into it. Getting inconsistent meaning, I was prone to all sorts of over-reactions to half-understood phrases, facial expressions, intonation, and behaviour.

Looking back, I saw that I had left him little alternative of how to be toward me and that my mother had provided him with a clear model and, in the absence of any other, he had followed it. Looking back, I saw that I couldn't blame him for his behavior any more than one could blame a racist who had been brought up by a Nazi.

"Ian," I said, waking him up in the morning, "I want to speak to my older brother." I explained to Ian that I had been writing a letter to James and assuming he was like he had always been. I explained that I thought he might have changed and that I had to be sure that he was still the person I wished to avoid.

Though I did not love him, like him, or even have any interest in him, I had come to have empathy for James. Like Ian, he had been bullied badly throughout school. Like Ian, he had been seemingly without any ability to reflect or see beyond the surface of things. Like Ian, James's life had been a showy, pretentious, and compulsion-driven one with lots of people who knew him with whom he was friendly, but few who were "friends." I looked back on James's life as I had looked back on Ian's. Ian had never had anyone like me in his life until he met me. James had had me in his life but I'd never let him in.

"I have to speak to him to be sure that I don't want to see him," I told Ian. "When I left, he had begun to change."

I dialed the number that my father had given me. James answered the phone. I was afraid of him, but not in the same way that I was afraid to speak to Tom. I was afraid of Tom because I feared he could affect me and because he looked for the you in there. I had no such fear of James. He never seemed to look for the anybody in anybody any more than he looked for the him in him.

"It's really good you called," said James. "I've been doing some serious thinking about you these last two weeks. I had so much to tell you but I couldn't write it because I couldn't risk someone else reading it. I was scared you'd just read it and think, oh that bastard. You were right about so many things. You've had the right idea." James burbled on and on. It was not at all like the him I had remembered. This was a person who was enthusiastic and sharing and not at all defensive. He had gone from being a person who was no more than all he'd built up in appearance to being a person with something more than what was on the surface.

"Are you following me, mate?" he asked, noticing that I hadn't said anything. I was so relieved. He actually gave a damn about whether I was keeping up. I asked him if he could speak a bit more slowly. "Oh, yeah, sorry," he said, "it's just it's so good to talk to ya." I couldn't believe it. There had been no scoffing or embarrassment at my difficulties. He had understood my needs and had consideration for them.

James felt I was free and admired that freedom. He could see I was my own person, untangled in anyone's web, no cog in the machinery of someone else's compulsions, no performer in someone else's melodrama. He explained how he was trying to be the same and was slowly getting there. He explained how he was still caught up in other people's webs but that at least he knew inside now what was going on. It seemed that he had come to have some idea of who he was and that he was on the edge of getting to like it. Before he hung up, he said "love ya," and though I didn't love him back, I knew he could probably accept that without, mistakenly, taking it as some reflection upon his worth. He had never said that before, or perhaps I'd never heard it. I really felt, though, that he probably meant it and that although he'd made little sense to me as we'd grown up, I had finally made some sense to him.

Though I didn't love him back, I no longer felt threatened by him. More than this, he was no longer the evidence that what was within my mother was such an unchangeable part of him and other "the worlders." Though it was all too late to develop a sense of family with these biologically related strangers, this biological family of five was no longer split down the middle. One part had been cut away from the apple but the rest was edible. I no longer feared these people, even though one of them would always be, in my view, too damaged to be salvageable without fear of the damage spreading. It made so much more sense that one person was damaged than that the whole world was unaccepting, pretentious, defensive, and compulsive.

━ ◢

The effects of my books had spread across the world. We were getting letters from professionals who were trying to develop devices, toys, approaches, and alternative environments to better accommodate the sensory and perceptual problems of the thousands of people in countries all around the globe who had some degree of autism.

A lady in America was developing toys that would catch the

interest of otherwise indifferent children by appealing specifically to their particular sensory fascinations, toys that would build bridges.

A man in Germany was trying to develop an auditory device to do the same things for auditory processing that the Irlen lenses had done for our visual processing.

The Irlen Centres around the world were moving from working with people with dyslexia and learning difficulties in general to taking up the challenge of working with functionally nonverbal children and adults with autism.

An Italian father of a nonverbal boy with autism had approached the Irlen Centre for training and, together with some colleagues, was setting up the first facility in his country to specifically address the perceptual problems of people with autism.

Universities all around the world were questioning their ideas and assumptions about "retardation." They were also looking at how they could lessen the load on people labeled retarded in order to help them function at a level they might otherwise be capable of without sensory, perceptual, or communication burdens.

In Japan, high-functioning people with autism were writing in fractured English with the use of their dictionaries. One wrote to tell us she had never had a friend and that everyone called her stupid. Through a pen-pal list for people like herself, she came to have more friends in a few months than she'd had in her whole life. Another wrote that she appeared to have lots of friends but nobody knew her. No matter how many things she appeared to achieve, she never felt any of the achievement, because she had never yet found a want within her and had just been reaching out blindly to the goals that she had been taught were worth achieving. A third voice in the wilderness of bustling Tokyo wrote to ask if she was the only Japanese person like herself who we'd heard from. Yet another wrote with a story like mine, of having left home at a young age, entered into a relationship just to get away, and then finding the world crumbling down upon her when she discovered she couldn't outrun her autism. These stories echoed those we received from people from other countries, backgrounds, and ages.

A large number of Australian people with autism had written me. For the first time, they were in touch with one another, forming their own support groups and starting up their own newsletter.

We kept a big list of all the people who'd written, from children and teenagers right up to a handful of people in their fifties and sixties with autism. When people asked if I knew of others like themselves, we would send them a list.

We put the Japanese people in touch with others to whom they could speak in their own language. We put people with sensory or perceptual problems in touch with others with those problems and did the same for people who had allergies and metabolic difficulties. We put people with personality difficulties or self-other difficulties in touch with those who shared these things. We put abused and self-abusive people with autism in touch with others like themselves, so they could talk things through with one another in ways too many of them never could with therapists. We put misunderstood, lonely, and bullied children and teenagers in touch with others like themselves, so that even if we couldn't change their lives directly, they might find a comrade with whom they could at least talk about things by letter. When we heard of older people with autism who had struggled with institutional life, drug therapies, or years of misdiagnosis, we put them in touch with others who'd been through those things. When we heard from people with autism whose parents were embarrassed, frightened, or ashamed of their autism, we put them in touch with others who could tell them how they either overcame the effects of their own parents' denial or had helped their parents over it. These people were the real experts for one another because they had shared one another's experiences from the inside.

Three people with autism—Jim Sinclair, Kathy Lisner, and I—had started an international organization, Autism Network International, or ANI, more than two years before. One of the things that the organization did was publish a newsletter called *Our Voice*. Its membership had grown to encompass people with autism from all around the world. People who had never had friends, had never been themselves with people who appeared to be friends, or were never understood by their friends had a social network through which they could share their interests, thoughts, and problems, and make contacts.

People with autism were giving public talks about their own condition instead of having others do it for them. They were appearing on TV talk shows and showing up at hearings, institutions, and organizations as advocates for one another.

Parents and professionals were turning to autistic people for advice when their own outdated theories didn't measure up or their techniques didn't work as well as they'd hoped.

Fewer people were scratching their heads at the word "autism" or hiding in shame at the thought it would bring blame or stigma upon them, their friends, partners, or families. People were reconsidering things that they'd done, as well as their assumptions, their prejudices, and their weaknesses, and the behavior that had sprung from these things.

More books and articles written by people with autism were cropping up in countries all around the world, some by people who had functional verbal language and some by people who didn't.

In the world of film, where before autisticlike characters had usually appeared without being identified as such, opening titles now directly stated the diagnosis. Hollywood seemed to have realized that there was interest in looking at "different" people in the movies. Hollywood had also bought the film rights to my own two books, so there was a film on the horizon.

The world was looking again at disabilities, at perception, at sensory problems, and at learning difficulties and so-called retardation. It was looking again at the whole idea of "normality," at equality, and at consciousness. Though I hadn't caused the snowball, I had thrown my share of snow onto it and there was no stopping it now.

———

A manuscript came through the post. It was from a young woman who, like Alex, had begun to reach for independence without a voice of her own. She was one of the regulars who had been writing to us for some time. Like some of the others who wrote, she had a university education but—unlike most of them—she was still functionally nonverbal. Her letter asked if I could read her manuscript. She wanted to get it published. She wanted to be a writer. She wanted her "voice" heard.

— ◢

Ian slept in a huddled bundle of duvet, secure in himself and secure here with me and the birds and the gentle sound of the wind that danced over the valley fields. I woke up snuggled next to him as though we were a pair of koalas.

I got up and went downstairs. My stomach was making noises, telling me I needed breakfast. I opened the fridge: avocado, tomato, egg. I had written a list of the possible combinations of things for breakfast; avocado and walnuts, tomato on Ryvita, omelette. None of those appealed. I looked through the glass doors of the kitchen cupboards, skimming over Ian's cereals. I couldn't eat those because of a severe allergy to milk and a lesser allergy to soy milk and coconut milk, and because nut milk and oat milk were really an acquired taste with cereal, one that I hadn't yet got with appreciation.

I opened the cupboard door to look at cooking ingredients. Among the wheat-free choices I could make were barley flour, millet, rice, and ground corn. I could bake some scones, make some millet or corn bread, or have some barley pancakes. The thought of pancakes with jam came up and it connected with a physical response that told me my taste wanted this. For once, one of my wants had got there quicker than all the stored personally disconnected "coulds" my defenses could come up with. I headed to the fridge for the sugar-free jam.

The idea of carrot pancakes jumped into my head with a compulsive ferocity. It had no connection with taste-want. No, I shouted mentally at the thought, I don't *want* carrot pancakes. The thought of apple pancakes then jumped in and then banana pancakes and then banana fritters. None of those connected with taste-want either.

It was hard to drive my body to make the pancakes that I wanted. All these compulsions drove me to carry out "their good ideas," the contents for which were in corners of the room, away from where I wanted to be to cook my pancake. I found myself heading in the wrong direction, unable to keep my body consistently on my track. When various thoughts competed, my body was poised to respond to all thoughts, not just the ones earmarked as "want."

My hand was on the jam jar now. A thought jumped in that the jam would have gone bad by now. I opened the jar and looked. It was fine.

Theoretically, bad jam went into the bin. Despite the fact I thought the jam was fine, my body was following through with the previous idea that the jam would be bad by now and the logical consequences of that thought.

My compulsions drove me to the bin with the open jar. I knew I didn't want to throw the jam in the bin. I'd headed for the stove where I'd cook my pancake and ended up at the sink instead. My hands were draining the juice off the jam for no reason that made any sense to me, but there was a vague thought hovering about that if food had excess juice, you drained it off.

Without the juice, the jam now globbed over onto the side of the jar, making it look like jelly and not jam and not so nice to eat. Distracted, my feet went to the bin and the jam that I wanted was tipped out of the jar and into the rubbish. The same vague thought had hovered that if something looks unappetizing and is probably bad then it gets thrown out.

I felt sad. I felt like some bastard had just thrown away something I wanted. Defiantly, I went back to the fridge and reached for a new jar of jam and opened it up. A thought happened that it was wrong to open up a new jar of jam (new things had to be

saved). The urgent and compulsive thought made me feel attacked for opening it up. There was another old jar of jam on the
shelf, older than the good one that had just been thrown out. It
was peach jam and I hadn't wanted peach jam.

A compulsive thought jumped into my head that it would be
good to finish off this old peach jam so it wasn't wasted. My hand
reached for it. Damn it, I didn't *want* peach jam. I wanted the jam
that got thrown away and, if I couldn't have that, the cherry jam
was my next choice even if it *was* a new jar.

I took hold of the cherry jam jar and took it out, closing the
fridge door like I wished I could on all the compulsions driving
me to pay attention to all their stored possibilities and rules about
jam.

I felt angry and my mind played out a stored picture from a TV
episode of *Cops,* where the police had been called out to a food
fight between a couple. The picture was of an angry person
throwing a jam jar across the room at the wall. Not my thought,
I thought, getting my mind on my track.

I willed myself to stay on track as I cooked my pancake. As I
cooked it, I had the lid off the jam and the knife already dipped
into it, waiting to spread it and giving signs to my defenses that I
knew what I wanted and was damned well going to get it. If only
I could get to the stage of spreading the jam, I would be okay.
Thoughts about grating carrot into my pancake jumped into my
mind. I mentally scoffed at the stupidity that my mind would
think that I possibly wanted grated carrot in a jam pancake.

The pancake was finished and though my defenses drove me
to feel guilty about using the new jam, I spread it and ate it down
vengefully. I was winning. This was *my* life.

I climbed the stairs and stood at the bedroom door. I looked at
Ian off in the world of sleep and knew that sleep was not a place
he went to, abandoning me in the process, nor probably was
death. I was not abandoned to my defenses and never would be.
I knew that even asleep, he had a mind in there. I knew that that
mind, though no more constantly aware of me in sleep than

awake, knew at least peripherally of my existence at all times. In knowing of his knowing, I felt the surety of my own existence.

This was a surety that the transient reassurances of the ever changing social-cladding of ego could never give. It was a surety bigger than feeling that I was my own body, with all of its emotional and physical sensations, and that I could express myself through it. It was a surety that I was an expressed whole self moving in a place where inner and outer worlds meet. It was a surety that Ian, as a separate person, carried—beyond my control—a continuous awareness of my existence, my being.

I looked at Ian. He did not idolize me for how my achievements might reflect upon his social worth. He did not back-pat himself by keeping me dependent or "charitably" carrying me for my disabilities. He did not possess me as a material object or own me as a tool to please his body or a house servant to take care of him. He did not value me for how I could be a reflection of him or for fitting his assumptions and mirroring his expectations. Looking at Ian, I knew that this awareness of my existence wasn't carried in his ego, but in his self; not in his mind, but in his soul. Looking at him and knowing that, I could accept that he and I were all the things I had been unable to accept: "family," "together," and "us." I knew that though defensive instinct and poor skills told me otherwise, I *was,* like others, a social being.

In that moment, I felt who we were. We were anybodies anywhere. We didn't need to be special in "the world." We just needed to be special to ourselves and to share our self-love without walls with at least just one other person.

Epilogue

A year after writing this book, I find myself having to write a postscript that I could never have anticipated. Ian and I separated and agreed we would not remain married.

I met Ian in the spring, a time of growth, and we weathered the changing of seasons that made up years until he left like the leaves of an autumn that arrived at the same time. What remained were the harsh and prickly sensations of change and lack of familiarity which were weathered alone through the winter that followed and gave birth to the spring, which brought with it clarity. Here, in that spring, a knowing that life taught me returned to me like an old friend; endings are the start of new beginnings for those who can mourn the past and let it go in order to look forward.

In life we are geared to look for the destinations rather than the journey itself. Ian and I were destined to journey together, but we didn't check the tickets. It turned out that that journey had us change trains and arrive at separate destinations. That journey was the heaven and hell which is the stuff of growth and development, however difficult and challenging. With Ian I learned about letting down walls, letting in pain as well as love, and through that, I better found the key to sharing my soul with others. Ian met me in my own world and together we built an island and each, in different ways, outgrew it. For my part, it was inevitable that I would build a bridge to the mainland.

That mainland is new under my feet, the shoes with which I tread it are not yet acquainted with its soil, not yet worn in. My life on that mainland will inevitably unravel in the summer and the seasons and years that follow.

. . . But that is a whole other story.

Further Information

• For further information about autism or Asperger syndrome, contact your local branch of the National Autistic Society.

• For further information about DMG (dimethylglycine) and other biological approaches to autism spectrum disorders, contact:

> Bernard Rimland
> Autism Research Institute
> 4182 Adams Avenue
> San Diego, CA 92116
> USA
> phone: 619-281-7165; fax: 619-563-6840

• For further information about B.I.R.D (Brain Injury Rehabilitation and Development), contact:

> The Clinical Director
> B.I.R.D.
> 131 Main Road
> Broughton, Chester CH4 ONR
> United Kingdom
> phone: 01244-532047 (Outside U.S., drop initial zero).

• Any person with autism or Asperger syndrome (a closely related developmental disorder) may wish to subscribe to an international newsletter run by people with autism (and closely related disorders within the autistic continuum). Subscription is open to children and adults of all ages from countries all around the world. The newsletter, called *Our Voice,* is for people with all levels and types of communication abilities and levels of functioning. For a subscription form, contact:

Autism Network International
P.O. Box 448
Syracuse, NY 13210-0448
USA

• M.A.A.P is a very positive and supportive international newsletter network for parents and professionals. Although it does focus on more advanced children and adults with autism and related developmental conditions, subscription is invited from those involved with so-called lower-functioning individuals. It has a lot of hope and good ideas to offer. For a subscription form, contact:

M.A.A.P
P.O. Box 524
Crown Point, IN 46307
USA